UNDER
FIRE

PEOPLE, PLACES AND
TREASURE

UNDER
FIRE

IN AFGHANISTAN, IRAQ
AND ISRAEL

An Eyewitness Account by
Dan Cruickshank
and David Vincent

BOOKS

This book is published to accompany a series of
documentaries broadcast on BBC2 in 2002/3
Executive producer: Basil Comely

First published in 2003
Copyright © Dan Cruickshank and
David Vincent 2003
The moral right of the authors has been asserted.

All photographs copyright © Dan Cruickshank

ISBN 0 563 48768 2

Published by BBC Books, BBC Worldwide Ltd,
Woodlands, 80 Wood Lane, London W12 0TT

Commissioning editor: Emma Shackleton
Project editor: Martin Redfern
Designer: Linda Blakemore
Cartographer: Olive Pearson
Production controller: Belinda Rapley

Set in Baskerville and Din
Printed and bound in Great Britain by
CPI Bath

CONTENTS

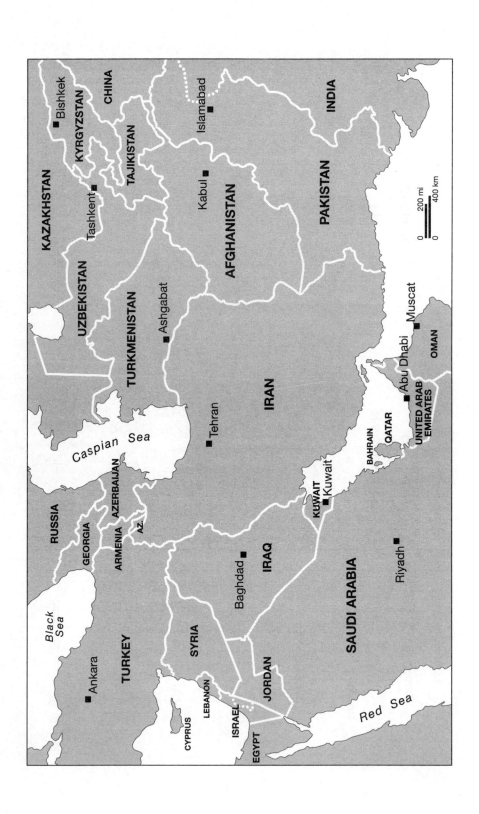

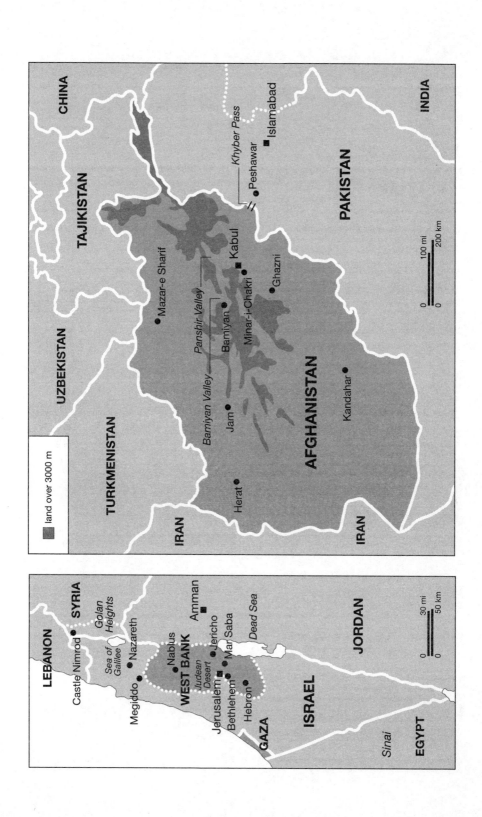

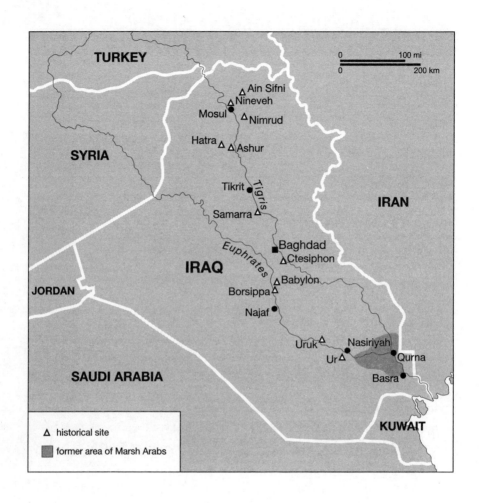

INTRODUCTION

MY FIRST ENCOUNTER WITH THE GIGANTIC BUDDHAS of the spectacular Bamiyan valley in Afghanistan was not promising. It was in the pages of Robert Byron's *The Road to Oxiana*, written in 1934. In this otherwise inspiring book of exploration he wrote of being sickened by the 'monstrous flaccid bulk' of the Buddhas while admiring the form and decoration of the ancient caves that flanked them, where 'Persian, Indian, Chinese and Hellenistic ideas all met at Bamiyan in the fifth and sixth centuries'. But despite Byron's strange revulsion – or perhaps because of it – the image of these remote, ancient and monstrous figures, the earliest personifications of the Buddha, was haunting. I longed to see them, as wonders from a long-lost and distant world, but it was not until 2000 that I again gave them very serious thought. This was when they were threatened with oblivion. Despite international protest they were indeed destroyed, in March 2001, at the hands of the fundamentalist Islamic Taliban regime which believed that the Buddhas – despite their venerable age and abandoned condition – were evil pagan idols and an affront to Muslims. Like many in the world I was shocked and dismayed by this brutal assault on art and history and, I suppose also like many, I tried to make sense of such crass vandalism by attempting to put it in context. It was akin to the iconoclastic madness that broke out in England in the 1530s and again in the 1640s when much that was of religious and artistic beauty was destroyed in the name of a Protestant and Puritan God, or to the ideological attacks that were mounted between 1955 and the 1970s on Buddhist monasteries in Tibet. But then, in September 2001, all abstract pondering ended.

The attack on the World Trade Center towers in New York and on the Pentagon in Washington DC on 11 September 2001 shifted the world perspective. The distasteful but remote excesses of the Taliban were suddenly seen in a new and dramatic light. Their actions were no longer perceived as the insular activities of a bizarre regime but as part of a fragmenting world of sinister and awful new possibilities. It was quickly decided that Osama bin Laden's al-Qaeda organization was responsible for the attacks of 11 September. Almost equally quickly, Western governments agreed that bin Laden was possibly nurturing nuclear material for use in future terror attacks, and was based in Afghanistan where he was being succoured by its Taliban regime. The fall of the Taliban, with Western aid, was now inevitable, and in late 2001 anti-Taliban Afghan fighters, with Western troops, moved on Taliban strongholds. By Christmas 2001 it was all over. The fundamentalists had been deposed, and, although bin Laden had not been captured, US and European troops were garrisoning Kabul and other Afghan cities – heralds, they claimed, of a new period of democratic freedom for a country that had endured nearly 25 years of continuous warfare.

This transformation of the status of Afghanistan raised intriguing possibilities. I knew that the Taliban attack on the Buddhas at Bamiyan had been but a final blow in a long pummelling of the country's culture. Afghanistan's position on the cultural and commercial crossroads of the ancient world had made it rich in cultural treasures of all kinds. The first sustained assault on these came in the wake of the Soviet invasion of December 1979 when, during fighting with the Afghan Mujahedeen, monuments were damaged and destroyed. But more terrible were the bitter years of civil war that engulfed the country between the Soviet withdrawal in 1989 and the rise of the Taliban in the mid-1990s. It was during this period that Afghanistan's heritage was systematically and cynically looted or carelessly destroyed by a series of wanton and tribally or ethnically orientated warlords all vying for worldly power and riches; and what little survived was finally to fall to the ideological excesses of the Taliban. Their inflamed interpretation of the Koran led them to believe that all images of living beings – be they ancient sculptures, paintings of men or beasts, or modern photographs – were sacrilegious and, along with profane music, fashion-conscious clothing and the shaving of faces, were to be destroyed or suppressed.

What, I wondered, were the consequences of this sustained attack on art and history for the ordinary people of Afghanistan? Was their sense of national identity undermined? Was their pride affronted? In a country torn by decades of war, privation, terror and suffering how important were history, beauty and art, and the memory that their land – now desolate – had once been one of the world's great repositories of cultural treasures? In January 2002 my chance came to find out. Basil Comely, an executive producer at the BBC, asked if I would like to go to Afghanistan to discover what had really happened to the Bamiyan Buddhas and the looted Kabul Museum with its world-famous collections including the Bactrian gold, the Bagram ivories and the Kunduz hoard of ancient coins, and to look at the human consequences of these cultural catastrophes. The answer was yes. The risks were assessed, a team assembled and a tough regime of training imposed. We learnt how to escape from a minefield using nothing but a pencil, how to behave at vehicle checkpoints or when abducted, and the best way to staunch the bleeding of a deep wound. Visas were obtained from the nascent Islamic state of Afghanistan, and in early March 2002 we flew to Kabul – almost exactly a year after the destruction of the Buddhas.

The story of the adventure that unfolded is told in the following pages, but the most powerful impression made on me at the time was the intensity of the feelings that most Afghans – many with little or nothing of worldly comfort or wealth – had for their cultural history, and the pain they felt at the passing of so much of it. Some of the encounters were strange, unexpected and intensely moving. There were those with the dignified Afghan men – Muslims of course – who expressed their horror at the sudden and mysterious destruction of the 1800-year-old Buddhist pillar known as the Minar-i-Chakri in 1998; the Hazara man, a Shia Muslim living in a 1500-year-old Buddhist cave in the face of the Bamiyan cliff, who recalled, with tears in his eyes, the circumstances surrounding the destruction of the giant and beloved Buddhas – 'This was a barbaric act'; and the Hazara woman who emerged from her

Bamiyan cave and told me the awful tale of how her baby son had been crippled by the Taliban, and how her heart bled for the loss of the Buddhas whom she saw almost as the protecting spirits of the valley. These mighty images were not worshipped as idols but had been rendered sacred through the veneration of ages and had, by their unique presence, made this remote valley a significant place in the world. Did Afghans care about history, beauty and art? This was an absurd question. In their poverty and want, history was as important as life itself. They knew the meaning and power of their ancient past, which was a source of great pride to them, and they bitterly resented the way in which they – as a people – had been, and were being, robbed of their memories. Who or what was to blame was more complex – lawlessness, vicious ideologies, intense poverty, foreign adventurers – and a subject of intense debate among Afghans. I left the country deeply impressed by the fortitude, courage and character of the people, and much concerned for their future. Appalling difficulties lay behind them, but it was clear that great difficulties also lay ahead.

A couple of months after I returned from Afghanistan a series of programme plans unfolded that had an almost fearful symmetry. I was to go to New York to start a year-long documentation of the plans to rebuild the 16-acre World Trade Center site in Lower Manhattan. The Western invasion of Afghanistan, in a quest to punish bin Laden's al-Qaeda and their Taliban hosts, had been the first dramatic consequence of the 9/11 attack on the United States. Now I was to see how New York was itself dealing with the aftermath of the attack.

Ground Zero had become the most significant urban site in the world, and it immediately became clear that the rebuilding of the Twin Towers must embrace and resolve an extraordinary range of concerns. The site lies in the financial heart of one of the greatest commercial cities in the world. The destroyed buildings had contained 11 million square feet of offices as well as vast amounts of shopping space and a complex transport interchange. In addition, with its pair of 110-storey towers, the World Trade Center had made a major contribution to New York's characteristic soaring and serrated skyline. A rapid rebuilding was vital for the prosperity of New York and to demonstrate to the world that this ghastly terrorist act had not succeeded in crippling the city. But because of the horrifying way in which the site had been created – 2800 people killed in the most frightful and terrifying circumstances, with 1700 bodies reduced to atomized fragments and not identified – the redevelopment had to be undertaken with great sensitivity and consideration. It was agreed that any new buildings had to be of the highest architectural quality, and that the mix of uses had to bring vitality to downtown New York. It was also agreed that the people of the city should be actively engaged in the debate about the rebuilding of the site – and that their views should be not only heard but acted upon. The rebuilding of the World Trade Center site was to be a great public enterprise, unprecedented in US history. Only if the rebuilding was 'done right' in form and content, and if it brought Lower Manhattan back to bright life, could a fitting memorial be achieved to those who had died. If this did not happen they would all have died in vain and, in a certain way, terrorism would be seen to have triumphed. The new buildings had to reconcile commemoration and commerce in a creative manner, and make a positive contribution not only to New York but to Western urban culture in general. A tall order indeed, especially since everything was to be driven by private capital and would ultimately be in the hands of businessmen whose aim was commercial profit.

I arrived in New York in July 2002. My mission was to observe, to insinuate myself into the extraordinary and complex system that was evolving to choose a brief, an architect and a scheme. I would be talking to the families of the bereaved, to architects, real estate executives, politicians, academics and, of course, to all manner of New Yorkers. So, having spoken to Afghans about the consequences of war, I now had the chance to discover how the people of New York had responded to an act of war, and to terrible and unexpected violence in the heart of their city. The Bamiyan Buddhas and the World Trade Center towers were hardly similar, yet in a strange and revealing way they were both symbols of the lands in which they had stood. If the Buddhas reminded Afghans that they lived in an ancient and once highly cultured land that had stood at the centre of the ancient world, the World Trade Center towers expressed certain American values. They were, indeed, towers to Mammon, the tallest towers in the city that is the epicentre of the US global capitalist economy. That, of course, is why they were attacked, and many New Yorkers I talked to felt that the attack on the towers was an attack not only on US values but on the American way of life, on freedom and democracy. I attended, indeed participated in, a series of public meetings in New York, between July 2002 and January 2003, during which the rebuilding of the site and appropriate forms of commemoration and memorial were debated in an incredibly heated and intense manner. Opinions were strongly divided. Many New Yorkers believed that the Twin Towers should be rebuilt exactly as they had been, not merely out of sentimentality but as an act of defiance, as the best way of telling the world that the only people who had died in vain were the terrorists. In a similar vein many of the Hazaras I spoke to in the Bamiyan valley argued that the two giant Buddhas should be re-created as the only way of righting a great wrong.

In February 2003 a scheme for rebuilding the World Trade Center site was finally chosen – after a competition by invitation among leading international architects – in a typically dramatic and intense New York manner. As well as the opinionated, vociferous and emotional citizens of New York, many organizations have a say in the future of the site. There is the New York Port Authority, controlled by the governors of the states of New York and New Jersey, which owns the site; there is the mayor of New York who has political control over the site; and there is a certain Larry Silverstein, the 70-year-old New York property tycoon who acquired a 99-year lease on the Twin Towers only weeks before they were destroyed and who will have command of the private capital to rebuild if his insurance claims, amounting to $7 billion, are finally agreed. In addition to these, given the site's immense international importance, there is Federal interest and money has been made available for the architectural competition and for the bereaved families and the memorial aspects of the scheme. Needless to say, agreement over a winning scheme was hard to reach. There was intense lobbying, nefarious behaviour and a growing sense of dismay that this great and noble enterprise – to revitalize New York and to commemorate the dead

– was sinking into a quagmire of commercial wheeler-dealing. The experts appointed by the mayor and the New York State governor are alleged to have selected one scheme, but then the governor and mayor intervened personally and picked another – the one designed by the Polish-born architect Daniel Libeskind. Six months after being chosen as the winner, Libeskind's scheme was already under strain. The tower he proposed – which at 1776 feet would not only be the tallest tower in the world but also commemorate the year in which America declared its independence – had been taken in hand by Silverstein, who argued that its construction should be overseen by his own architects and that it should be constructed not where Libeskind envisaged it but on a part of the site that would give the tower's office content higher value. Driven by market forces and built as a private commercial venture, the reconstruction of the World Trade Center site could yet become a sordid tussle and take at least 20 years to complete – hardly the vision for a fitting memorial to the dead that galvanized and inspired New Yorkers during the grim weeks after the attack.

While documenting the cut and thrust of rebuilding the World Trade Center site I was also drawn into another part of the world that was to be transformed as a direct result of the attacks of 9/11. In November 2002 I flew into Baghdad from Jordan with a small BBC team, joined now by David Vincent. The Afghanistan programme, broadcast on BBC2 in the early summer of 2002, had led to a series entitled *Under Fire*. Its aim was to investigate regions of the world where art, culture and history were in the firing line – where they were actual or potential victims of political, ideological or nationalistic upheaval and violence. I wanted to record buildings, and cultural institutions like museums, that were threatened by the same obliteration that I had seen inflicted in Afghanistan, and to talk to people about the meaning and power of history and cultural memory. In late 2002, as a Western invasion of Iraq seemed an alarming probability, no country was a more urgent or topical focus for the series. Iraq – known in ancient times as Mesopotamia – is the cradle of world civilization, the place where dramatic leaps of the human imagination led to the invention of writing and the wheel, and to key developments in literature, art, theology and mathematics. That November, I was acutely aware that Iraq's historic buildings, its museums of international importance and its 10,000 recorded archaeological sites were of the highest quality and significance – and also terrifyingly vulnerable to the violence and chaos of war.

The story of our adventures as we travelled through Iraq – from Mosul and the Kurdish Autonomous Region in the north to Uruk and Basra in the south – is told in this book. By the time the journey ended it was clear that the Iraqis – a proud people with a powerful sense of, and love for, the exceptional history of their ancient land – wanted both peace and to be rid of Saddam Hussein and his bullying Baathist organization (although, of course, no one ever dared say this directly). But, perhaps paradoxically, no Iraqi I met wanted to achieve this liberation by suffering the humiliation of a foreign invasion. It seemed clear that bitterness and violence would follow a Western attack which, even if militarily successful, would mark the beginning – rather than the end – of the battle for the hearts and minds of the people of Iraq. Despite being disparate in their religions and even in their ethnicity, all Iraqis I met appeared united in their conviction that a foreign invasion would be an unbearable provocation.

With David and the rest of the *Under Fire* team I returned to Baghdad in April 2003, a little over a fortnight after the city had fallen to US troops. The aim this time was to discover what of historic importance had been destroyed or damaged during the war and, in particular, the truth behind the sensational announcement, issued by the Iraq Museum staff days after the US Army had taken Baghdad, that 170,000 objects in its collection had been stolen or destroyed.

Between these two visits to Iraq we went to Israel and the Occupied Territories, arriving in Tel Aviv on 20 March 2003 just as the land invasion of Iraq got under way. Israel, along with the Occupied Territories of the West Bank and Gaza, is one of the most historic regions on earth. Many of the major civilizations of past millennia have passed through it, fought over it or ruled it. A land holy to all three of the world's great monotheistic religions – Judaism, Islam and Christianity –

it is now a place where conflicting claims to the land, both Israeli and Palestinian, are based on history. So here, like nowhere else on earth, history itself can be a direct victim of violence. Both sides have attacked, damaged and destroyed historic buildings and sites in the course of military action. But both sides have also attacked history in attempts to exact revenge and, more subtly, to distort evidence of early occupation. In the cycle of violence and hatred, Muslims have attacked ancient synagogues, while Jews have threatened, damaged or destroyed Muslim or Palestinian sites and buildings: each side has used the outrages committed against it as justification for committing outrages of its own. Ancient, historic and sacred buildings – like the 2000-year-old Tomb of the Patriarchs in Hebron and the 1300-year-old Dome of the Rock in Jerusalem – have been battled over, divided and threatened, or have become the scene of terrible massacres. The Israelis are battling to sustain a state, the Palestinians are battling to establish a state. Both want essentially the same land; both feel that history and precedent establish their right to that land; and, the final tragedy, few Israelis or Palestinians – Jews or Muslims – believe that their respective and potentially conflicting interests and aspirations can be reconciled in the same country. The Holy Land – racked by hatred and violence – was the most unholy place the *Under Fire* team visited and, given the bitter and seemingly implacable nature of the conflict, remains one of the most terrifying places on earth.

Attacks on history, art and cultural identity remain an urgent and alarming issue across the globe. This book tells the story of three locations – Afghanistan, Iraq and Israel and the Occupied Territories – in which culture was, or still is, under fire. What follows, a collaboration between David Vincent and myself, is an eyewitness account of an extraordinary period in the history of world culture.

Dan Cruickshank, London, July 2003

CHAPTER ONE

AFGHANISTAN: AFTER BAMIYAN

IT WAS ONE OF THE MOST HORRENDOUS CULTURAL OUTRAGES ever perpetrated by mankind, and yet the world seemed powerless to do anything. When grainy images of the destruction of the imperious Buddhas carved out of the rockface in Bamiyan, north-central Afghanistan, flashed across our television screens the universal reaction was one of stunned disbelief that the Taliban, the fundamentalist Islamic rulers of the country, had actually carried out their threats against these ancient colossi that had withstood even the might of Genghis Khan. History had been dragged ruthlessly into the front line, and sacrificed to political and religious ends, in possibly the worst vandalism since the destruction of the Buddhist monasteries in Tibet by the Chinese or the despoliations of the Khmer Rouge in Cambodia. Sometimes the human race's ability in construction seems to be matched only by its brutality in destruction.

In retrospect, this was only a rumble heralding the thunderclap that was to follow almost six months later to the day – a cultural disaster setting the scene for the vast human catastrophe witnessed in New York and Washington DC on 11 September 2001. At the time, though, all that was clear was that a people's art and cultural heritage had been reduced to dust and rubble in a land devastated by war and poverty. After over 20 years of bloody civil wars and anarchy Afghanistan was back on the front pages, and for all the wrong reasons.

During the first and second centuries AD Afghanistan was a major cultural and commercial crossroads of the world, bridging the great empires of the East and West; the historian Arnold Toynbee called it a 'roundabout' civilization. The Silk Road from China to Europe passed through Afghanistan, and over hundreds of years waves of rampaging armies, such as Alexander the Great's troops in the fourth century BC, swept through its harsh terrain; all left their mark on this strange, tribal land. Although the country was brought to its knees in the US-led war that followed the attacks on the World Trade Center, in truth the mortal blows had already been struck. While the Taliban, as allies of Osama bin Laden, were quickly dispersed by Western military might aided by Afghan Northern Alliance forces, the scars these hardliners left on Afghanistan's people and culture would take far longer to heal. Incensed and alarmed at how the will of a few could defile centuries of art and achievement in a land as culturally rich as Egypt, yet mostly unexcavated, plans were made to travel to Afghanistan as soon as it was safe to do so.

The intention was to examine the destructive legacy of the Taliban not just in Bamiyan, but also at other sites of historic significance such as the little-known but valuable National (or Kabul) Museum, which was reported to have been seriously looted during the civil war between 1990 and 1996; the fabled Buddhist pillar known as the Minar-i-Chakri; and the ancient minarets of Ghazni. Cultural artefacts, ranging from entire buildings to the most delicate of objects in the museum, had been targeted for decades by both foreign and domestic vandals, originally as plunder and latterly for ideological reasons. What remained of this neglected yet important heritage? What had happened and what had survived? How were the battered Afghans reacting to their plight? And to what extent, living as they were with the appalling consequences of war and poverty, did they care if their history had been obliterated? In addition there had been rumours of lost treasures, such as the priceless Bactrian gold which had not been seen since 1999. The team, led by Sam Hobkinson from the BBC Arts Department who would film the trip, would attempt to track down the gold in order to offer some prospect for the survival of culture – and hope – in Afghanistan.

In January and February 2002 life was still far from stable in the country, and reports were coming through almost daily of heavy fighting in remote regions. Local warlords controlled key areas, despite the fact that an interim government had been set up under Hamid Karzai, and anarchy bubbled dangerously close to the surface of everyday life. But since there seemed to be no prospect of improvement in the near future the chance had to be taken now. Direct entry to Afghanistan from the West was not possible, which was how the team found themselves on board a very small piston-engined plane flying in from Islamabad in Pakistan. It was March 2002, but it could have been 30 years earlier at the time of the Vietnam War. The other passengers included a mixture of hacks with their battered camera equipment, stoned or drunk – sometimes both – loitering for a mission; and some slightly desperate freelancers hungry for a story – perhaps the last throw of the dice in a dwindling career. Dangerous locations attract these sorts. As the plane bumped along over the Khyber Pass – right now perhaps one of the most dangerous places on earth – below lay the magnificent Hindu Kush range. Raw, elemental and drained of colour, this ribbed and ragged terrain showed little or no sign of human life. Yet these had been battlegrounds for centuries past, and were still rumbling with the violent quarrels of disparate groups.

'Kabul … is a fast-growing city where tall modern buildings nuzzle against bustling bazaars and wide avenues fill with brilliant flowing turbans, gaily striped *chapans*, mini-skirted school girls, a multitude of handsome faces and streams of whizzing traffic.' This is how Nancy Dupree begins the section on Kabul in her guidebook *An Historical Guide to Afghanistan*, originally published in 1970. Like Baghdad, another city torn apart by war, in the 1970s Kabul was a thriving, ambitious place, intent on gorging itself on Western tastes in clothes, cars and lifestyle. A few decades later, Dupree's mini-skirted schoolgirls would have sent the Taliban into fits of incandescent rage.

Strategically situated in a narrow valley along the Kabul River high in the mountains near the Khyber Pass, the city has a 3000-year history marked by frequent destruction and rebuilding. The country has been invaded by, among others, Alexander the Great, the Arabs, the Mongols, the Persians and the Moguls, and Kabul has been the capital since 1776 when Afghanistan's Persian ruler, Timur Shah, moved here from the southern city of Kandahar. However, it has never been secure in its position as the seat of power, due to continuous intertribal tensions and the regional pull of the older cities of Kandahar and Herat. It was occupied in 1839 by British forces, who were fearful of the Russian influence in Persia and Russian designs on India. They withdrew from the city after a bloody uprising in 1842, but returned to avenge their losses, during the course of which the famed Kabul casbah was tragically blown up. A second Anglo–Afghan war broke out in 1878 over rivalry between the British and the Russians for political influence in Afghanistan in what became known as the Great Game, a phrase coined by Rudyard Kipling. A short period of British rule followed before the kingdom of Kabul was handed over to a tribal leader, Abdur Rahman, in 1880, although Britain retained the right to control Afghan foreign affairs. Only after the third and final Anglo–Afghan War, in 1919, did Afghanistan achieve full independence.

As modernization grew apace during the twentieth century, the country continued to wrangle with Pakistan over the region known as Pashtunistan. And in December 1979 the Russians occupied Kabul, turning it into their command centre during the ten-year conflict between the Soviet-allied government and the Mujahedeen rebels. It fell into rebel hands after the collapse of Mohammad Najibullah's puppet government in 1992. As these forces broke up into rival warring factions the city suffered increasingly, with little or no breathing space in which to regenerate its resources and infrastructure. Between 1992 and 1996, 60 per cent of the city was destroyed and 25,000 deaths occurred. In 1994, one attack alone, a vicious assault by an alliance of warlords, is said to have killed more Afghans than even the Russians had managed. The fight for Kabul only ended in September 1996 when the city was taken by the Taliban. After the Taliban themselves had fallen in November 2001, following heavy attacks by opposition forces and US aerial bombardments, Kabul spent several months in a state of uneasy limbo under the interim government of Prime Minister Karzai. An atmosphere of suspicion and sporadic violence now prevailed, and military intelligence strongly suggested that it would get worse before it improved. It was a sobering thought with which to land at Kabul airport.

Despite the appalling pounding that the city had taken, evidence of which was immediately apparent to new arrivals, life was flourishing even among the ruins. Kabul's outskirts may have been lined with burnt-out tanks and armoured personnel carriers, but its streets were still crammed with people, many on bicycles or in horse-drawn carts, an appreciable number with guns. There were also coffee houses open and cartloads of fresh provisions for sale, and even chickens having their throats slashed in the Islamic halal tradition, their blood running into the gutter. In parts of the city the wrecked buildings stretched for hundreds of metres and gave the appearance of being uninhabitable, yet on closer inspection they turned out to house families too poor to move or rebuild. Whole quarters had been laid low by the fighting that had gone on almost without a break over the previous 25 years, and in this regard the long, straight thoroughfare of Jade Maiwand, now shattered, was a particularly impressive sight – a post-war modernist paradise littered with signs for aid agencies.

The guesthouse where the team would be staying was modern but organized in a traditional defensive manner and, like its neighbours, stood within a walled compound entered through a stout gate. In the event of a grenade or rocket attack the house was low enough and set far enough back from the wall to minimize damage – or at least that was the theory. A chequerboard of such strongholds on the edge of the city had been visible from the air and initially this had been puzzling; but now the reason became evident. This was the pattern of life in Kabul: defence as a way of everyday existence in a permanently feuding city. The guesthouse was clean and even had a good supply of hot water. There was also a resident family of servants including an excellent chef, late of the French Embassy, who over the following days would produce an amazing variety of dishes. The guests ate these culinary creations with a mixture of astonishment, satisfaction and guilt. What was left on their plates could feed an Afghan family for days, and the cost of each meal could sustain them for weeks. Foreigners might be there on working assignments, but their position was still very much one of privilege.

The next day, news filtered through of a rocket attack two days previously on Kabul airport, aimed at the military forces based there. This had not been reported in the media and, locally, a coup was feared.

Just a matter of time, was the verdict of the British forces based in the capital. Accompanying this piece of information were reports that the road from Bamiyan to Jam had recently been booby-trapped with anti-personnel mines. It was important not to take any risks in this environment: one could be lulled into complacency very quickly once things became more familiar, but this could prove lethal in a city and country that were still extremely volatile. In a country as unstable as Afghanistan, security was a constant preoccupation.

The Taliban, the recent rulers of this poor, ravaged country, were drawn mostly from the majority Pashtun ethnic group. The name translates as 'Students of Islam', and they emerged as a cohesive group under their reclusive, one-eyed leader Mullah Mohammed Omar in 1994, when Afghanistan was in a state of near anarchy, in reaction to the irreligious and amoral activities of the Mujahedeen guerillas. Of all the myths that quickly arose around the fledgling movement, Ahmed Rashid gives most credence, in his comprehensive account of the period, *Taliban*, to the story that neighbours told Omar of a warlord who had abducted two teenage girls and was detaining them at a local military camp where they were being subjected to horrific abuse. Omar reputedly rounded up 30 Talibs and attacked the base, freeing the girls and hanging the offending commander from the barrel of a tank. A few months later he was reported to have rescued a young boy from two commanders in Kandahar who were squabbling over him. On neither occasion did Omar demand any reward for his actions – only that people should lead a strict Islamic existence. As time went on and the Taliban's reputation grew, the Pakistan government asked them to protect its convoys passing through to Central Asia from attack by Mujahedeen forces; and within weeks of this request Omar's men took the city of Kandahar. It was to be less than two years before they also had control of Kabul.

In one sense, the arrival on the scene of the Taliban had certain beneficial effects. The values they initially promoted were generally perceived as unremarkable, imposing peace and stability and putting a stop to the destructive, self-seeking activities of the warlords. Their rigid standards of morality and behaviour, though hardly progressive, were not exceptional in the Muslim world, and were essentially an echo of the codes of moral and religious conduct that had long prevailed in Saudi Arabia, where Wahhabism had flourished since the eighteenth century. Founded by Muhammad bin Abdul Wahhab to cleanse Sunni Muslims of what he perceived to be the taint of Sufi mysticism, Wahhabism was a belief in the power of the primitive in a world as close as possible to that into which the Prophet was born. It was, put crudely, a 'back to basics' campaign with its intolerance of modern life and of profane art and beauty. All images of living things were forbidden, and veneration of the tombs of holy men was regarded as idolatry. In their strict application of morality and theology in the formulation of a social code and law the Taliban had much in common with the English and American Puritan sects of the seventeenth century, who wrapped up their bigotry in the nobility of a big moral idea. And, with a sponsor such as Osama bin Laden basing the headquarters of his al-Qaeda network in the country, they did not want for either money or international publicity, though that relationship would ultimately bring about the regime's downfall.

Nothing gripped the imagination of the West as much as the primitive and brutal repression of women and culture under the Taliban. Women were regarded as a threat, a presence that could undermine the fanaticism that underpinned men's devotion to radical Islam. The dubious pleasure, if such a thing were allowed, of administering the increasingly severe edicts fell to the Department for the Promotion of Virtue and Prevention of Vice, or Amar Bil Maroof Wa Nahi An al-Munkar, headed by the much-feared Maulvi Qalamuddin. The young men, often uneducated, who formed his religious police patrolled the streets of Kabul, Herat and Kandahar with their guns and sticks, ready to lash out at anyone, particularly women, who broke the taboos. Services such as hairdressers and bathhouses were closed down, sacrificed to a hard-line dogma. Some of the regulations, broadcast daily on Radio Shariat, were scarcely credible; among the activities banned were listening to music, shaving beards, keeping birds, flying kites (a popular spring activity in Afghanistan), idolatry, gambling, Western hairstyles, religious chanting, dancing at weddings and playing drums.

Women had already been suppressed by the Mujahedeen, who had taught young men that a woman who showed her face publicly was a loose woman. Now, before going out in public, women were forced to put on an all-enveloping burkha, and wear flat shoes and no make-up, to escape the wrath of Qalamuddin's enforcers. And it was not only women's rights and legitimate aspirations that were being trampled upon: the education and health system of Afghanistan had collapsed since women were no longer allowed to teach or nurse. Married women accused of adultery, and unmarried women suspected of having sexual relationships with men, were summarily executed. The punishments that the Taliban inflicted were out of all proportion to the alleged crimes, utterly barbarous and – by all standards of international law and morality – illegal. The Koran and the Hadeeth, the collected sayings of the Prophet, were deliberately misinterpreted to support a wide range of social and religious suppression. In truth, the Taliban were meting out punishments for 'crimes of vice' in accordance with Pashtunwali law, and their ranks were swelled by the products of war, poverty, illiteracy and male isolation, who brought an oppressive zeal to the streets of these previously tolerant cities. Hardly any of the measures, which were described by the Taliban as a reversion to traditional life according to strict Sharia law, had been insisted upon by any previous rulers. Indeed, as far back as 1959 the idea of purdah for women had been made optional: they had begun to enrol at Kabul University, as well as entering the workforce and the government.

The vehemence with which the religious police restricted people's appearance and behaviour was applied also to the arts and media as fundamentalists seized ever greater control. Magazines were closed down, along with other branches of publishing, as well as film, television and the performing arts. On that first morning in the city a quick visit to the Kabul Theatre confirmed the moribund state in which live performance found itself after more than two decades of war and unrest. What had been a decent-sized auditorium was now little more than a shattered shell, bombed out and looted, with the reliefs of dancers on the walls of its façade ripped from their fixings. Only the traces of their once-graceful poses bore testimony to the intended purpose of the building; a sophisticated, cultured community had been robbed of yet another form of artistic expression.

Outside was a postcard seller plying a trade that had been prohibited under the Taliban, and his wares proved curiously poignant. Under a sign reading 'Afghan Cards and Postcards Available' was a jumble of faded, dog-eared images of better times. Dan spotted a promotional card for Afghan Airlines, a pink-fringed photograph, obviously taken many years before, of a dozen or so air hostesses lined up smiling in their neatly tailored uniforms. There were other cards promoting tourism in the country, featuring stereotypical images, such as camels and tour buses, representing different eras of transport. The postcards were all 'new' stock; they had never been purchased or sent but were left over from an optimistic print run. Dan bought a selection, which felt like taking away Afghanistan's past in a box, yet there seemed no danger of the stock dwindling. And as for the tour buses, a number came to light over the next few days, burnt out at the roadside or abandoned in fields, stripped of any reusable parts.

At another tiny stall further along the ramshackle, busy street there were piles of books for sale, including old guides to Afghanistan. This was manna for Dan, who bargained with the vendor and came away cradling a small library. The books revealed the country's striking cultural life prior to the Russian war – here was a nation continuing to absorb influences from outside, and with seamless ease, into its own personal and national identity. Of particular value were the old guides to the Kabul Museum and the historic sites, illustrated with colour photographs of the colossal Buddhas at Bamiyan, still *in situ*, and arte-facts from the museum itself – Greek, Roman and Hindu work, the stupendous Bagram ivory panels (now looted), all proudly confirming that it had been no backwater collection but rather one of immense international importance. The press had reported bleakly on the huge losses endured by the museum, making these documents all the more valuable as a record of Afghanistan's intensely eclectic civilization.

When the Taliban decided to act against portrayals of living beings the National Gallery of Afghanistan, with its collection of paintings and drawings, was an obvious place to be targeted by the religious police once the Bamiyan Buddhas had been destroyed and the statues in the Kabul Museum broken up. Deeply aware of this risk, the curators were determined to act to save at least some of their collection. But when the team arrived at the gallery, at first it appeared as though they had not acted quickly enough. The floors were piled up with paintings that had been ripped apart, their frames little more than firewood, and any images viciously scratched out. Little seemed to have evaded the Taliban's uncultured grasp, and the director of the gallery, Abdul Fatah Adil, pointed to a series of prized items that had been defaced. 'This is a painting of an African man. It was presented to the gallery by an African artist,' he said softly, putting it back on the stack with touching care. 'And this one, this painting shows a man studying.' What he described was barely discernible on the small, square canvas, but he clearly retained a precise image of each painting catalogued in his mind's eye – the one thing the Taliban could not eliminate. He had not been present when they had done their work, and despite knowing what was about to happen, he was unprepared for what he subsequently found. 'When I came here, as an Afghan, I had tears in my eyes, believe me,' he disclosed. You did not have to be Afghan to be moved by the scale and wantonness of the destruction, and it was not easy to relate to the mindset of those responsible. Relentless in their prosecution of the edict against the representation of living things, the Taliban had made regular visits to the gallery to ensure compliance, and, similarly, had destroyed throughout Kabul films, drawings, books, statues, musical recordings and photographs. Over 1000 films, for instance, were thrown on to a bonfire at Afghan Films, the government-run national film studio and archives.

Yet despite the Taliban's best efforts, ingenious, if highly dangerous, ruses had sometimes succeeded in concealing items from their censorious eyes. Some paintings had survived at the gallery thanks to the guile and deft brush of one man. Dr Yousef Asifi, a medical doctor who also happened to be one of Afghanistan's leading artists and had exhibited internationally, had been desperate to preserve as much of the collection as possible. Rather than hide the canvases, he carefully painted over the offending parts with watercolours: to the untrained eyes of the Taliban officials they appeared inoffensive, and so evaded their hammers and knives. Walking through some of the rooms in the gallery, Dr Asifi, a smallish, unassuming man, demonstrated his camouflaging skills. When gently wiped with a damp cloth, an innocuous-looking landscape revealed a group of people and some sheep in the foreground. In several other paintings a human figure or animal was magically brought back to life with one small swipe. Hugely effective and miraculous to observe, it represented at least a small victory in this one-sided cultural war. Although justifiably proud of his work, Dr Asifi was also very aware of the risk he had taken: 'If the Taliban had caught me, it would have cost me my life,' he admitted. In the world of medieval wretchedness the Taliban wove around Afghan society, there was no hint of exaggeration in this analysis.

Dr Asifi's disguise work, which he had been allowed to carry out after telling the Taliban it was a programme of restoration, could be viewed as among the most valuable he had ever done; he estimated that he had saved approximately 80 pictures. Nor was it the first time he had resorted to this ruse: four years previously, he had managed to save 42 paintings at the Foreign Ministry in a similar fashion. However, the most depressing statistic is that, despite this subterfuge, the Taliban still managed to lay waste to nearly half of the gallery's total collection of 800 paintings – and Dr Asifi knew of at least 26 of his own works that had been destroyed. His actions may have provided a chink of light, but it was in a vast and disturbing gloom.

The Taliban decree against freedom of artistic expression had resulted in an exodus of writers and artists, unhappy to leave their homeland but fearful of arrest and worse if they stayed. Visual artists took to producing anti-Taliban works in neighbouring countries such as Pakistan, but they were fighting from a position of weakness. After the bitter-sweet experience at the National Gallery, the next place to visit was perhaps the one that, apart from the Bamiyan Buddhas, was said to have suffered most in terms of needless, vicious damage. It was time to see what remained of the Kabul Museum.

After more than 20 years of war and civil unrest not only did Afghanistan's present and future lie in ruins – so did its past. Darulaman, the location of both the great royal palace and the museum, had been laid out in the 1920s just after Afghanistan had been liberated from the British Empire. Once an emblem of a fresh beginning, it now stood deserted, stripped of its majesty and bearing the scars of two decades of suffering. Described in the 1970s as a 'luxurious park' containing neo-classical villas and palaces, it was now little more than a wilderness of rubble and undergrowth. And the museum itself offered a bleak, culturally apocalyptic vision, far worse than could have been anticipated.

Until 1992 the Kabul Museum had been home to world-famous items such as the Bagram ivories, the Kunduz hoard of coins, the Bactrian gold and some of the finest Buddhist statuary anywhere. Covering more than 50,000 years of the region's history, from cave dwellers via Hindu, Buddhist and Islamic cultures up to the Durrani kings who came to power in the eighteenth century, its collections consisted of frescoes, bronzes, glass and statues relating to cultures from Central Asia, India, China, Egypt, Greece and Rome. It had been the most comprehensive collection of the artistic output of these civilizations anywhere in the world, and in *An Historical Guide to Afghanistan* Nancy Dupree called it 'one of the greatest testimonies of antiquity that the world has inherited'. Yet now the place was little more than a shell: no windows, no roof.

Dr Omar Khan Massoudi, the museum's director, had agreed to show the team around the damage. Above the main door hung a banner that plaintively read, 'A nation stays alive when its culture stays alive', a noble sentiment and yet, as Dr Massoudi pointed out apologetically, 'This is what happens to a museum during wartime. All the rooms are like this. It is truly heartbreaking.' There was little or nothing to suggest that this had been a museum gallery. Suddenly Dan spotted one of the items he had dreaded finding in this state. Could that be the famed statue of King Kanishka, the foremost king of the second-century AD Kushan dynasty and the propagator of Buddhism in the region? Positioned at the entrance to the museum, he had been without his head and torso for many centuries but, before his demise, had been noted for his generous pantaloons and outsized feet. Now he was little more than a pile of limestone rubble. To add insult to injury, according to a museum official, the Taliban had laughed as they smashed up his 1800-year-old form. Its destruction was an enormous tragedy, all the more so for being premeditated.

It is true: no Afghan institution has suffered quite so much in the recent past as the Kabul Museum. Surprisingly, it was not the war against Russia or the ensuing three years of communist government which followed that resulted in losses – the invaders took nothing, and in fact repainted a couple of exhibition rooms. However, in the civil war fought by rival Mujahedeen factions that followed between April 1992 and 1995, when Muslim guerrilla groups funded by the West captured Kabul, the museum was continually taken and then retaken, used as a military base and plundered each time, losing in total around 70–80 per cent of its collection. It was a time of cultural pillage comparable to the wholesale ransacking of the museums of Germany and Russia during World War II, terrible deeds, the true extent of which we are only now beginning to learn. Buyers in Japan, Europe and the USA made small fortunes, sometimes large ones, dealing in Afghan antiquities as thousands of works found their way on to the international black market, often looted to order by the Mujahedeen. It got so bad that at one point the United Nations Educational, Scientific and Cultural Organization (UNESCO) was unofficially advising Westerners leaving Afghanistan to take as many items as they could, in order to safeguard them. Then disaster struck, as Dr Massoudi related: 'It was reported on 13 May 1995 that rockets had hit the museum, and it was on fire. It had a wooden roof, so the display cabinets and the treasures were on fire. I heard it on the radio, on the BBC.' The missiles had also destroyed a fourth-century AD wall-painting and buried the collection in debris, while the main structure of the building had been perforated by gunfire. Today, the first floor still stood open to the elements as its roof had proved too expensive to replace. Sunlight streamed in through the apertures which once had been windows, the bare stone of the walls framed by dazzling blue skies as rich as the museum was dusty and grey. These were no longer galleries; in fact they were hardly even rooms.

At Dan's request, Dr Massoudi showed him the room that had once displayed the world-famous Bagram ivories. This series of exquisite Indian panels made to decorate furniture, dating from the Kushan Empire (c.135 BC – AD 241) and excavated by French archaeologists between 1936 and 1946 at a site 50 kilometres north of Kabul, had vanished, looted during the civil unrest and for the most part smuggled out of the country to dealers in London, New York and Tokyo. One buyer had gone public: Naseerullah Babar, a retired Pakistani general and former Minister of the Interior, admitted that he paid $100,000 for a piece from the Bagram collection, but claimed he acquired it for 'safe keeping' – though there were strong rumours that the basement of his house was a repository for looted Afghan treasures. Indeed, according to one dealer, during President Bhutto's regime in the 1970s Afghan antiques 'flowed through Pakistan like a river'. London dealers affirmed that they had been offered other examples of the ivories from contacts in the border town of Peshawar, but the whereabouts of the majority of the collection was a mystery. All Dr Massoudi knew was that in late 1993 a UN representative had visited Kabul and been taken to the museum by representatives of the then government. The first thing he had wanted to see was the Bagram collection; he had had to report that 'most of the Bagram items, including the ivories collection, have been looted'.

Other major items that had disappeared included the entire coin collection, one of the oldest and largest in the world, including the Kunduz hoard of more than 600 Graeco–Bactrian coins dating from the third and second centuries BC; some Greek–Buddhist stucco sculptures and schist reliefs dating from between the first and third centuries AD; Hindu marble statuary from the seventh and ninth centuries; and fragments of wall-paintings from the Bamiyan valley. If a museum is defined by its collection, then this building would now be hard to classify as one, such was its barrenness.

Another burnt-out room had once featured exhibits from the Bamiyan region, but friezes, statues and ceramics – objects that had once seemed indomitable, unassailable – were now reduced to rubble. Dan asked the director what the losses from the museum meant to the people of Afghanistan. Did they feel that, having lost their history, they had also lost their memories? 'Without a doubt, this is a very sad time for the Afghan people, who have lost their culture and their history,' agreed Dr Massoudi. 'If a building is destroyed you can rebuild it, but if your national heritage is lost you can't bring it back.' But hope for the museum's future lay in the vast untapped riches at sites yet to be discovered and excavated, despite years of illegal digging and looting that the interim government was apparently taking firm steps to deal with.

While the looting that took place between 1992 and 1995 had seriously depleted the stock of priceless artefacts, the Taliban's iconoclastic fury had also contributed to the museum's losses – ironically, after they had put an end to the looting with their severe, Sharia law penalties for stealing. It was the same belief system that subsequently led them on their smashing spree, and Dr Massoudi introduced Yaha Yaha Zada, a curator who had actually witnessed the Taliban's attacks. The circumstances under which the Taliban came to the museum were duplicitous, according to Zada. 'It was an ambush attack, if I may say so,' he began politely. 'They told me that they wanted to see the treasures of the museum and this interest made me feel quite happy, as a couple of days before, the Taliban Minister of Vice and Virtue came and promised to help the museum, telling us that it would be reconstructed soon. All our problems were over, he said.' But this was not what transpired when a delegation from the ministry, including the Culture and Information Minister and the Finance Minister, arrived on 4 February 2001. Mr Zada offered to show them the galleries, but they were more interested in the stores, the contents of which they proceeded to smash up with hammers; the shards were now stored in boxes for possible future reconstruction. He had tried to protest, but an official warned him to keep quiet or he would himself be hit with a hammer. In an attempt to avert at least some of the damage Mr Zada told the Taliban that many of the objects were from the Islamic period rather than Buddhist, which seemed to have saved some of them. He was emphatic that he could not stand by and do nothing, despite threats to his personal safety: 'I decided, even if it cost me my life, to save them, as I had lived and worked with these statues for 18 years, and had come to love them.'

It was an extraordinary situation to find himself in: by slowly winning the trust of the Taliban, he was able to decide which pieces were saved and which destroyed. The ones to be saved were quickly packed and taken to a safe store in the centre of Kabul, at the Ministry of Culture. This man, whose life had been immersed in the conservation of these important historic items, must have felt an incredible mixture of exhilaration and abject sadness. 'I loved these objects like my own children,' confirmed Mr Zada. 'To see them broken in front of my eyes was the most tragic day of my life. But anyone, Afghan or non-Afghan, would have felt the same pain – it would have been a painful sight for any culture-loving human being.' He then pointed to the remains of a statue that had been selected by the Taliban for obliteration. 'After three days they saw this statue, found in Kunduz province. It is made from marble, and so when they hit it by hand they could not break it. So they brought a much bigger hammer with which they hit it very hard.' Mr Zada pointed out the damaged areas, hacked apart with brute force, and continued: 'I was made to watch while they smashed away at it all day with the large hammer and a pickaxe.' He tried turning the face to the ground when they finished for the day, in the hope that they might miss it the following morning. But while the statue had been attacked, he did not feel it was purely the depiction of living objects that drove the Taliban. 'They were not interested only in the destruction of the figures or statues, but they wanted to destroy all historical heritage,' he concluded sadly.

Mr Zada then indicated a series of wooden boxes containing shattered statues and sculpture, abstract features jumbled into a Picasso-esque vision. Even these tiny, delicate Buddhist faces, over 1500 years old, had not escaped the ire of the Taliban. It was humbling to hold these remnants of beauty, no longer worshipped and no danger or threat to anyone, yet battered by the hubris of man, dressed up as religious zeal. It was beyond comprehension that human beings should exert such brute strength on the fruits of the human imagination, and it was hard to look at their fragmented faces and not feel ashamed. Yet these were not mute objects: their features quietly spoke of beauty in the face of adversity, our own moral adversity. Dan asked Mr Zada how he saw the future for the museum and its massively depleted collection. The answer was more optimistic than might have been expected. 'Our plan is the reconstruction of the Afghan National Museum. We hope to repair and recover items, in order to show the world that our culture is alive.' The museum would open again at some point in the future, he was sure.

Kabul Museum staff are being helped in this mammoth task by the Society for the Preservation of Afghanistan's Cultural Heritage, which from its base in the notorious Pakistani clearing house of Peshawar, just east of the Khyber Pass, is trying to stop the looting and dispersal of artefacts. In addition, an Afghanistan Museum in exile, as it were, was set up in the late 1990s in Bubendorf, a village outside Basel in Switzerland, by an architect named Paul Bucherer. Made up entirely of donations, the collection in the whitewashed chalet already includes more than 2000 objects, and is receiving backing from both the Swiss government and UNESCO. Bucherer, dubbed the 'Oskar Schindler of Afghan art', views his venture as a 'basket' for reclaimed Afghan artefacts, and he has a further ambition: to re-create the Bamiyan Buddhas. This aim is increasingly unlikely to be achieved, but his unusual museum will be a valuable resource when the Kabul Museum is finally in a position to open its doors again.

Outside Kabul was one of the wonders of the ancient Afghan world. The Minar-i-Chakri – the Tower of the Wheel – was built as a 25-metre-tall pillar crowned by a lotus motif and, suggests Willem Vogelsang in his book *The Afghans*, 'by the Buddhist symbol of the wheel (Sanskrit *Chakra*)', which would explain its name. Constructed in the second or third century AD, the stone and mortar edifice was a landmark for Buddhist pilgrims who visited the area for its host of shrines and stupas. The pillar itself was a representation of the Buddha at a time when it was not the practice to depict him as a living form – unlike at Bamiyan, for example. According to reports, this wonderfully engineered and sophisticated structure had collapsed in March 1998 in suspicious circumstances. Was it true that the Taliban had only been attacking depictions of living things? It appeared that all monuments to the past were fair game in their unforgiving eyes.

In the blazing sun the team's vehicles, accompanied by armed Afghan guards, lurched over the unmade roads that radiated from Kabul, US Chinook military helicopters whooshing overhead as a constant reminder of the instability that reigned beyond the capital. Not long into the bumpy journey there was a vehicle checkpoint, and to go further needed the local military commander's goodwill. He was not at present around, so the checkpoint guards and village elders offered traditional green *chai* and conversation to fill in the time until he returned. Dan explained his mission to them, and asked how they saw their country's heritage. One man in particular was eager to share his thoughts: 'We are very happy that you are here to tell the story of what has happened to our cultural heritage – it is such a cruel way to treat any historical subject.' He conceded that he was unhappy at the actions of the Taliban, something he could not have admitted a few years before, and saw it as his responsibility to pass on his memories in time-honoured fashion: 'What a man remembers, he tells his son, and he in turn tells his son. I will have to tell my children of the wonders of this country and its history. They can destroy our buildings and monuments, but they can't destroy our minds. We all have memories, and history now lives on in them.'

After several hours the commander, Engineer Afzal, finally came back. An architect trained in Saudi Arabia, he claimed to have fought the Russians in the 1980s, during which time he lost three brothers, and had then confronted the threat of the Taliban. He told Dan that he thought the interim government were 'bad people', just a small clique running the country. In response to the request to pass through into his area he decided to come along too. However, having started he suddenly remembered that the road ahead might be mined – a likely proposition, as it is estimated that over five million landmines are still buried in Afghanistan – and at the same time he recalled an urgent meeting in Kabul. The rest of the party continued to bump along the track until no further progress was possible in the vehicles, then continued on foot along barely visible paths, walking on rocks where practicable and keeping an eye out for mines. The air was getting thinner with the increasing altitude and the sun was now overhead, making everyone hot and breathless. To add to the difficulties, the guides did not even seem very sure where the Minar-i-Chakri actually was.

Finally, after an hour and a half of increasing sweat and scepticism, there it was. But the remains of the enigmatic pillar were now a mere stub with a pencil-like point 6 metres high, and a pile of stones and rubble around its feet. No preservation work had been carried out since the 1970s, and in recent decades the area around the tower had often been on the front line between warring factions – indeed, during the 1980s bored Soviet troops had used the pillar for target practice, and the ground was now littered with the remnants of exploded plastic mines. Before it fell into such a ruinous state the Minar-i-Chakri was a marvel of ancient architecture. Around it would once have stood a major Buddhist monastery, though nothing of that had survived into modern times. The loss of the pillar was tragic. Who was responsible? Had the Taliban indeed committed yet another cultural atrocity?

When Dan asked some men in the local Chakri village what they remembered of the night of its collapse their answer was inconclusive. 'At night-time we heard an explosion. The next morning, we walked up to the Buddhist pillar and found it destroyed. We don't know who did it, but this was during the Taliban time.' It seemed hard to believe that a structure that had stood for nearly two millennia should suddenly fall down in such a way, but two possible explanations put forward were that the heavy rain and snow that week had weakened an object already in dire need of repair, or that robbers had been hoping to find treasures hidden within it. 'With the Minar-i-Shakari, the world's cultural heritage lost its last great example of an incomparable piece of architecture,' wrote historical writer Chris Dorn'eich in a letter to the Society for the Preservation of Afghanistan's Cultural Heritage. The villagers were similarly moved. 'We are very sad. It was such an important thing for us, and so valuable.'

Back in Kabul, Nancy Dupree, whose book remains one of the most important and influential guides to the country, shared her memories. Now 74, Nancy has led an extraordinary life, much of it devoted to Afghanistan and its people. Louis Dupree, a Harvard archaeologist and specialist in the ancient cultures of Afghanistan, was her second husband. They married in 1966 and travelled throughout the country for much of the 1970s. Louis' death in 1989 only served to deepen

Nancy's devotion to Afghanistan, its people and its culture. She lived in Peshawar on the Pakistan border, where she worked assiduously for the Society for the Preservation of Afghanistan's Cultural Heritage, and made regular visits to Kabul. Her reputation spread far and wide: award-winning American playwright Tony Kushner wrote a play, *Homebody/Kabul*, based on her guidebook, and her eccentricity was legendary; in interviews, she was famous for referring to King Kanishka as her 'boyfriend'. In a *chaikhana*, a traditional Afghan tea house, this feisty woman explained the origins of her love affair with Afghanistan. Like many passions, it had started at a cocktail party, back in the 1960s. Abdul Hab Tarzi, head of the newly created Tourism Department, in response to her complaint that the region was under-resourced for visitors, had quipped, 'You're quite right. Why don't you do something about it?' Nancy accepted the challenge and never looked back, publishing *The Valley of Bamiyan*, the first of her books, in 1963.

The Kabul she came to be so fond of in the 1960s and 1970s was a world away from the impoverished city of the early twenty-first century. 'It was a fun city, a wonderful place to be. We had all kinds of restaurants, ski lodges, swimming pools, tennis tournaments – we lived a very hectic life because we were so busy enjoying ourselves doing all these things. But of course what was it that we were enjoying? We were enjoying it because we could relate to it – it was all Western.' This lifestyle was not without its downside, as she realized with hindsight. 'Part of the problem, why we have had this 25 years of chaos, is because the upper elite since the 1920s were so Western-oriented. They turned their backs on the value system of the majority of the people.' Back then, nobody worried about the loss of Afghan culture – 'Everybody was too busy having a good time.' Life was a social whirl, at least for the privileged. 'We used to have dinner parties, dancing all night by a full moon, and then the hard core would stay for sunrise breakfast.' Nancy paused at the memory before continuing, nostalgically, 'I don't know how we got any work done!'

Nancy had first seen the giant Buddhas of Bamiyan in 1963, and had proclaimed them 'one of man's most remarkable achievements'. She had also been lucky enough to see the cave decorations before the

Taliban wielded their hammers and pickaxes. Her comments highlighted how vulnerable the decorations were, even to the gentlest of forces. 'Well, they were always a little patchy. Where the colours remained they were very vivid. Considering their age and the fact that there had been little conservation, they were in very good shape, but the paint was starting to flake off and they needed to be restabilized. Even the flight of a bird going past is enough to flake it off.' Later, in the 1990s, the Mujahedeen – who had a considerable track record of looting from museums and archaeological sites – had used the caves to store arms. It must have been utterly frustrating for a principled woman such as Nancy to see the past pilfered and despoiled in such a brutal and opportunistic way. And as if that was not enough, 'Pakistani dealers were unfortunately using my guidebook as a catalogue, saying get me one of those, or two of those.'

Contrary to public perception in the wake of the attacks, Nancy insisted that when the Taliban first came to power they were 'very, very supportive, but hardliners started to take over the cabinet. A very simple example is that we used to have Radio Afghanistan. All of a sudden, it's Radio Shariat.' Their actions and decrees went beyond even the strictest interpretations of the Koran and, according to Nancy, were far more sinister in intent: 'They were wrapping up things in the mantle of Islam, but really they were trying to wipe out this Afghan identity.' Despite the horrors of the Mujahedeen and the disastrous actions of the Taliban, Nancy still felt positive. 'I think the Afghan character is still here,' she said. 'I always said these Afghans are not extremists. One of the characteristics of their culture is tolerance. I call it an ethnic mosaic, and that is why so many were terribly distraught at this attempt to diminish their Afghan identity.' The international fuss when the Taliban announced their intention to destroy all the country's Buddhist statuary, including the Bamiyan colossi, was 'music to their [the Taliban's] ears. At one level, the bigger fuss that was made to save the Buddhas, the more likely they would be destroyed. So they went up there and they made an example to the world, saying we're in control. This goes on, you know, to September 11.' Despite the cultural loss, Nancy believed that the niches in which the Buddhas had stood retained their mystical allure. For years she had talked of writing an update to her guidebook, and had sought funding to do so. Was this still in her mind? She chuckled. 'I don't know if the old girl can do it.'

Inspired by Nancy, the next day preparations began for the 12-hour drive to Bamiyan. Perhaps no other mission on this trip was as complicated – or as emotional. Crammed into two four-wheel-drive vehicles, the party set off northwest from Kabul for the Hindu Kush mountains, which tower over the city at a height of nearly 8000 metres. After the noise and bustle of Kabul the road grew steadily rougher and more potholed, and each kilometre exacted its toll of bruises.

The province of Bamiyan was severely hit in 1997 by Taliban restrictions on supply routes, which denied its inhabitants essential food and aid. The appalling consequence was that many of the region's 300,000 Hazara inhabitants were forced to eat grass in an attempt to survive in what was known nationally as the Hunger Belt. The Taliban, drawn from the Sunni Pashtuns, saw the Shia Hazaras as *munafaqeen*, or not true to Islam, and so felt at liberty to treat them in this harsh way. Indeed, 80 per cent of Afghans are Sunni – though they belong to the Hanafi sect, the most liberal of the four branches of Sunni Islam – and their relationship with minority sects such as the Shia Muslims and the Sufis is fractious, though in the past there has been a degree of tolerance on both sides. Put simply, the major difference between the two schools of thought is that adherents of Shia Islam believe the true successor to the Prophet Muhammad to be his cousin Ali, a hereditary succession, whereas Sunni Muslims believe that the Caliph Abu Bakr followed Muhammad, according to more democratic principles. The Hazaras, a resilient people who had remained effectively independent until 1893, successfully resisted all attempts by the Taliban to take control of their valley, but their reward was a slow strangulation. Small but strong, the Hazaras bear their history in their faces, their characteristic Mongol features telling of their past when Genghis Khan's invading army interbred with the local Tajik people. For at least a millennium the Bamiyan valley was a major trading post on the Silk Road, linking the West and Central Asia with India and China. It was a crossroads of commerce, culture and religion, which explains how the two giant

Buddhas, the smaller one 38 metres high and the taller one 55 metres, had come to be carved in its northern rockface, probably in the third and fourth centuries, by the Kushans, a dynasty that arose in northern Afghanistan and Gandhara in the first century AD and grew rich through its position on the trade route. The Buddhas were in fact part of a chain of carvings that stretched as far south as Sri Lanka. King Kanishka pioneered Mahayana Buddhism, which gave prominence to the life of the Buddha and for the first time depicted him in human form – though, as Nancy Dupree was quick to point out, 'the Buddha never claimed to be divine'. The coins of the period bear images of Greek, Iranian and Hindu deities, as well as the first figurative representations of Buddha. All we know for certain is that the carvings were there by AD 632, when the Chinese pilgrim Xuanzang visited Bamiyan, and noted the Buddhas' existence along with ten monasteries and over 1000 monks.

It was proving no easy task to reach this remote enclave. Six hours into the journey, disaster struck. A front wheel on one of the vehicles buckled in a particularly jarring pothole, and had to be hammered back into shape in a local village. This was precisely the kind of mishap that could prove catastrophic. Any delay could result in the journey being completed in the dark – a dangerous thing to do in bandit-infested Afghanistan. While a small crowd of men worked on the vehicle Dan contented himself with a little shopping, indulging in a traditional brown Afghan hat and finding a small hut that sold pop-music cassettes. This had been a practice banned under the Taliban, and the vendor confirmed that he had been a refugee in Iran until very recently, when it had felt safe enough to return. Eager to keep up with what was hip on the Afghan music scene, Dan purchased a cassette of a popular young male singer which was to form the soundtrack for the rest of the drive. But even these amusements could not distract from the march of the clock: with a 10 p.m. curfew the team either had to be at Bamiyan by that time or they would have to face a night sleeping at the roadside, with gangs of armed bandits roaming about. By the time the wheel was pronounced usable again the sun had begun its startlingly swift descent. The next few hours would be an anxious time that would test everyone's resolve.

After what seemed an age the vehicles reached the Shiber Pass, where the dust track narrowed still further and small rocks were spat over the edge and into the black void of a 300-metre drop. It would have been hair-raising even in broad daylight and without a deadline. The situation was not improved by the drop in temperature that had occurred with the hour and the altitude, resulting in icy conditions and blustery winds on the steep ascent into the Hindu Kush. The hands of the clock were creeping towards ten, and further vehicle checkpoints were expected. The security men began to advise what to do in case of incoming fire: 'Run back along the road, keeping the vehicle between you and the gunmen.' This was getting serious. But in the nick of time Bamiyan magically appeared, and the trucks drew up at the door of the small lodgings house just five minutes before curfew.

By six the next morning the temperature had risen only slightly, but the light was already absurdly clear and radiant. Determined not to waste a minute, the team dressed quickly and went out on to the plain below the cliff in which the Buddhas had sat for so long. Hazara people were already going about their morning tasks, their scarlet clothes brilliant against the deep hues of the sandstone on, and in, which they lived. Then the huge niches that had enclosed the Buddhas loomed into view. Only then, at the site in which they had stood for over 1500 years, was it possible to begin to grasp the reality behind the shaky footage and the acreage of words that had flowed in lament after their destruction.

The smaller Buddha had been to the right, the larger to the left about a kilometre away. The television shots of the explosions came to mind, the debris and sacred dust billowing into the crisp mountain air, literally a smokescreen for this woeful deed. How much energy must it have taken? This was no fleeting whim: to destroy these two solid figures was a task that absorbed the Taliban soldiers for days. Nearly a year ago to the day, it had taken 25 charges of explosive to finish off the larger Buddha after shelling with artillery and tanks had failed. Men had swung on ropes to lodge dynamite in the crevices of the Buddhas, as the only way to topple them seemed to be to penetrate their very fabric.

This had not in fact been the first attempt to defile the images. In 1998 a Taliban commander attacked the smaller Buddha with explosive charges, and fired rockets at the groin area of the larger one, before depositing two burning tyres on its lip. However, he had been prevented from further desecration by Mullah Omar, who in 1999 issued an edict declaring that the Buddhas should be protected and that illegal digging for artefacts at sites across Afghanistan should cease. It is easy to forget that when the Taliban first seized power they were protective of the Buddhas. Mullah Omar seemed fully aware of the potential income from tourism, and while there was still a chance that the Taliban could somehow coexist with the outside world, he seemed willing to turn his blind eye to such arguably idolatrous icons.

Many, including Nancy Dupree, believe that the turning point came when the Taliban was infiltrated by Arabs such as members of Osama bin Laden's al-Qaeda network, who were absolutely determined in their iconoclasm. According to a report in *The Times* on 24 November 2001, a document had been discovered in a house used by Arab, Chechen and other foreign fighters, which tried to persuade the Taliban to blow up the Buddhas in order to be faithful to the fundamentalist view of Islam, something to which Mullah Omar was keen to remain allied. Even then he might have held firm had it not been for the February 2001 decision of the United Nations, urged on by Bill Clinton, to impose fresh economic sanctions on Afghanistan. At this time only three countries officially recognized Afghanistan, the country was about to enter its third year of devastating drought, and the Taliban had actually been complying with UN demands to eliminate the vast poppy fields in the plains which had fuelled the country's illicit drug trade. It was all too much for Mullah Omar, who declared: 'All we're doing is breaking stones.' And so on 27 February 2001 he gave orders for mass cultural destruction, using these chilling words: 'All the statues in the country should be destroyed because these statues have been used as idols and deities by the non-believers before. They are respected now and may be turned into idols in future, too.' Despite there being no Buddhists left in Afghanistan, and despite the potential revenue from future tourism, their fate appeared to be sealed.

The news came through while a team of Western diplomats were examining the previous decade's destruction at the Kabul Museum, and their reaction was one of deep shock as they had only that morning been reassured about the safety of the most significant heritage in Buddhist statuary. Despite last-minute efforts by a clutch of countries, including Pakistan, Saudi Arabia and the United Arab Emirates, to persuade the Taliban to change their minds, on 1 March 2001 the countrywide process of destruction began, using everything from hatchets to rocket-propelled grenades and artillery. Three days later the Taliban announced that two-thirds of the country's statuary had been destroyed. UNESCO spokesman Koichuro Matsuura accused them of cultural criminality, saying that 'the perpetrators of such an irreparable act would bear a heavy responsibility before the Afghan people and history'; India denounced the purge as 'a regression into medieval barbarism'; and newspapers reported that Houshang Mahboubian, a London dealer in antiquities, had offered £3.4 million for the two giant Buddhas. But it was too late for moral or financial incentives; the edict had been pushed through by Mullah Hason Turabi, the Taliban's Chief of Religious Police. A fog of confusion and misinformation descended while the Taliban moved into Bamiyan. Rumours of their efforts to obliterate the Buddhas circulated throughout the art world until 11 March, when the Taliban reported that the task, under the supervision of Defence Minister Mullah Obaidullah, had been completed to cries of 'Allah Akbar' (Allah is great). Ten days later, the Taliban reportedly slaughtered 100 cows and gave the meat to the poor as an act of atonement for having taken so long to destroy the statues, and the heavy rains and snow that soon followed were interpreted by the Taliban as a sign of approval from Allah.

Rarely can physical absence have created a more powerful sense of spiritual presence. The niches in which the huge Buddhas had stood still defined their existence, and it was impossible not to feel immensely moved by their naked vulnerability, which was not purely metaphorical: the niches themselves had been severely compromised by the explosive assault, and the whole cliff face was in danger of collapse. But, for now, with small birds darting in and out of the artificial caves that had housed the priests who once tended the Buddhas, the scene appeared untarnished by time.

Unable to resist the lure of the site, Dan picked his way over to the remains of the closer Buddha, or at least to those not taken by looters to be sold on the black market. He picked up a large fragment, about the size of a hubcap, and felt suddenly humbled by the reality of what he was holding – a shard of history itself. Some of the larger pieces of the Buddha had been pushed together and covered with tarpaulin to protect them, and Dan went over, curious to see what remained. He lifted the flap of the covering, only to reveal a rifle-propelled grenade nestling amid the rubble. The shock on his face was immediately evident, in self-reproach as much as fear. Was this a booby trap? It was certainly a vivid reminder that this was still a very dangerous country, with mines and ordnance everywhere. One false move, one careless step, could have severe, even fatal, consequences.

A local man, an elder with a grey turban and tapered silver beard, described how terrible it had been when the Taliban arrived. 'As soon as they entered any Hazara home, they asked us to leave. They asked us to put our shoes on, saying we had no right to live here. Then they put all our belongings in the backs of lorries and everything went. People's belongings, animals and money. They were only allowed to wear the shoes, nothing else. I saw it all.' So most of the inhabitants, or at least those who had not already left voluntarily, seem to have been moved out before the explosions began, though a few were said to have been either beaten up or murdered by the Taliban. Despite having moved away to other villages in the region, the Hazaras could still hear the explosions very clearly. And the brutality of the Taliban was related by a local mother, bitter anger still creasing her strong, handsome face. 'We were forced out at gunpoint. They took my child from me and threw him on the ground, hurting his leg and breaking it.' She pointed to her young son, seated on a mat near her. 'They did it on purpose,' she continued. 'We did not know what to do. And when we went for treatment, we did not have enough money to pay. When we finally came back here we took him to hospital, but now he can't move his leg at all.' It seemed an appalling story of casual cruelty, and the poor boy would carry for the rest of his life a reminder of what happened that day in Bamiyan.

One man had actually witnessed the explosions, and even been pressed into helping. Dan talked to him in the coolness of his primitive cave-dwelling. 'When the people had gone away from Bamiyan,' the man said, 'the Taliban could do what they wanted to. The first thing they did was to fire rockets and bombs at the statues, very high-explosive ones, but that didn't work. Later, they brought six lorries of explosives. They forced me and some others to go with them as prisoners. They made us carry the explosives up and down, setting them in various bits of the Buddhas. They were Arab and Pakistani engineers who controlled the explosions. This procedure took 25 days to one month from the first explosion. When the first explosion happened, the whole region was on fire, so strong was its force. It felt like the whole mountains were lifted off the ground, and the whole of Bamiyan was on fire.' It must have been an incredible thing to witness – both horrifying and, in an awful sort of way, compulsive. The man went on to confirm that some of the bigger fragments, and decorations from the niches and the little rooms that led off them, had been taken away in the days following the destruction, bound for the bazaars of Pakistani frontier towns such as Peshawar. 'The pieces were sold – put in vehicles and then sold. I was very angry. We all were, but we were not able to say anything. What could we say? There was nothing we could do about it. They [the Buddhas] were a symbol for Bamiyan, for Afghanistan, and I think, for the world. This was a barbaric act.' It was, indeed, a tragedy of the highest order. What the world had lost was a ground-breaking cultural hybrid, a unique fusion of Greek with classical Indian and Central Asian art.

Despite the daunting 38-metre height of the smaller Buddha, devout pilgrims used to climb a staircase inside the cliff, a sacred route flanked by numerous decorated rooms and chambers, and pass behind the Buddha's head. Dan could not resist the temptation to clamber up and pass his hand over the ornamentation, the details scooped out of the surface to give the subtle appearance of texture and life when viewed from afar. As he examined the empty niche more closely he noticed with excitement that some of the Hellenistic drapery design had survived; over what had been the statue's right shoulder, it would have originally been painted a sacred blue, in contrast to the deep red of the larger Buddha's attire. In fact, the surfaces of both statues would have been brilliantly coloured and the niches covered in detailed paintings, very different in appearance from the crumbling sandstone that remained. It was hard to imagine that at its peak, over 1500 years earlier, the whole cliff face would have been painted with roof beams, doorways and windows, an incredible man-made mega-structure making up a thriving, polychromatic monastery. Now the small Buddha possessed a ghost-like quality.

It was time to investigate inside. On the east side of the niche, through a now half-buried doorway, was the rugged, precarious staircase that led pilgrims to a chamber or sanctuary. Here there were still some magnificent remnants of the paintings that had adorned its walls. Rows of Buddhas and bodhisattvas (Buddhas-to-be) were depicted sitting majestically in their dark, purplish robes, offering some idea of lost glories. They had all had their faces hacked off, but Nancy Dupree's book confirmed that this had been so for a long time – probably the act of some early Muslims. The technique used to prepare the walls was like that for the surface decoration of the carved Buddha: a mixture of mud and straw was applied, followed by a coat of fine plaster made from gypsum – a technique still used in Afghan village houses. Such echoes spoke of the vitality that would have informed these vestibules and grottoes, and of the wealth of veneration that would have brought the walls and ceilings alive. Higher up, past walls cracked by the blasting, other cells gave hints of their former glories in patches of flaking green or blue. But some of the vast number of cells and caves had not fared so well, with layers of soot and grime that had accumulated over the centuries concealing the ancient Buddhist artwork. In her guidebook Nancy Dupree talked of seeing elephants, exotic birds, winged horses, wild boar and the ranks of Buddhas and bodhisattvas, decorated in a palette of burnt sienna, green, lapis-lazuli blue and yellow ochre.

By this point the air was becoming very thin, and it was impossible to know to what degree the integrity of the stairs and their supporting structures had been compromised by the Taliban's dynamite. It was heavy going, and risky, but after a final short scramble there was the entrance to the gallery which until only a year before had passed behind the Buddha's head. This was as far as it was possible to go; since the destruction visitors could no longer reach the other side and its labyrinth of cells and sanctuaries. Light-headed and overwhelmed, trapped between exhilaration and despair, the team looked out over the Bamiyan plain from the Buddha's perspective – a shockingly wide and all-encompassing vision offered by this sacred vantage point. Suddenly the sense of loss was acute, the folly of man ghastly. As Nancy Dupree had maintained, the site still radiated a powerful sense of mysticism, undiminished by bombs, rockets and explosions, but it spoke, too, of other forces that could be brought to bear in the name of religion. For everyone, but for Dan in particular, this was without doubt one of life's most moving experiences. The anger would ferment, but the primary emotion was of regret and mourning for the loss. 'Poor benighted fools,' Dan muttered into the thin, cool air.

The return journey to Kabul was quiet in every sense. The Taliban had sought justification for their iconoclasm and social repression in the scriptures of the Koran, the word of God as revealed to the Prophet Muhammad, and in the Hadeeth, Muhammad's own utterances. Perhaps a visit to a crowded Kabul mosque might help to track down the relevant passages. Here the mullah, himself dismayed by the Taliban's destruction in the name of God, drew attention to the following passage, translated from the Arabic, from Sura 22, Pilgrimage (al-Hajj) of the Koran: 'Guard yourself against the filth of idols, and avoid the utterance of falsehoods. Dedicate yourselves to God, and serve none besides Him. The man who serves other deities besides God is like him who falls from heaven and is snatched by the birds or carried away by the wind to some far-off region. Even such is he.' Taken literally, the sentiment obviously tallied with the second of the Ten Commandments from Exodus 20 of the Old Testament – 'Thou shalt not make unto thee any graven image' – yet its application in Afghanistan had been against objects that were no longer worshipped, as even Mullah Omar had admitted. The Bamiyan Buddhas, like the statuary in the Kabul Museum, were cultural objects, to be revered for historical and aesthetic reasons rather than religious ones.

On the issue of female modesty, these words come from the Koran's Book of Light 24:31.

And say to the believing women that they should lower their gaze and guard their modesty; that they should not display their beauty and ornaments except what (must ordinarily) appear thereof; that they should draw their veils over their bosoms and not display their beauty except to their husbands, their fathers, their husband's fathers, their sons, their husband's sons, their brothers or their brothers' sons, or their sisters' sons, or their women, or the slaves whom their right hands possess, or male servants free of physical needs, or small children who have no sense of the shame of sex; and that they should not strike their feet in order to draw attention to their hidden ornaments …

The application of seventh-century values and attitudes to late twentieth-century societies could never be easy, and the difference between modesty and invisibility is wide. In other Islamic societies, numerous 'secondary laws' have been handed down by clergy and judges over the years to deal with modern situations not addressed in the Koran, but the Taliban's resistance to progressive thought rendered the Afghan people cruelly muted, both culturally and personally.

In a desire to explore further the aspects of life affected during the Taliban's rule, the team went out on to the streets of Kabul in search of some vanity. Perhaps the most obvious area of living representation suppressed by the religious police was portrait photography. This seemingly innocuous service had been chased from the streets, but had now crept back into business as enterprising photographers re-established their pavement studios. So Dan perched himself on a seat and posed for what until recently had been seen as a sacrilegious act. With one hand the photographer held up a piece of cardboard to ward off the glare of the sun, and with the other he removed the cap from what was essentially a pinhole camera to allow in a little light, then quickly replaced it. After this he dipped the photographic paper in a tray of chemicals, then pressed it between sheets of cloth to dry and develop. The result was eerie – three striking images of Dan resembling the austere images of the late nineteenth century in their ghostly monochrome. It was photography laid bare, as magical and innocent a creation of an image as one could hope for.

Despite the relative comforts of the guesthouse, it was perhaps time to address the matter of personal grooming. A shave was in order, and it did not take long to chance upon a barber. Hair had been one area over which the Taliban had imposed considerable restraints: a man's beard was supposed to be the length of his fist, and failure to comply with this diktat had severe consequences. But since the fall of the Taliban in November 2001 hairdressing establishments had started to open up again. So Dan entered a reassuringly busy example, redolent with the smell of cheap cologne familiar from such premises the world over, and took to the red leather chair. Before he could utter a word of caution he had been lathered up by an eager young attendant, who then unfolded a lethal-looking cut-throat razor. Admirably stoical in his submission, within a couple of minutes Dan was shorn of a couple of days' stubble. After a delicate trim of the nostril hairs, it was time for a haircut. Rejecting the 1970s'-style coiffure suggested by the barber from a faded promotional photograph on the wall above the mirror – perhaps the Taliban had had a point about American haircuts – Dan settled for a tidying trim.

Further down the busy street was a shop displaying an array of Afghan jackets, hippy-looking sheepskin coats with thick, shaggy fur trims, such as had not been seen in the West for decades – since the era of the barber's photos, to be exact. And hanging beyond the jackets was something to excite any seeker of original merchandise: a series of hand-woven Afghan carpets, which on closer inspection were not perhaps as traditional as had first appeared. Integrated into the traditional geometric patterns were tanks, 50-calibre Russian machine-guns and rocket-propelled grenade launchers – an extraordinary cultural representation of the country's recent history. The shop contained a remarkable selection of rugs and carpets, all displaying an infinite variety of military hardware, nationalistic rhetoric, and maps of the country, mainly to celebrate the so-called victory over the Soviet forces. One particularly eye-catching design used AK47 assault rifles as minor details, alongside ranks of armoured personnel carriers and mosques arrayed in pleasing geometric formation. What used to be the template for Sufi symbolism and Islamic art was now used to celebrate military might and human triumph. This was belligerent imagery beautifully executed, and the way in which the weapons and armoured vehicles had been reduced to abstract forms epitomized something of contemporary Afghan existence, in which the gun was venerated almost as much as more traditional emblems.

Browsing over, the next stop was Ghazni, south of Kabul. After the uncertainties of Kabul and Bamiyan, there was little doubt here: the south was Taliban territory, its heartland, and already there had been rumours of re-emerging splinter factions and cells of resistance. While the sun burned more fiercely than ever, the attitude of the local people became cooler to the point of hostility. This was the true remnant of the decades of conflict, and specifically the last few months of bombing, and to Westerners it felt uncomfortable.

Located on the Kabul–Kandahar trade route on a high plateau beside the Ghazni River, the city of Ghazni, 130 kilometres southwest of Kabul, revolves around a major market for sheep and wool – the famed Afghan sheepskin coats hail from its workshops. Its strategic position meant it had become a military target during the Russian war. Centuries earlier, from 994 to 1160, it had been the powerful capital of the Ghaznavid Empire, which encompassed much of northern India, Persia and Central Asia, stretching from the Tigris to the Ganges. It was destroyed by Genghis Khan in 1221, but prior to that many sorties into India were launched from the city, resulting in the spread of Islam. The question in everyone's mind concerned the condition of Ghazni's giant minarets, built by Sultan Masud (1099–1114) and Bahram Shah (1118–52), which had supposedly served as models for the enigmatic, isolated minaret of Jam in a valley to the east of Herat in the northwest of the country. They were all that remained of a sophisticated mosque complex that had once stood at the heart of ancient Ghazni. But in what state were they standing now – if at all?

The minarets first appeared through the haze of a sandstorm. Worryingly, they appeared to be surrounded by an ex-Taliban military camp. Groups of men with AK47 assault rifles hung around the centuries-old structures, their militaristic apparel incongruous against the minarets' decorated brickwork. These were dangerous times to be outside Kabul and, well-intentioned though the team's mission was, this was not necessarily apparent to local militia, intent on rooting out what they perceived as the enemy and assuming control once more. Indeed, a few days earlier a US helicopter had been shot down in a battle being waged around neighbouring Gardez. So both parties exchanged suspicious glances and there was no option but to remain at a safe distance.

The minarets – one of which had been reduced to about half its original size, the top half of the cylindrical and fluted shaft having fallen off – had been damaged during the war against the Russians, and they were still in the middle of a war zone. All around lay evidence of this – not only burnt-out tanks, armoured personnel carriers and field guns, but also ominously active and undamaged vehicles. The Americans had bombed very close to the site in their efforts to remove the Taliban, and the minarets seemed to have been incredibly lucky – though for how much longer was questionable. Like the minaret at Jam, they remained in a state of near-collapse as looters had in recent times undermined their foundations in their frenzied search for treasures. Dr Mohammad Popal, the chancellor of Kabul University, had observed that looters were 'an organized Mafia' who were now the biggest threat to Afghan culture, since the relative peace in the country made it easier for thieves to operate in remote regions such as these. If the bombs did not get the historic sites, then the looters would. The deprivations of war had rendered so many Afghans homeless and hungry that the chance of earning a few dollars through digging was not to be passed up, despite the jeopardy in which it put the country's cultural heritage. It was entirely understandable, but no less tragic for it.

In their way the minarets had been pioneering structures, the first on such a scale in Afghanistan. Their intricate geometric decoration was carried out in moulded brick, and the brickwork was more than merely structural and included epigraphic friezes in square kufic and Noshki script, as well as panels of floral designs. Ghaznavid construction of this kind showed how Islamic architecture integrated design and decoration to make it intrinsic to a holy building rather than merely aesthetic, with the detail absorbed into its very fabric. The lower shaft of the damaged minaret, jagged as a broken tooth, had an eight-pointed star base, with Masud's name inscribed in kufic script at the top of the shaft. The use of fragile bricks, combined with the severe frosts experienced in the region, had always presented a considerable problem of preservation even before the threat of bombs and looters' spades. It was a miracle that such proud, beautiful architectural monuments were still standing, even in a dilapidated state, given their position at a location of continued strategic and military significance. However, it was evident that, unless international aid and expertise were applied soon, these lonely masterpieces, and their more spectacular relation in Jam, would soon submit to the ravages of time and conflict.

The journey back to Kabul was broken at a vast, shimmering lake lying among a cluster of rugged hills. With the snow-capped mountains of the north in the far distance, it felt as timeless and unspoilt as Alexander the Great would have found it when he and his army marched through these lands over 2000 years ago. It was hard to reconcile such serene beauty with the savagery of war that had threatened it on so many occasions, and so recently. Suddenly the birdsong was interrupted by the distant drone of a helicopter, which grew ever louder until an American Black Hawk rose dramatically from behind a mountain, literally throwing a dark shadow on this oasis. Here was the reality, that with such an idyll went the harsh machinations of human strife and conflict; Afghanistan remained caught in the brutal aftermath of the bombing – not at war, but certainly far from anyone's notion of peace.

The last remaining mystery of Afghanistan's lost treasures is probably the most perplexing. The Bactrian gold, a hoard of 26,000 gold artefacts, was unearthed in northern Afghanistan by a Russian archaeologist, Victor Sarianidi, in 1978, and was so called after the ancient name for this region. One of the greatest archaeological finds the world has ever known, it was comparable with Howard Carter's discovery of the tomb of Tutankhamen in 1922. The first-century AD collection included intricate ancient Iranian and Kushan ornaments, statues of creatures and goddesses, necklaces, dress ornaments, pendants, hairpins, buckles and even a crown set with pearls and turquoises. This fabulous wealth of treasures, its unique fusion of classical and Oriental influences so characteristic of Afghanistan, was believed to be the funerary goods of wealthy tribal elders at the royal burial site known as Tillya Tepe or the Golden Mound. There had been nothing conspicuous about the tomb, which is why it had survived so long without being discovered or looted.

Formerly kept at the Kabul Museum, the hoard had been moved to a safer storage place by 1991, and it was now rumoured to be in secure but secret storage elsewhere in Kabul – evidence pointed to it being in the vaults of the presidential palace and the adjoining National Bank. There were other alarming theories, though. Ibrahim Stwodah, the General Director of Kabul University Libraries from 1970 to 1978, had heard whispers that the artefacts had been moved to Russia by the Soviets. More disturbingly, others claimed that the Taliban had offered the hoard to their sponsor, Osama bin Laden, as collateral and, according to claims heard by Robert Kluyver of the Society for the Preservation of Afghanistan's Cultural Heritage, bin Laden had arranged for it to be smuggled across the mountains to Pakistan to be sold. Yet others asserted that the Taliban had destroyed the treasures. The team was hoping to be able to track down this elusive collection of riches and confirm for the Afghan nation, and the world, that it was still in existence and safe. But it would not be easy. Nancy Dupree had been very circumspect about its location: 'I agree with the members of the present government, that we keep a very low profile on it. You lose things you don't have to just because you can't keep your mouth shut.' And even she had never set eyes on the collection.

Wasey Ferouzi, Director of the Archaeology Centre of the Academy of Science, was polite and welcoming, but he laughed quietly when asked where the Bactrian gold was and said that he could not reveal this. He added that it had last been seen in 1999 by a delegation of archaeologists, who had confirmed that at that time the collection seemed to be intact. Since then no one had, to his knowledge, seen it, or was in a position to state firmly that it had survived both the bombing and the Taliban. When Dan asked him if it was in the vaults of the presidential palace or the National Bank, or at the Ministry of Culture,

Mr Ferouzi would not be drawn, saying only that it was indeed in one of those places but he could not reveal exactly where, due to the security situation in Afghanistan. This seemed eminently reasonable, even if it did not exactly shed light on the situation.

Rumours and counter-rumours abounded. It was said that former president Najibullah had sealed the hoard in seven trunks and hidden them in a vault carved out of the rock underneath the presidential palace. The vault itself was protected by a steel gate secured by seven locks, with keys held by seven people dispersed throughout the world. At least three of the keyholders, including Najibullah, had subsequently died. Another popular fable circulating in the bazaars and coffee shops of Kabul was that the Russians had a duplicate set of all seven keys; in a slight variation, some sources asserted that renegade Soviet troops had broken into the vault in the final hours before Kabul was abandoned, and replaced most of the treasure with fakes. Other reports claimed that the legendary guerrilla commander and former Defence Minister with effective control of Kabul, the late Ahmed Shah Massoud, who had resisted first the Soviets and then the Taliban for years, had confirmed that the treasure was in the presidential palace basement in a safe with a steel gate, but also that the Taliban had got control of it. There was one other possible suspect, if in fact the gold turned out to be missing. Gulbadin Hekmatyar had been appointed Prime Minister in 1992 by President Burhannudin Rabbini. A cynical and savage opportunist, Hekmatyar, supported by the Pakistani authorities, turned against the government in early 1994 after failing to acquire sole and supreme power. After waging terrible campaigns against Kabul he was brought back into the fold in June 1996 to counter the Taliban, and was once more appointed Prime Minister. But despite his efforts the Taliban gained control of Kabul, and Hekmatyar escaped to Tehran. He certainly had the opportunity and the lack of principles, if not the resources, to acquire the gold during his time as Prime Minister, and certainly if it was missing he would have to be a prime suspect.

Carla Grissman, a distinguished art historian and member of the Society for the Preservation of Afghanistan's Cultural Heritage, spent many years documenting the country's disappearing cultural history, particularly after the looting of the Kabul Museum in the early 1990s by the Mujahedeen, and has kept a close eye on all the claims and rumours concerning the Bactrian gold, which she helped to catalogue. According to Grissman, several Afghan governments tried to blow up the vault in the presidential palace but, as far as she knew, without success – testament, perhaps, to the workmanship of the German company that built the vault in the 1960s. Grissman handled the objects herself, back in 1978, just after their discovery. She recalled how very close to tears everyone in the room had become, with the Afghans feeling that this was incontrovertible evidence that theirs was a civilized country. The whole affair was taking on the trappings of a fairytale.

The next stage was to have a meeting with the civil servant in charge of Interim Affairs, to see if the administration could be persuaded to allow cameras into the presidential palace. Prime Minister Karzai was to be personally consulted, which inevitably meant that nothing would happen quickly. The obligatory tea was served, and after several hours in the small ministry office word came back that the team was to be allowed into the presidential compound. This was very promising – the more so as previous journalists had failed to get even this far. The gates to the palace were heavily guarded and the search for arms was thorough – even the security man from the ministry was frisked, an indication that no one was yet to be trusted.

Once inside, the team was taken to what was known as the Palace of the Heart's Desire, a neo-classical villa built in the early twentieth century by an English architect, pleasing to the eye but, it soon became apparent, not the building with the vaults. Then, inside the main presidential palace, and tantalizingly close to the possible site of the hoard, an argument broke out among the Afghan entourage. It seemed that entering this building was a step too far. Further attempts at negotiation failed as the man from the ministry remained firm and the team was politely ushered from the building, having probably been closer to the Bactrian gold than any Westerners for many years. Emotions were mixed: there was disappointment at having got so near and yet having failed to confirm the continued safe storage of the treasure; but at the same time understanding of the Afghans' wariness even to admit its existence in a country still too unstable to allow the location of such tempting artefacts to be identified. Without any firm evidence, it was only possible to hope that the hoard remained intact; certainly there was nothing other than unsubstantiated rumour to suggest that it had been looted or taken away. The Russians had tried to smash through the concrete surrounding the vault and there was reportedly a large hole to prove it, but if they had been unable to get in the chances were that the Afghans too had been unsuccessful. All that could be hoped was that one day circumstances in Afghanistan would be stable enough for a major operation to be mounted to open the vaults, and reveal once more to the world the golden treasures of the country's cultural heritage.

Thwarted in that quest, the team was determined to see at least one item of beauty that had evaded capture by the Taliban, though, for security reasons, it was clearly tricky to get to see any of Afghanistan's greatest riches. After patient yet persistent negotiation at the Ministry of Information and Culture, a decrepit-looking place in the centre of Kabul, the authorities agreed to produce one heroically saved item from the Kabul Museum. This was to be the first time it had been shown to the outside world since the Taliban began its purge over a year before. The storage rooms contained over 200 crates that had been evacuated from the museum to the Kabul Hotel before arriving at the ministry. Unfortunately, the Taliban had managed to breach the rooms and smash certain items. Dr Massoudi, the museum director, explained that the museum staff had been unable to keep the location secret from the Taliban, who had smashed the locks, entered and broken numerous pieces. Mr Shiraz, a museum employee who had been forced to witness the brutality, had been distraught. 'When they broke these pieces I felt faint, I was sick at what I saw, as they destroyed the artefacts we had been preserving. All these things were our heritage and history,' he continued, 'yet in front of us, they were destroying it with hammers.' Mr Shiraz explained that he and his colleagues had always believed that the Taliban would fall sooner rather than later, which was why they had always tried to defy them in cunning ways. This drive to prolong the process as much as possible, in the hope that even a few artefacts might be preserved, was heroic, displaying more than anything the passion the Afghan people feel for their culture and history. Boxes of carefully gathered shards were labelled 'Items broken by the Taliban', and put aside for future restoration. With time and money they could once again be more than the sum of their parts.

It seemed amazing that anything might have escaped the Taliban's hammers, but Dr Massoudi moved on to show Dan an incredible survival: a Roman-style wine bowl dating from the second century AD, excavated in Kunduz in 1965. It depicted a wonderful Bacchanalian scene, with exotic bare-breasted dancing girls handing out drinks to louche reclining men, lascivious musicians regaling them with no doubt lusty tunes, and general naked frolicking. The scenario on all four panels of the bowl was one of decadence and indulgence, and therefore a particularly miraculous survival. How had the museum staff managed to fool the Taliban? With a bit of quick improvised thinking, apparently, and feinting. 'We covered the images with cotton wool, paper and Sellotape,' said Mr Shiraz, 'and diverted the Taliban's attention to the bottom of the bowl, claiming there were no images of living beings on it. Had the Taliban noticed the erotic imagery,' he went on, 'they would have smashed it instantly.' It was a brave and clever deception, and showed the true dedication of the museum staff to their objects, even at great personal risk. The world owes them a debt of gratitude.

It was the eve of the Islamic New Year, and there could perhaps be no more uplifting way to conclude the trip than to share in its celebration. The Taliban proscription of religious chant and ceremony had affected no group more than the devotees of Sufism, *Tasawwuf* in Arabic, the branch of Islam that originated in Central Asia and Persia and celebrates the spiritual mysticism of the Koran rather than its more prosaic laws and teachings. The main two schools of Sufism in Afghanistan are the Naqshbandiyah and the Qaderiyah, but all the faiths are guided by a Sheikh, who is like a Hindu Sadhu or guru and sometimes achieves the status of a saint. This was the first time the Afghan Sufis had been able to practise their traditional rituals since the Taliban's rise to power.

Sufi means 'wool' in Arabic, and refers to the rough woollen coats traditionally worn by its adherents, who express their devotion to Islam through music, movement, chanting and shaking in order to get closer to God by stripping away the rational. They draw on many spiritual sources and embrace all the techniques that lead to enlightenment – including dancing, controlled breathing and chest-beating, mortification of the flesh, contemplation and meditation. Sufis also believe in tolerance as a means of gradually bringing people to a greater spiritual awareness. Through their theology they map the stages of a mystical quest for the ultimate goal of unity with God. That quest can be ecstatic, emotional and deeply profound. Ancient Sufi poems often take the superficial form of a love story, relating the agony of separation from the Beloved and the joy of finding Him, these romantic narratives serving as metaphors for the spiritual search for enlightenment. In the poems the Divine is the man and the seeker the woman, whose identity merges with that of her lover as unity is achieved. Worldly concerns are gradually discarded and renounced in the search for mystic realization, a journey referred to as the path or *tariqah*. It is hard to imagine anything the Taliban would detest more, especially as the tombs of Sufi saints are objects of veneration and perceived as centres of spiritual power.

Bright flags and religious banners festooned the Sufis' houses as they gathered outside for prayer. The Sheikh, Mir Ghulam Sarwar Quadary, delivered a volley of plaintive, lilting chants, a *zikr* or remembrance of God, and the young men grouped around him began to accompany his voice with their own rhythmic chants and movements. Although a little self-conscious at first, they quickly forgot their audience. As they rocked with intense fervour to the sheikh's lead, their guttural syncopation and controlled breathing were formidable to behold, and not a little fearsome in their primal display of raw emotion.

A man who introduced himself as Hasibulla and said he worked at the Interior Ministry confided, 'In the five years that the Taliban were here, we have not seen a day like this, but today is a day of honour. We have come to see our people and our country, and this is a place of happiness for us.' The street was becoming busy with eager families, men and burkha-less women together, arriving to worship. A woman called Gulmakai shared her thoughts on the occasion: 'We are very happy that we are allowed to work, and are free now to celebrate New Year in peace,' she said excitedly. There was little to say, beyond an acknowledgement that the passing of periods of adversity, something with which Afghanistan is all too familiar, brings releases such as this.

In the candlelit interior of one of the houses a group of men were sitting cross-legged in a circle while one of their number played a *tambur*, a long-necked stringed instrument like a lute, and another pounded *doira* – hand drums – with his palms and fingers. Strains of devotional music drifted through the air as the men immersed themselves in the ritual, gently swaying to the heady lilt of the tune. In this atmosphere there was one white-bearded elder to whom all eyes were irresistibly drawn. Shaking his head slowly to the beat he was completely mesmerized as he advanced along his *tariqah*, and as he lost himself within his trance tears ran from his tightly closed eyes. This was what had sustained these durable people through hardship and repression: the belief that one day they would be able to commune with their God in this intimate, wonderful manner. And, ultimately, this was proof that culture, in all its various forms, could not be vanquished, however harsh the measures meted out by any regime. Certainly, in the case of the Taliban the destruction of the Buddhas had been catastrophic for the world, and the looting of Afghanistan's outlying archaeological sites was an ongoing disaster, as it was in so many impoverished countries with rich histories of ancient civilizations; yet this proud nation of disparate tribes and sects was too enmeshed in its history and traditions not to retain its sense of cultural identity, even in the face of regional political fragmentation. It was not invincible, but it would take more than the barbarous edicts and beatings of the Taliban or the callous, organized pillage of the Mujahedeen to silence Afghanistan's unique culture and heritage.

'Kill a man's cultural history and you bury him twice,' wrote journalist and author Rosemary Righter in 2001 as news filtered through of the imminent destruction of the Buddhas. While looters continue to rape the remote landscapes of Afghanistan, using the trade routes established by drug smugglers in this poppy-rich land, the lifeblood of this nation, orphaned by bloody conflict to paraphrase former UN Secretary General Boutros Boutros-Gali, is being slowly drained away. Its strategic significance, the key to its importance in ancient times, has tragically become its Achilles heel. The destruction of the Buddhas, and even the fate of the contents of the Kabul Museum, seized the headlines but the widespread smaller acts of illegal excavation that go on unnoticed remove for future generations, in Afghanistan and outside, an understanding and appreciation of the great peoples that came together in this land. It would be wrong, therefore, to take the actions of the Taliban or the Mujahedeen out of context, to ascribe exceptional degrees of evil to individuals or groups – in 1885, for example, a fifteenth-century mosque in Herat was destroyed by the British, and in 1843 they blew up the old casbah in Kabul. There are always reasons, but there are never excuses.

Returning to the UK via Pakistan, it was easy to take comfort from the re-emergence of life in Afghanistan, from the Sufis' reawakened celebrations, the plans to renovate the Kabul Museum – or even the opportunity to shave or have one's photograph taken. The Culture Minister, Dr Sayed Taheen, has declared, 'Each time after destruction our people have managed to survive, and to revive what they lost. I'm sure we'll do it once more.' While these are worthy sentiments, what had also become clear – and it was something that would be borne out, with more public consequences, in Iraq in 2003 – was that 'post-conflict' could be far more deadly and destabilizing than conflict itself. In his 2003 book *Bush At War*, which looked at the first 100 days after 9/11, veteran American journalist Bob Woodward reported that just prior to the bombing of Afghanistan Bush asked his war cabinet: 'Who will run the country?' 'We should have thought of that,' was the alleged response of Condoleeza Rice, National Security Advisor to the President. The Western-trained and -funded Mujahedeen had grown bitter when abandoned by the West at the end of the Russian war, and the consequences were appalling for Afghanistan and its people. Once again, following the ousting of the Taliban in November 2001, the West has been judged by many to have neglected to plan for the aftermath, despite constant promises to the contrary. This is the origin of Boutros Boutros-Gali's remark about Afghanistan being orphaned: once the high drama of intense military engagement is perceived to be over, the West looks to new distractions and abandons the previously favoured child to its own devices. Devices which, in so many cases, are malevolent and devastating.

The Bamiyan Buddhas have been the focus of much international attention since their demise on 11 March 2002. Many ideas about what to do with the empty niches have been put forward: some want to see them rebuilt using the Greek restoration process of anastylosis, while others call for the niches to be left symbolically empty and the remaining fragments to be displayed in a new museum in the Bamiyan valley. A Japanese team of designers has even suggested employing a display of lasers to bring the Buddhas back to virtual life, as happened with the 'Tribute in Light' display at the Ground Zero site in New York. More importantly, work is under way to reinforce the now structurally compromised niches. Putting the Buddhas back in the cavities would help to support them, but it seems that for the foreseeable future the aim is stabilization. The frescoes in the caves are being conserved by teams of experts, and the local Hazara people are being moved out of them in an attempt to preserve what is left. They are being given land – harsh, mostly barren land, admittedly, but appreciated by the Hazaras after their persecution at the hands of the Mujahedeen and the Taliban. Elsewhere, though, the minarets at Ghazni remain highly vulnerable in a region heavily mined and full of gangs of bandits, and families with lethal cultural weapons such as spades and pickaxes. To much of the world, the war in Afghanistan is over; in truth, it has barely scratched the surface. To quote from the final couplet of Bertoldt Brecht's play *The Resistible Rise of Arturo Ui*, 'The bastard son is dead, but the bitch is still on heat.' Too bad, then; an impatient world, still traumatized by the 9/11 tragedy, had in late 2002 turned its attentions to the Middle East, to an old familiar foe.

CHAPTER TWO

THE LOST CITIES OF IRAQ

'WHEN YOU RETURN, I want you to come back and see me, and tell me just how beautiful my country is,' said Dr Mudhafar Amin, Head of the Iraqi Interest Section at the Jordanian Embassy in London. The aim of our projected visit was to see the treasures of ancient Mesopotamia, of the great empires of the Assyrians, Babylonians and Sumerians, before the imminent attack by American and British forces intent on discovering Saddam's alleged weapons of mass destruction and possibly ousting the regime. We wanted to find out what the Iraqis felt about their immensely important cultural and archaeological heritage, and to what extent it defined their national identity. We had read of the vulnerability of Iraq's historic sites during the first Gulf War of 1991, and were anxious to show the world the devastation that could take place in this unique country, the cultural mother of all other nations.

All we needed was the Iraqi government to give its blessing to our project. After our return, *The Times* was to allege that we had been invited to make the programme by the Iraqis. But although it is standard procedure when dealing with totalitarian regimes for official permission to be granted in the form of a state invitation, it was in fact the BBC that first approached the Iraqi authorities. It took two months for a reply to arrive. Now at last our visas had been issued and a letter of introduction in Arabic supplied. Entering Saddam's Iraq seemed the easiest thing in the world, we thought. It was the last time we were to entertain that feeling.

A few weeks later, on 12 November 2002, we flew into Saddam International Airport from Amman in Jordan. As we stepped out of the plane, the first sight to greet us was the slogan 'Down USA' painted on the floor of the walkway. Rumours had been rife that morning of a possible rejection by the Iraqi government of UN Resolution 1441, which called for the country to surrender its weapons of mass destruction. With demands for *baksheesh* ringing in our ears from the customs officers, soldiers, porters and airport officials, we loaded our bags into the two large vehicles waiting for us and headed for Baghdad itself.

We were booked into the Al Rasheed Hotel, on the west bank of the Tigris. As we drove through the airport, and then along the deserted highway to the city centre, large neon signs proclaimed ominously of the Al Rasheed: 'It is more than a hotel.' Later, in the northern city of Mosul, we saw a sign atop a decaying 1960s' concrete block for a central hotel which prided itself on 'A Mixed Reception'. The Al Rasheed had been for many years the choice of the world's media, their presence only outnumbered by the eavesdroppers who lingered in its marble foyer under airbrushed portraits of Saddam. The hotel's other notable feature was the mosaic of George Bush senior that graced its threshold. Gap-toothed and leering, it bore the legend 'Bush is Criminal', and had been designed by a leading Iraqi artist, Leila Attar. During our time there we were told by more than one Iraqi that she had been killed by the Americans in retaliation. I found this hard to believe, but back in England the newspaper archives revealed that she had indeed died in June 1993 when President Bill Clinton, in the belief that Saddam had planned the assassination of Bush senior when he visited Kuwait in April that year, ordered 23 missile strikes against an Iraqi GID defence complex in the prosperous Baghdad suburb where Attar lived. She died, along with her husband and maid, when a stray bomb hit her house.

Times had been hard, even for the Al Rasheed. The economic sanctions of the previous decade had stripped bare the concept of luxury, and the rooms, in their 1970s' Cold War splendour, spoke of a different time and clientele. We had been warned that our rooms were likely to be bugged, particularly on the lower floors – we were on the second – and there were highly visible cameras in the corridors, as well as a bellboy on each landing. In the rooms themselves, guests had only to pick up the phone to hear the feedback from the microphone within it. We had to take care with everything we said. But despite our unease, and the confirmation that Saddam had indeed rejected the UN resolution, the next few days promised the intensity of Baghdad allied with, we hoped, our first forays into the desert and perhaps a glimpse of the wondrous arched vault of Ctesiphon. Through the Press Centre we were assigned Thaer, a gentle if worried-looking journalist who was to be our government minder and fixer. His task was to make sure we did not film anything that could be construed as detrimental to the image of the Iraqi government or people. And so, accompanied by Thaer and our driver Khalil, a walrus of a man already devoted to our as yet unintelligible mission, we set off in the obligatory four-wheel-drive GMC to try to find the pulse of this sprawling, intriguing metropolis.

Known to Arabs as the City of Peace, Baghdad was founded by Mansur, the second Abbasid caliph, who ruled from 770 to 775 AD. On the west bank of the Tigris he created what is known as the Round City, famed for its double brick walls, moat and towering inner wall. Four major radial roads led out through processional gates, and at the centre was the caliph's palace, distinguished by its green dome. The famous Baghdad of the *Arabian Nights* is the one of Harun al-Rashid, the fifth caliph, who made it one of the most opulent, progressive cities in the world, at the centre of commercial and intellectual life in the Middle East. After Harun's fall the Round City was destroyed and life moved to the east bank. Centuries of sack and ruin followed, interspersed with periods of stability and regrowth. The Mongols under Genghis Khan's son Hulagu and later his descendant Tamurlane, then the Persians and finally the Ottoman Turks took control, the latter remaining in possession of Baghdad for 400 years until World War I.

Great cities are often defined by great rivers and Baghdad is no exception, with the Tigris a constant presence, cutting a swathe through the urban sprawl. Much of today's Baghdad, which grew enormously in the late twentieth century, is of a reasonably standard, modern Middle Eastern design, though significant examples of its rich architectural heritage remain, such as the traditional houses with their splendid overhanging balconies known as *shenashil*. During the Ottoman era there was little urban planning, and most of the streets were narrow lanes and alleys that met in haphazard fashion. While Sa'doun Street has become the major thoroughfare, al-Rashid Street, in the heart of the city, still retained the bustle of the markets, and its colonnaded splendour offered an echo of past glories. Constructed in 1916 and originally named al-Shara al-Jadid, or New Street, it was paved by the British the following year after they took the city from the Turks. Off this elegant thoroughfare we visited the long-established book market on al-Mutanabi Street in search of literary treasures. There all manner of traders bring their wares to spread out on the pavements and road, though almost nothing we saw was published after 1990. The range was vast, from old official tourist guides and lush photographic records to a 1980s' Argos catalogue and an even earlier *Shoot!* annual. The guides offered a poignant glimpse of an Iraqi international identity long disappeared. 'Who else can fly you from Baghdad to the USA with no change of plane? No one,' proudly proclaimed Pan-Am. One picture showed a jumbo jet flying over the vaulted roof at Ctesiphon, neatly capturing the marriage of ancient and modern that in those days Iraq was so keen to promote.

The book street was only one of Baghdad's myriad open-air markets, and we were to discover the intense sensual experiences of its others, including the spice market and the animal market, where one man in particular, obviously a local favourite, drew crowds by placing scorpions in his mouth. This side of social interaction is perhaps the last to disappear, but also often the first to reappear, on the streets of a war-torn city. On sale in the various food markets (which also offered a nifty line in poisons), were gargantuan carp from the Tigris which flapped in shallow bowls, ready to be selected and then killed and gutted on the spot, fresh cheeses brought into the city by farmers, and bundles of vivid green herbs and leaves. There was little doubt of the region's vast agricultural resources, despite the economic sanctions that had strangled much of its infrastructure.

Before venturing into the desert to see the remains of ancient civilizations we decided to visit a couple of sites that spoke of more recent history. It is no secret that Saddam Hussein, despite the human rights abuses and murders committed by his regime, was an enthusiast for the heritage of Iraq and ensured that money was spent on conservation and on the perpetuation of its culture. His principal motivation was to ensure that he took what he saw as his rightful place in the pantheon of the region's great leaders, especially Nebuchadnezzar, king of the Neo-Babylonian Empire from 605 to 562 BC. Thus he funded a series of vanity projects such as his countless private palaces, all lavishly appointed in terms of 'dictator chic'. On the edge of the city, occupying a vast site next to a motorway, the lavish Umm al-Ma'arik, which roughly translates as the Mother of All Mosques, was built to celebrate what he saw as his finest hour – victory over the Americans in the first Gulf War, or the Mother of All Wars as he referred to it. Its soaring, peacock-blue-tiled minarets are modelled on Scud missiles on their launch pads in a dramatic attempt to link religion and battle, and to underline Saddam's own Muslim credentials. They are each 43 metres high, a reference to the 43 days of US attacks on Baghdad in 1991. In a further provocation, the golden dome of the mosque has the Arabic word 'La' spelt out on it – a defiant 'No' to foreign attackers. Indeed, the hand-scripting of the mosque's 605-page Koran is said to have been done with 50 pints of Saddam's own blood. The building, reputed to have cost tens of millions of dollars, certainly smacks of egotism on Saddam's part but also symbolizes his fear of the growing influence of Iranian Islamic fundamentalism. Nearby, we saw the early stages of construction of what Saddam had proclaimed would be the largest mosque in the world, now destined never to be finished.

A far starker consequence of war awaited us in another part of town. The Amariyah bomb shelter, a squat, ugly, 1980s' concrete construction in a leafy, prosperous suburb, was the scene of a catastrophe during the first Gulf War when it was hit by American bombs, killing the vast majority of those asleep inside. Despite the anger and grief of the bereaved it has been kept as it was after the bodies were removed, and its stark, brutal presence is deeply moving. On the afternoon of our visit, there was a local power cut. Daylight flooded into the gloom through the bomb's entry hole, which was fringed by the bunker's steel reinforcing rods that had been splayed inwards by the force of the impact like wicker canes. Amidst the posters proclaiming, with conscious irony, 'Long Live Iraq', flowers had been placed in memory of those who had died.

Intesar Ahmed was the keeper of the site and its guide. 'It was on

13 February 1991,' she told us 'at about four o'clock in the morning, when the shelter was suddenly attacked by two bombs, guided by laser, each weighing 2 tonnes, and dropped by an F1-11. The first bomb pierced the roof of the shelter, which was 2 metres thick and made of reinforced concrete. Next there was a big explosion inside the shelter. The voice of the explosion was very strong, and 408 people, women and children, were killed. All civilians.' Dan was struck by the simple strength of her narration. Clearly this was her script as a guide, but no amount of repetition could strip her story of its tragedy. 'The bodies of the dead stuck to the walls so strongly they made shadows on them,' she continued. 'Also, arms and legs of children were found blown out of the shelter. There were only 14 survivors, who luckily were sleeping near the door and were blown out by the force. Four minutes later there was a second bomb, like a napalm bomb, that caused terrible smoke and a heat of over 400°C, like an oven.'

The scene must have been unimaginable. How could it have happened? Dan wondered. 'The US said they had bombed it as a military installation, but four days later the Pentagon admitted their mistake and apologized. But it was too late.'

Dan asked where Intesar had been that day. She said that, with her husband away fighting, she and her daughters had stayed at home, 'because the voice of the bomb was very terrible. We hid together ... and prayed.' She paused to collect herself. 'It feels like I live inside a cemetery. It's very difficult, but maybe I have a message, a mission, to tell the world what happened here, that this is the result of war.'

It is impossible to hear a phrase such as 'the voice of the bomb' and not be chilled at its grim poetry. Here was an example of the terrible human casualties of war, the collateral damage that so rarely makes the headlines. Even in war, a country can never be an abstract commodity; it is always a people too, and it is always people who die. Dan asked if Intesar was afraid of further conflict. 'Yes,' she replied, 'and I ask, why make another war? I'm certain we haven't any nuclear weapons. I'm sure, because we've seen war, and lived war, and we hope for peace only.' Admirable, passionate words that spoke of the fragile optimism and pride within this determined woman.

After this shocking memorial we wanted to visit a site south of Baghdad that had captured the visual imagination of the world for centuries, but which by its very structure would be highly vulnerable to any stray bombs. Ctesiphon was one of the great cities of ancient Mesopotamia, built on the banks of the Tigris by the Parthians in the second century BC, as the capital of their empire. The city was captured by Roman and Byzantine forces five times and finally fell to the Islamic Saracens in AD 637. Soon afterwards it sank into ruin, hastened by the proximity of the newly settled Baghdad. More recently, it was the site of a major battle in World War I, when in November 1915 the Turks drove back British troops advancing on Baghdad.

Today, all that remains are the extensive brickwork ruins of what was probably a palace or great banqueting hall called Takhti Khesra, dominated by one of the most stunning and visually arresting architectural structures in the whole of the region: a vast, unsupported vault, which the Iraqis claim is the widest single-span unreinforced brick-built arched vault in the world, dating from the Sassanian period of the third or fourth century AD. In architectural terms a parabolic arch, it spans 30 metres, and to stand beneath its towering presence, nearly 37 metres above, is to feel the wonder of our world. All that prevents the tonnes of honey-hued brick from crashing down is man's understanding of the inherent structural integrity of natural forms, and a certain faith. The arch embodied the virtues of strength and fragility that define so much of human existence, and it was hard not to think of it as a symbol for the country as a whole: so advanced, so civilized, and yet so fragile and threatened, tottering on the edge of oblivion. If anything were to happen to this wonderful expression of engineering and belief, the nation itself would seem doomed. Indeed, the brickwork reportedly suffered a stress fracture as a result of heavy bombing nearby in 1991, though this did not seem to have compromised its stability.

Saddam's relationship with Iraq's historic sites has at times seemed oddly strategic. A French-built Osirak nuclear reactor, destroyed by the Israelis in 1981, was placed perilously close to Ctesiphon, and in April 2003 it was reported that Iraqi military vehicles were being sheltered amongst the ruins.

That evening we persuaded Thaer to take us to the famed Khan Mirjan restaurant, a photograph of which had seduced us in Gavin Young's book *Iraq*. A fourteenth-century coaching hall or *khan*, it was built around a huge central hall with a high vaulted ceiling and has two balconied floors overlooking the main floor. The only completely roofed *khan* in Iraq, in 1935 it was saved from neglect by the authorities and turned into a museum of Arab antiquities before becoming an upmarket restaurant. In the photograph you can make out a dusky, romantic space lit by candelabra, with customers seated on deep cushioned benches, serenaded by a live band. In the 20 years or so since it was taken, however, a change had occurred. On our arrival, as the only guests that night they turned on the electricity to lift the gloom a little, but though the building had retained its beautiful structure only a few tables graced the draughty floor, lit by bare bulbs. Scratchy taped music started up, but nothing could lift the sense of melancholy. And the food was awful. As a symbol of Iraq's luxuries and facilities that had decayed through lack of visitors, it could hardly have been more powerful.

While our time in Baghdad and its environs had been enlightening, giving an authentic flavour of Iraqi urban life, we were keen to start our survey of the important archaeological sites in the north and south of the country. The Director-General of the State Board of Antiquities had to give written approval before we could visit them, and, having received from us a very generous donation in US dollars, he was now seriously considering picking up his pen. We decided to visit him at his office, in the Iraq Museum in Baghdad. This was a place we had wanted to visit anyway, since its unrivalled collection of treasures from Iraq's rich history made it one of the most important museums in the world. We would ask its staff what plans they had for the collection in the face of war, and perhaps see some of its most notable pieces.

The weather was still hot, about 30°C, and so it was with some relief that we entered the cool, marble entrance hall of the museum's administrative block. There were the obligatory long, faded leather sofas and chairs on which we would later have to wait hours for permission to film the museum's galleries. But luckily we managed to locate Dr Donny George, the charismatic Director of Research, who in recent years had been the public face of the museum due to his excellent spoken English. A small bear of a man with thick grey hair, he led us into his office and immediately offered us fresh filter coffee.

In 1975, a decade after it opened its doors, the Iraq Museum published a catalogue of hundreds of its most valuable items. Still the most definitive public record of its collection, it included these words from the then Minister of Information: 'The relics of the past serve as reminders of what has been before, and as links in the chain of communication between past, present and future. The society which possesses many and fine museums has a correspondingly stronger historical memory than the society without them.' These fine words are hugely fitting for the national museum of a country with a history as distinguished as Iraq's, incorporating as it does significant empires such as those of the Sumerians, Akkadians, Babylonians, Assyrians, Chaldeans, Parthians, Sassanians and Abbasids, as well as prehistoric cultures.

After the 1991 Gulf War the museum remained closed for nearly ten years. When it finally reopened this was mainly thanks to its loyal staff, many of whom were working unpaid and with only limited supplies. Among its highlights are the Assyrian galleries, with their carved reliefs and giant winged bulls, familiar to visitors to the British Museum; the Hatran galleries, with their wonderful carved statues and heads cele-brating the dead of this desert city; and the captivating Sumerian rooms, with their unearthly, moon-eyed statuettes and 8000-year-old lizard-headed Ubaid figures. There are also galleries displaying wonderful medieval Korans and early Islamic artwork and crafts. We were eager to capture the sense of this priceless collection and, in filming something of its wonder, to demonstrate to the West the potential tragedy if anything happened to it.

Dr Donny was keen to discuss the international importance of his institution. 'I would say the Iraq Museum is one of the best museums in the world,' he began. 'It's a rare museum that contains all these proofs of human culture and civilization in one place, and what's very important is that all the objects were gathered only in Iraq. Nothing is from outside Iraq.' Given the value of the collection, Dan asked what precautions the staff were taking in the event of an attack. Dr Donny looked weary but answered with quiet assurance. 'It's a very hard time, but we've had this time before – during the Iran–Iraq War and the Gulf War. We have trained people to evacuate everything, and to protect the objects that we can't move, such as the statues and Assyrian reliefs. We have a lot of places for evacuation, and we know how to protect these things. The small pieces will be put into boxes, and we have secure places to distribute them, as we did in the last war. They were 100 per cent protected then; nothing was lost from the Iraq Museum. We hope that if it starts, we will have enough time to evacuate everything. But if they are going to be hit,' and here Dr Donny lowered his voice and fixed his gaze, 'I wish to be here to catch the bomb.'

It would not be the only time on our trip that we heard such passionate, stirring sentiments. But, Dr Donny went on, the 10,000 and more registered archaeological sites throughout the country also remained deeply vulnerable – and that huge figure did not include as yet undiscovered sites. It seemed reasonable to claim that a bomb falling almost anywhere in Iraq risked landing on a site of archaeological inter-est and importance. It was no wonder that ordinary Iraqi citizens felt a greater sense of importance about their homeland's history than did their counterparts in many other countries. What vexed Dr Donny was the difficulty of convincing international aid and support agencies of the need to protect even the major sites.

'We've been applying for the major sites to be registered on the World Heritage List, but they've always been rejected. Imagine that – Babylon is not registered on the list! Or Nineveh, Nimrud or Samarra. The only site currently registered is Hatra. We believe it is a political battle. We do our best to protect our sites, with guards and archaeologists living there, but international aid through UNESCO would be very important to us.' He delivered the words calmly, but was clearly angry and frustrated. And with the lack of resources came looting, Dr Donny admitted. 'Particularly after the Gulf War, when with the very hard sanctions some people, particularly in the south, were driven by poverty to loot some sites and regional museums. We also have evidence of European people sitting in Saudi Arabia, in Jordan, Turkey and Iran, directing Iraqi people where to dig. At the same time the riots started in the south, and nine of our museums were hit, meaning that more than 4000 pieces were lost from Basra, Amara and Kufa, and from Kirkuk in the north. The looters were Iraqis,' Dr Donny conceded, 'but they were guided by Iranian officers, we believe. But the dangerous thing is that we don't know what was lost from the archaeological sites that were not registered.'

We had heard rumours of pieces being looted to order – this was common at sites of historical importance anywhere. And the remoteness of some of the Iraqi sites meant that they were deeply vulnerable. Clearly, economic deprivation was driving Iraqis to pilfer their own culture, but to what extent were they being organized by outside forces? Dr Donny didn't hold back from blaming outsiders, particularly, unsurprisingly, the Americans at Ur, where he alleged they stole objects from the royal palace during the 1991 Gulf War. 'And not only that, but I have counted myself where they have fired 400 shots from a heavy machine gun on a tank into the southern wall of the ziggurat at Ur. Just somebody sitting behind a machine gun, shooting on that wall. Just imagine that cruelty against history.' Though undoubtedly well rehearsed, Dr Donny's words rang true. Ur was to be one of the final destinations on our trip, and we were anxious to witness this damage for ourselves. If true, it would constitute outrageous, wanton vandalism.

One aspect of Iraqi cultural heritage that has attracted the attention, and usually derision, of the outside world has been its reconstruction policy – Saddam has undertaken to restore certain sites, such as Babylon, to their former glory. To many observers this has seemed little more than another form of vanity project, destroying or concealing authentic archaeological evidence, but a different perspective could be identified within Iraq. 'I would love people to know the Iraqi opinion about this,' Dr Donny said when pressed. 'We believe that we are still part of the same historical cycle. Also, we have solid evidence that in all Iraqi history kings were always proud to reconstruct the ancient cities. For instance, the ziggurat at Ur was started in about 2000 BC, but the one you see was reconstructed by Nebuchadnezzar during the Neo-Babylonian period, about 1500 years later. We have written evidence that the kings were asking future kings and princes, if they saw that an ancient building was crumbling, to reconstruct them, and to put documentation there to show that this building had been constructed in your time.' This was certainly the line Saddam Hussein had followed, in particular at Babylon, where bricks stamped with his name exist alongside those bearing the name of Nebuchadnezzar. When Dan put it to Dr Donny that surely there had to be a compromise between political statement and ancient artefact, he continued to follow the Baath Party line. 'We are rebuilding the palaces and temples of our great-grandfathers. We are doing as much as we can to protect them for the coming generations. But of course, we are not reconstructing everything. We do a lot of studies, and if we don't have good reasonable evidence we don't do anything. That is very important. We have the example of Babylon. German archaeologists excavated it and then left it open, so it was turned into a quarry for bricks for local building. Ten or 20 years ago it was a completely destroyed city, and you could not picture it, so we started work to show Babylon to the Iraqi people.'

We had yet to visit Babylon, though the photographs of the reconstruction work there did not fill us with as much optimism as Dr Donny evidently felt – or felt it politic to express. But perhaps the more salient point was that we in the West have largely forgotten the historical wealth of Iraq, and as a result the sites are vulnerable to attack, intentional or otherwise, because if we don't know we don't care. Dr Donny reckoned he knew who was to blame. 'This is the fault of the media. Because of the war, people think of Iraq as a desert land, with military camps and factories for weapons of mass destruction.' He had experienced Western ignorance at first hand. 'Sometimes I'm in Europe giving lectures, and I talk about normal life here, the cultured life, the classical concerts we have, the art exhibitions. No one believes me! We have the Iraqi National Symphony Orchestra, fine art institutions, four or five television channels, but nobody believes it. You are here in Baghdad – you can see for yourself. And it's not just the sites: major things started here, such as writing, cities, empires, laws, even the wheel. The Industrial Revolution in Europe depended on our inventions and discoveries. History started here, but no one wants to remember that. In Iraq, our people know this. They know who they are.'

Dan moved on to the current political climate, and asked Dr Donny how he, as an Iraqi, understood the situation. He answered with measured conviction. 'Everybody should defend themselves. And if Iraq builds up an army, this is normal to defend itself. I'm an archaeologist, not a politician, but I feel this is self-defence. We have a saying, "Even a cat, if cornered, scratches."'

Behind Dr Donny's warmth and professional wisdom, much of what he had said toed a line that seemed designed not to offend his superiors, which seemed eminently sensible. His passion for his subject and his country ran deep – how hard it must be for a man of his intellect and abilities to have to subordinate his own beliefs to those of the state.

While we continued to wait to hear from Dr Jaber Ibrahim, the Director-General of the State Board of Antiquities, we managed to gain brief access to the exhibits. Our movements were tightly monitored by the staff, understandably nervous of any foreign media, but we were able to spend some time in the Assyrian, Sumerian and Hatran galleries. A few display cases were already empty, suggesting that a start had been made to the evacuation plan, but enough items remained to tantalize. Dr Donny had proudly informed us of the museum's education policy, and indeed in gallery after gallery we were swamped by school visits. Whether the immaculately turned-out Iraqi schoolgirls absorbed their history lessons as Dr Donny intended, or preferred to giggle and gossip, is not the point. A museum is defined as much by its visitors as by its exhibits, and what we were witnessing were the wonders of ancient Iraq alongside the inheritors of that land.

Eventually, we received word that the Director-General had at last sanctioned our trip, but our fixer, Thaer, cautioned us against too much haste: individual letters now had to be typed to present to each local authority. Three hours later they were in our hands, and we were eager to depart. Thaer suggested we interview Dr Jaber as a 'thank you' for the consents, but enough time had already been lost and we declined. Within six months the tables were to be turned, and it would be we who were eager to interview the Director-General and he the one to play coy.

Back at the hotel we checked out, after sending our driver, Khalil, into the back streets to change money for us. He returned laden with plastic bags crammed with 250-dinar bills, and we paid the cashier in tottering wads of notes. Just then a crowd of dark-clothed Westerners marched through the lobby, putting themselves between us and the small middle-aged man at their centre. It was 18 November, and Hans Blix and his weapons inspectors had arrived in town to continue their searches after a gap of four years.

The road north of Baghdad is new and in our GMCs we made quick progress. The various palaces and military buildings gradually gave way to small towns interspersed with scrubby desert. Our first stop was to be the great Assyrian capital of Ashur, 300 kilometres north of Baghdad and 11 kilometres south of Mosul. We had discussed Ashur with Dr Donny, as the Western media had reported that the Iraqi government intended to build yet another dam on the Tigris, which would threaten to submerge this ancient city. The official Iraqi line, which Dr Donny somewhat unconvincingly related, was that the area was seriously short of water because Turkey was withholding vital supplies. He admitted that some parts of Ashur were likely to be affected, but said that a wall would be built to protect the majority of the site from the water. Perhaps finding it hard to balance political and personal beliefs, he asserted that such a major historical city 'cannot be allowed to be drowned under water, ever'. The threat was a real and urgent one.

Ashur had long been a human settlement before it became a city, mainly due to its proximity to the river Tigris, which now lies east of the ruins but originally ran to the north. The city was founded in about 2500 BC, probably by settlers from Syria or from the south. Named after the Assyrians' national deity, it was the religious centre of their mighty empire and thrived as a merchant city for centuries until it was finally sacked by the Babylonians in 614 BC. Though the seat of Assyrian power had been moved to Nimrud in the ninth century BC by Assurnasirpal, Ashur continued to be the place where Assyrian kings were crowned and buried. In the second century BC it was again inhabited, if briefly, but then lay buried in the sand until it was excavated stratigraphically between 1903 and 1913 by a German expedition led by Walter Andrae. The inner city was encircled by walls with a total length of 4 kilometres, while to the east massive quays were built on the river by King Adadnirari I in the thirteenth century BC. At this time, Ashur contained many temples dedicated to a variety of gods including Ashur, his consort Ishtar and Nabu, the god of writing. Three major palaces have also been uncovered.

As we crossed the dunes, passing grazing camels and teams of archaeologists at work on the western side of the city, we saw the main object of our attentions in front of us. The ziggurat at Ashur, dating from 1200 BC, is an imposing and moving presence. Built as temple-towers across Mesopotamia from approximately 2200 to 500 BC, and constructed from mud bricks with kiln-fired glazed bricks used on the façade, pyramidal ziggurats were probably not places of public worship but were rather perceived as the house of God. From a four-sided mud-brick platform the bricks would rise in steps, to culminate at the summit in a small shrine reached by a series of ramps, symbolic stairways to heaven. Each time a temple was rebuilt, the remains of its predecessor's walls would act as the foundation. Over time, many of the surviving ziggurats across Iraq and Iran became covered in dust and sand, and now resemble huge mounds rather than man-made constructions. This was certainly the appearance of the one at Ashur, its imposing dimensions looking mighty indeed in the largely flat landscape.

With our boots clinging precariously to the parched brickdust we clambered to the peak of the ziggurat, and were rewarded with a clear indication of Ashur's strategic power. The origin of Iraq's former name, Mesopotamia, is Greek, from *mesos* meaning middle and *potamos* meaning river – the land between the rivers. The history of this land and its people dates back further than 7000 BC, and the secret of its success is irrigation. The alluvial plains enclosed by the Tigris and the Euphrates and their tributaries are sun-baked and arid in summer, yet with the addition of water they become fertile. The abundance of wildlife was what first attracted people to the region, and the undulating plains in the north proved perfect for keeping cattle and planting crops. Such comfortable living conditions were conducive to innovation and discovery, and today, as Dr Donny had emphasized, we credit the Mesopotamians with having invented writing (in the form of the wedge-shaped script known as cuneiform), mathematics, the wheel, the concept of the city-state, and agriculture. These may seem big claims, but for centuries this land was alive with cultures and peoples who had the natural resources to think beyond the hand-to-mouth needs of their nomadic ancestors or those who eked out an existence in harsher climates. Mesopotamia bore witness to what people could do with time on their hands and ready materials.

Like all great rivers, the Tigris possesses a chameleon-like ability to change its appearance. Whereas in Baghdad it looks dubious and untrustworthy, at Ashur it conforms to a stereotype of ancient beauty. Reed beds line its shore and shrill, brightly coloured birds dart over its surface. The mood seemed timeless and peaceful until broken by the thud of a low-flying jet, reminding us of life both elsewhere and, regrettably, here. Looking back across the expanse of the city of Ashur it was easy to identify the route of irrigation canals, the harbour and the plan of the buildings, which stretched for hundreds of metres in their partially excavated, slowly reclaimed form. It was hard to imagine the disruption to this scene that a new dam on the Tigris would cause; the irony, at the time of this visit, was that the imminent war might put paid to those plans while jeopardizing the site in quite another way.

It took only a short while to reach Mosul, the main city of northern Iraq and our temporary base. It seemed a pleasant, prosperous city, lacking the choking, stifling smog of Baghdad and retaining a characteristic charm, particularly in the winding alleys of its Old Town. The deserted fairgrounds and parks lining the Tigris bore testament to the city's role as a summer resort for those wishing to escape the intense heat further south. We were staying at a huge, ziggurat-shaped hotel on the edge of town, its beige interior torpor relieved only by the tape stuck to the windows to prevent shattering in the event of an explosion, and by a sign to the *saigon*, or shelter. We were almost the only people staying there; next morning, when we arrived in the dining area to find no breakfast, a waiter calmly explained that the kitchen staff had not thought it worth preparing for a mere 26 guests.

Chivvied on our way, we drove the short distance to one of the most evocative names in Mesopotamian history: Nineveh, once administrative centre of the Assyrian Empire and now gaudily over-restored in parts, in keeping with the theory espoused by Dr Donny. It had its heyday in the seventh and eighth centuries BC, but even then, as Gavin Young noted in *Iraq*, the city was at least 4000 years old and the origins of its name are Sumerian. Sennacherib, who ruled from 705 to 681 BC, was responsible for the elevation of Nineveh to the capital of the civilized world, as his soldiers built fortifications, dug gardens and constructed a dam. It was his palace at Nineveh, with its 71 chambers, that provided the winged bulls and relief-carvings depicting scenes of Assyrian life, often military, brutal and in dramatic, comic-strip detail, that now reside in the Iraq Museum and the British Museum. They were excavated in 1845 by Sir Henry Layard, who also discovered parts of the library of a later king, Assurbanipal. On Assurbanipal's death in 626 BC the Babylonians launched a war against the Assyrians. Some 14 years later the Babylonians along with other peoples from the East, the Medes and Scythians, destroyed Nineveh, which was left as a haunted ruin and memorial to a forgotten civilization.

For most schoolchildren of an earlier generation, the name of Nineveh was associated with the Old Testament prophet Jonah, who was supposed to have gone there, on God's instructions, after being swallowed by a whale and then saved by being vomited up. God told him, 'Arise, go to Nineveh, that great city, and cry against it; for their wickedness is come up before me' (Jonah 1:2). His tomb and shrine can still be seen on the hill known as Nebi Yunus; it stands behind metal bars within a mosque, as Jonah is also venerated in the Koran.

By one of the 15 reconstructed city gates we came upon a shepherd with his flock, surrounded by his children and a pack of barking dogs. We tried to ask him how he felt living on such a historic site and his answers were friendly but pragmatic: he lived in a tent there because he could not afford a house. Later examination of the tape revealed that he suspected we were there to tell him off, which probably curtailed his comments. Khaled, our new fixer as Thaer had been recalled to Baghdad, could not understand our wish to speak to ordinary Iraqi people. He was reluctant to initiate such encounters, saying that if we wanted to know about such sites we should talk to the museum directors. His unease was palpable, as he had been instructed always to present

Iraq's best face to the foreign media. This was his job, and we understood that, yet we preferred to seek out the feelings of the local people. If historic sites were at risk, then of course archaeologists and curators would be upset, but our mission was more to discover the connection of the ordinary people to their heritage and culture. That day Khaled displayed his impatience by repeatedly detailing the undeniable riches of his country and challenging us to match them in Europe. Nevertheless he proved a capable fixer, intelligent and sensitive, if inclined to worry.

He led us to another reconstructed gate, and this time we were fortunate enough to discover two winged bulls *in situ*, still guarding the entrance to the empty space that had once been the Great Hall. One was propped unceremoniously on concrete blocks and the other had lost its proud head, but here were the symbols of the palace of Sennacherib where they belonged, welcoming visitors to the proud Assyrian city of Nineveh. So much history, and all completely unprotected – it was as frightening as it was exciting.

The third of the triumvirate of great Assyrian cities was Nimrud. Like Nineveh, the place had been settled for millennia before it was developed as his capital by Shalmaneser I, who reigned from 1273 to 1244 BC. Assurnasirpal II also reigned from here, preferring its strategic defensive position to that of the city of Ashur, but the Nimrud that mostly remains is the legacy of his son, Shalmaneser III (858 – 824 BC), who built its magnificent ziggurat, and the fortified temple of Ninurta at its side, beside the palace of his father on the east bank of the Tigris nearly 40 kilometres southeast of Mosul. Every king, as at the other Assyrian capitals, sought to outdo his predecessors in terms of grandeur and construction. Named after Nimrod, the father of Ashur and said to be a great-grandson of Noah's, the city was known in the Bible as Calah or Kalhu, and contained temples, palaces and countless gardens. Among the most notable buildings was a temple to Nabu, the god of writing, that contained a cuneiform archive. Sacked twice by the Medes between 614 and 612 BC, it was then virtually abandoned apart from a brief Greek occupation around 150 BC. Today, the remains are reached via a winding road through numerous small settlements, though the site itself continues to occupy a lonely, remote position with sweeping views of the plains, interrupted only by the occasional tell (mound) signifying another forgotten building or complex.

When we arrived, a team of local archaeologists and workmen was hard at work reconstructing a gateway at the base of the ziggurat. Excavations at Nimrud were begun by Layard, but significant discoveries arose from the activities of Sir Max Mallowan after World War II. Mallowan, first director of the British School in Iraq and a trustee of the British Museum, was usually accompanied by his wife, the crime writer Agatha Christie, who wrote in the shade of the site's Dig House. Her novel *They Came To Baghdad* describes the experiences of a young girl coming to Iraq for the first time to join a dig – with suitably sinister consequences. Another novel, *Murder in Mesopotamia*, uses the country as its setting. In her autobiography Christie declared 'how much I have loved that part of the world', and it is clear that she viewed archaeology as complementary to her art.

While Layard and his team were responsible for discovering the great winged bulls, Mallowan found smaller treasures at Nimrud, including the now famous carved ivory showing, with almost sensual horror, a Nubian being mauled to death by a lion, which at the time we were there was in the collection of the Iraq Museum in Baghdad.

In the grounds of Assurnasirpal's palace we were immediately struck by the sight of the reliefs, damaged and few in number, familiar from the Assyrian galleries at the British Museum but here perfectly in context. It felt like glimpsing a lion in the wild having previously seen one only in the confines of a zoo. Despite being over 2800 years old, the scenes of martial life and recreation retained their original vivid immediacy. Every sinew and contour on man and beast had been rendered with mesmerizing precision. Incredibly, we saw huge slabs that had been taken from the walls and were now just propped up, surely tempting to light fingers – though it would need many of them. We thrilled at panel after panel of intricately picked-out detail, lovingly rendered, adorned with great swathes of cuneiform script bragging of conquest and triumph. Walking through such splendour we had an intoxicating sense of living history, of the importance of these artefacts and buildings not just in terms of historical record but also as testament to the swagger of man and his ability to inspire awe by means of construction. Yet the protection given to this site seemed minimal, despite Dr Donny's assurances in Baghdad: the compound fence had a padlock on its gate, but this would be unlikely to deter a resolute gang of thieves.

From the top of the ziggurat – a great dollop of crumbled brick now 17 metres tall, though when built it would have been twice as high – we spied a small Bedouin encampment almost in the shadow of Nimrud. This seemed a good opportunity to discover something of the modern life of these nomadic people. As we approached, the scene could have been timeless – provided one ignored their white Toyota pick-up trucks. Ragamuffin children darted in and out of the tents, which were divided into two sections: one for the women, who cooked, washed and tended to their broods, and one for the men to sit shaded from the sun and take tea while discussing the world. Outside, their sheep wandered in search of any grass left on the parched land. Three of the men seemed happy to talk, and invited us into a tent to drink tea. As the swinging tray of glasses arrived, Dan asked them to explain how important it was to them to live so close to one of the world's earliest cities. 'This is the civilization of Iraq, our heritage,' proclaimed Mohammed al-Azawi, a serious young man who squatted beside us. 'We are proud of this place, of these ancient monuments.' These families went wherever there were fresh pastures for their sheep and flowing water, throughout Iraq and into Iran to the east, Turkey to the north and Saudi Arabia to the south. The men saw their existence as a simple way of life, and in answer to our questions about how vulnerable they felt in Iraq, to internal or external powers, they reiterated what sounded like a mantra: 'Our lifestyle will stay the same, and we will pass it on to our children.' It is precisely this obduracy that is likely to see their desire maintained, as it has been for thousands of years.

And then the conversation turned to the mainstays of life: sheep and women. One of the older men, Nazar Ahmed, revealed with a twinkle in his eye that as Bedouins they liked to have more than one wife – as many as four, if they could. However, when it came to everyday living 'our life revolves around sheep and rain'. This dismal analysis was briefly enlivened when it became apparent that Dan was being offered a wife by the Bedouins. He claimed to be seriously tempted, but the associated prospect of sheep and rain was perhaps less appealing and he politely declined. Before we departed, another old member of the tribe was called upon to recite a poem in honour of our visit. He was charmingly shy, and for a while it seemed as though he might be unwilling to perform, but after some goading he suddenly fixed his stare and began an old poem in praise of the Lord. For several minutes he recited his verse in a languid, rhythmic lilt. We were entranced; just as the nomads knew no solid foundations for their living quarters, so they retained their art, their poetry, only in their hearts.

Our next destination was the mountains that fringed the region to the north. After the scrubby desert around Nimrud, we were greeted by cool breezes and shocking blue skies as our vehicles wound their way into the scree- and tree-covered heights. Our destination was Mar Matta, the monastery of St Matthew in the Mountain, a small fourth-century building set dramatically on the face of a mountain called Maqluub and home to a dwindling community of Syrian Orthodox monks. Although today we think of Iraq as purely Muslim, it was once Christian, and Christianity has retained its traditional stronghold in the north, surviving by always being outspoken in favour of the Baathist regime. Being a Christian did not seem to be a professional hindrance: Tariq Aziz, then the Deputy Prime Minister, is a Christian, as, incidentally, is Dr Donny George. We were keen to find out to what extent antagonism towards the West in recent times had been reflected in the Iraqi Muslims' attitudes towards their Christian compatriots. Iraq is still officially a secular state, but the rise in Islamic fundamentalist feeling has not left it untouched. Several notable churches remain in Mosul, such as Chamoun al-Safa and the Syrian Orthodox Ma Tomba, but the Christian villages on Mosul's fringes, tucked away in the mountains, are less populous than they were. Christians used to make up almost 1 million of the 23 million Iraqis, although that number has fallen to less than 800,000 in recent years as many have left for Europe and the United States.

St Matthew, a Turkish monk fleeing persecution, was reputed to

have come to Maqluub as a hermit, and the monastery was founded in
AD 363. At its peak it housed more than 7000 monks, but from the ninth
century onwards it suffered attacks from the region's rulers. Today it has
only three residents. St Matti, as the saint is affectionately referred to
locally, is renowned as a great healer, and pilgrims of all denominations
flock to his tomb. Saddam Hussein himself visited on three occasions,
and according to the monks made a large donation which helped
maintain and repair the sandstone building. The site, though idyllic and
seemingly remote, lies well within the northern no-fly zone patrolled
daily by American and British planes. Before leaving the UK we had
read reports that in 1999 Allied missiles had hit the monastery, causing
structural damage. It is also situated close to the Kurdish Autonomous
Region, which for years has been in conflict with Saddam's regime.

We found little of material worth left at the monastery. Inside the
huge outer doors and up flights of worn stone steps were a series of
spartan cells, their walls covered with graffiti and their furniture often
broken. In one room Dan spotted two framed pictures for veneration:
one of the Virgin Mary, the other of Saddam Hussein. The cloisters
were dusty and empty, and apart from the caretaker there seemed little
sign of life. We entered the church that stands above the rock-hewn
chapel containing the shrine of St Matti, its coolness welcome after the
desert sun. As we admired the architectural features of the church,
almost Gothic in feel and incorporating Islamic pointed arches, we were
greeted by the English-speaking Father Bihman Samarchy, the youngest
of the three remaining monks.

It is easy to forget that Islam, established in the seventh century AD, is
derived from the scriptures of the Old and New Testaments, venerates
both Jesus and the Virgin Mary, and for centuries was renowned for its
tolerance. For the vast majority of Muslims throughout the world, this is
still the case. Yet when asked about the relations between Muslims and
Christians in the region Father Bihman became reticent, though his face,
spoke volumes. 'I don't know ... not all people ... some Muslims are
good, and others ... maybe.' He let his voice trail away, but the meaning
was unmistakable. Despite the rhetoric from both the Christian Church
and the government, it was perhaps inevitable that this tiny outpost and

its larger, if diminishing, community in Mosul and throughout Iraq should find tension in its relations with the Muslim majority.

The clanking of a bell meant it was time for prayers, so we followed Father Bihman into the chapel. Here he joined Father Adda and Father Paulus for a chanted ritual in the ancient biblical language of Aramaic – to a congregation of four Englishmen and their two Muslim drivers. This was a glimpse of life in Iraq before Islam. As their voices echoed around the building it was possible to imagine that this refuge, which had already survived for 1600 years, would surely live on despite whatever might be thrown at it. Yet in truth it remained deeply vulnerable, and no amount of patriotic rhetoric or history could protect it against bombs and angry mobs.

That evening, once dusk had fallen, we went to a restaurant in Mosul to break the Ramadan fast with our drivers and fixer. While we ourselves had not been completely strict in our observation of it, during daylight hours we had restricted ourselves to water, a little fruit and the occasional furtive energy bar. As soon as the sun went down, though, life changed in Mosul, as in every other city, town and village in Iraq. All along the main thoroughfares restaurants displayed spits of roasting chickens, and people crowded the tables as agile waiters threw down plates of salads, pickles and enormous flatbreads in front of their customers. This was followed by chicken or lamb, usually served with rice – though one night, in a fit of bravado, Dan ordered sheep's testicles. He was rewarded with a plate of a dozen or so, which he manfully gobbled. Once the main course had been consumed, the men sat back and reached for their cigarettes, and the smoke of the spits mingled with their tobacco fug. Lively arguments broke out, and a discernible relaxing of mood occurred. Understandably, our drivers became irritable by about four o'clock each afternoon, having forgone food and water since dawn, yet it was almost miraculous how their faces relaxed, and their manner changed, as soon as their bellies were full.

The next day, in order to take a further look at the religious communities of northern Iraq, we travelled to the border of the Kurdish Autonomous Region to visit the Yazidis. We had first read about this so-called devil-worshipping sect in Gavin Young's *Iraq*, in which he delighted in their various eccentricities as outlined in a Yazidi text:

> Lettuce was forbidden us, because it resembles the name of our prophetess Laetitia. Butter beans and dark blue were also forbidden. We do not eat fish out of respect for the Prophet Jonah, neither do we eat gazelle, since those herds belong to one of our prophets. The sheikh and his disciples abstain from the flesh of the cock, in deference to the peacock angel … And the sheikh and his disciples refrain from pumpkins. It is forbidden for us to make water in the standing position or put on our underclothes in the sitting position, or be alone in the privy or to wash in the bath. It is impermissible to pronounce the word 'devil', which is the name of our God, or any word that is near it such as 'evil', 'shovel' or 'snivel'. Neither may we say 'curse' or 'accursed' or any words near them.

This seemed too good an opportunity to miss, even if it did read like something from a *Monty Python* sketch. Unfortunately the Yazidis' place of pilgrimage, the tomb of Sheikh Adi, was now under Kurdish control and inaccessible without the right paperwork, which we were told could only come from Baghdad. However we could visit Ain Sifni, a non-descript, whitewashed town that skirted the boundary on the Iraq side. As we entered we were approached by a gaggle of excited children and a young man named Adnan Haji who offered to take us to the house of the head Yazidi. Arriving at a two-storey building, we climbed the stairs to a spacious roof terrace that led on to a long meeting room with chairs and tables. A stocky man in dark glasses and long robe, walking with a stick, entered and was announced as the Baba Sheikh Haji Karto. He answered our questions via our fixer, though he slipped easily between Arabic and two Kurdish dialects, making it hard for Khaled to follow. What we were told was that the Yazidis had no recorded history, and that there were 79 worlds in their religion. As for the mysterious Black Book or Mishaf Rash, which was said to contain the sacred writings of Sheikh Adi, Baba Sheikh informed us that about 300 years earlier it had been taken by a European man, and they did not know where it was now.

When we asked about the role of the peacock in their worship, we were told: 'In our religious ceremony, the Peacock Angel is the one we kneel and pray to as a prophet. We venerate him. After that comes the Prince or Emir, then the Baba Sheikh, and then the Qawal, who performs the music. The Peacock Angel is our living God, like your God. Some people involve personalities in religion, but we tend to stay away from individuals and politics. Even President Saddam Hussein is a leader of Muslims only, but the Peacock Angel is a god for everybody.'

The Yazidis' beliefs fuse various aspects of Zoroastrianism, Christianity and Islam. They believe they were created separately from other men, and are descended from Adam only. Linked to the extreme Shia (Ghulat) sects, there are some 300,000 adherents; about half reside in Iraq, and the rest live in Syria, in the former Soviet Union and as refugees in Germany. The sect's founding figure, Sheikh Adi, was a twelfth-century Sufi mystic whom his followers believe was the final manifestation of the Peacock Angel. The Emir is the secular head, while the Baba Sheikh is in charge of religious matters. Although persecuted over the centuries for their closed community, in particular by the Ottomans, they now, Baba Sheikh claimed, live in peace with their Iraqi brothers. However, our fixer Khaled had been nervous when we said we wanted to meet the Yazidis. 'It is dangerous to go there,' he protested. 'They will kill me. I am scared of them.'

Of their various beliefs, the matter of devil-worship is easily cleared up: God is good – therefore there is no need to worry about him. Instead the Yazidis venerate the Peacock Angel, who was cast out of heaven for not worshipping Adam. The ban on eating lettuce is harder to pin down. According to tradition, the devil once hid in a cabbage patch; a more earthly explanation is that the Ottoman caliphs carried out several massacres against the Yazidis in the eighteenth and nineteenth centuries and thousands were killed in the lettuce fields that once dotted northeastern Iraq. These mysteries only add to the Yazidis' allure which, it has to be said, outstrips their rather shabby reality.

Dan was intrigued by their ban on dark blue as a mark of respect for the peacock. Was this really true? The young man, Adnan, replied: 'For us, our God is beloved, and the blue colour is a symbol of him and we respect it. It is a holy colour.' At this point Dan could not hold back. 'But you're dressed in dark blue from head to foot!' he blurted out. Adnan looked at him, impassively. 'No I'm not. This is green.' It seems that even the archaic practices of a dwindling, vulnerable religion can fall victim to the diktats of fashion.

Dan asked the Baba Sheikh if his people felt threatened by the future. 'Of course we feel fear from the war,' he admitted, 'but this is a state affair, between the Iraqi government and the Americans. We hope that God will bring us peace and we hope to live in peace with Arabs and Turks, Muslims, Christian or Kurdish. But,' he added darkly, 'We are all Iraqis, and our soldiers will be martyrs in the war.'

Like the Christians, these strange people feel compelled to over-emphasize their loyalty to the Baathist regime in order to avoid per-secution. They claim to be, and may well be, loyal Iraqi citizens, but sitting where they do, perched precariously between the Kurds and the Muslims, they cannot afford to be complacent. Add to this the stricture that Yazidis are permitted to marry only within their own caste or clan and one starts to feel alarm for their future, at least in their present, cocooned state in Ain Sifni.

Back in Mosul our next task was to visit its Museum of Civilization. The main regional centre for the Iraq Museum collection, it is ideally located to display exhibits from Nineveh, Nimrud and Hatra, and reports in the British media had suggested that the staff had already started to put into effect their evacuation plan for the collection in the event of military threat. Behind the reception desk sat two women, who introduced themselves as Bernadette Hannah Mety and Saba al-Omari, both curators of the collection. They agreed to show us around. Saba, whose English was more fluent than her colleague's, was our guide.

We started on the ground floor in the Hatran gallery, where at first glance few precautions seemed to have been taken against the imminent outbreak of hostilities. This meant that we were able to see the museum's wonderful collection of 2200-year-old sculptures of lions and human figures: heads without bodies, and bodies without heads. One cracked statue lay on its side on a wooden pallet, but we were unable to ascertain whether it was being taken away for storage or for restoration.

Saba explained that at this level there were three sections – Hatran, Assyrian and Islamic – and upstairs a Prehistoric section which was not open to the public 'because of the circumstances'. Despite this statement she and Bernadette would not at first admit that the staff were taking precautions against possible aerial attack. Clearly a plan had been drawn up, but we could understand her reluctance to reveal too much to us. However, as Dan gently persisted in his questioning the two curators gradually relaxed, admitting that there were secret arrangements in hand and showing us display cases in which colour photographs had replaced the exhibits – gold coins that had been moved into secure storage.

We asked if there were many visitors these days. 'People come,' Saba said slowly, 'but they are poor, and can't even afford the admission price. If they have money, they prefer to buy food. People have been very badly affected by the blockade, the sanctions.' Next door, in the Assyrian gallery, larger items such as the winged bulls and carved reliefs from Nineveh, Nimrud and Khorsabad remained on display because their immense weight would make them difficult to move – or steal, we hoped. Their presence gave an impression of business as normal, but once again the smaller items had been moved to a 'secret location'; they included the pieces from the golden treasures of Nimrud, discovered in 1989, and now, Saba assured us, 'not in the normal store'.

At this point it struck home just how terrible it was that this threat existed, and that decent, caring professional people were forced to work in such a defensive, pressurized way. When we said so Saba smiled politely and agreed but an awkward silence followed, as the complicated dynamic became apparent – despite our obvious good intentions and our expressions of anger and sympathy, we still represented the threat, however indirectly. Who could say what these highly educated, polite women were thinking: the Arab tradition of discretion and respect rendered them inscrutable.

Passing into the Islamic gallery, we found a thirteenth-century white marble doorway from Mosul, some spectacular carved wooden doors from Samarra and yet further empty cases. A small pile of storage trunks lay on the gallery floor, presumably waiting to be filled with further exhibits. Then, suddenly, a jet plane roared overhead. 'We're used to that,' Saba remarked. 'The jets never stopped from the last war. They are American jets, from the north, sometimes from Turkey. They fly over Mosul especially. And the vibrations of the missiles shake the building … but we are ready to fight, whoever attacks us.' Her steely words shook us somewhat. Once again we were confronted by the strength of the Iraqi spirit in the face of military aggression, and caught a glimpse of the anger that filled so many hearts. Saba, however, was not finished. 'Life is meaningless to us, the Iraqi people. She's a Christian' – she motioned to Bernadette – 'and I'm a Muslim, but life is meaningless to us. We will protect this museum,' she continued grimly, 'to the last drop of our blood.' Her words fell away into a nervous laugh, but the spirit of passionate defiance was undeniable. She went on. 'People are afraid of us because of the bad propaganda. But we love people – we are not like that. We even welcome American visitors – we know they are an innocent people. We hate the decisions of the American authorities, but not the people.' This was an interesting comment. Saba was making an obvious but important analogy between the Iraqi people – perceived in the West, she believed, as wicked – and the American public, whom she was acknowledging as separate from their political leaders. Her tacit plea seemed to be that others shouldn't judge the Iraqi people by the actions of the country's leader.

What we had witnessed was history and beauty under direct, accountable threat. It was hard to imagine how frustrated these brave women must have been feeling, and what they and their colleagues had endured for so long. They were doing everything within their power, but their collection remained incredibly vulnerable. As Saba had pointed out, even the vibrations from the planes and their bombs rocked the building; one stray shell, and the visible remains of thousands of years of Iraqi history – of world history – would be obliterated. These empty cases and dark spaces spoke of the museum's plight as eloquently as if they had been full. We all fervently hoped to see them filled again, but knew in our hearts that this could be a long time away.

From the imminent first war of the twenty-first century we moved back in time to those fought in the twentieth. Since arriving in Mosul, we had from time to time asked Khaled if he knew where the British Commonwealth cemetery was. Iraq had, of course, had strong links with Britain, having become a British mandate after the defeat of its Turkish overlords in World War I. The country was eventually granted independence in 1932, but under the terms of the treaty British military bases were retained and an agreement was set up to train the Iraqi army. During World War II British forces had to put down a pro-Nazi revolt among Iraqi army officers and protect areas in the north.

There are over 54,000 Commonwealth war dead buried or commemorated at 13 locations in Iraq. The majority died during the Mesopotamian campaign in World War I. Mosul War Cemetery contained 191 burials from that time, all Indian soldiers but only six identified. After World War II, when Commonwealth forces occupied the city for four years, the remains of some 145 war dead from that conflict were brought into this cemetery from Mosul Civil Cemetery, Kirkuk British Military Cemetery and Kirkuk Muhammadan Cemetery, where maintenance would not have been possible. Bearing these historical connections in mind, it seemed worthwhile to film the cemetery to capture something of a bygone age.

But Khaled became unaccountably shifty whenever we asked to see it, and we grew suspicious. Eventually he gave in to our persistence and reluctantly agreed to take us there, though on condition that we did not film. We travelled across town and drove into what looked like a lorry park on a sandy industrial estate. The sign in the bricks of the wall read 'Mosul War Cemetery', but it seemed to be a mistake. Only when we looked more closely were we able to ascertain that this area had indeed once contained war graves. Now only a couple of memorials remained, and even they bore graffiti; all the gravestones had been broken off and the cemetery was almost razed to the ground. Indeed, at one end football goalposts had been painted on the wall.

This was a shock, but the keener Khaled was to move us on the more determined we were to delve further – and to run the camera surreptitiously. In the far corner, an enterprising hermit had fashioned some of the discarded gravestones into a shelter in which to live, and Dan read the details from one of the stones: 'Royal Artillery D. O'Connor, 27 June

1942, Aged 42'. We were not meant to witness this, and we could clearly see why. Such desecration was sad to behold. Across Europe, it is a depressing fact of modern life that war cemeteries often bear the brunt of the anger of political extremists and vandals, but such actions seemed out of character for the Iraqi people. Of the many we had so far met, a lot held strong views on the Americans and, to an extent, the British, which we could fully understand, but without exception they had treated us with courtesy and respect. This show of wanton aggression suggested that beneath the well-mannered Arab demeanour lurked a reservoir of anger and resentment. On the way back we were all chastened and silent; Khaled could barely meet our eyes.

Later, back in Britain, we got in touch with the Commonwealth War Graves Commission, who confirmed that Mosul War Cemetery was in a 'far from ideal' state, and that, in their opinion, 'the cemetery's deterioration occurred post-1990'. They based this view on the fact that 'the cemetery was in good order until the Gulf War because we had a UK member of staff based in the region … He was fortunately away on annual leave when hostilities broke out and it was another six years before we could return to the country. During that visit our staff reported the cemetery in its present condition.' Thankfully, they were able to confirm that this was a rare occurrence in Iraq and that normally the biggest threat was the harsh climate. As to what might be done, the Commission's representative was positive: 'Although the headstones are no longer in place at Mosul we are still able to identify the individual burials because just below the soil our headstone beams are still in place. The burials themselves have not been disturbed and the boundary of the cemetery remains secure from the urbanization that now surrounds it.' Perhaps at some stage new headstones can be affixed. Until then, the cemetery serves as a warning of how quickly hard-earned goodwill can be shattered.

We finally took our leave of Mosul, this prosperous northern metropolis with its unrivalled historic riches and wealth of human life, built up over the centuries but now hanging by a thread. Our next stop was the ancient Parthian city of Hatra, capital of the first Arab kingdom. An hour or so south of Mosul, off the main north–south highway, the site lies in a gentle depression in the windswept, scrubby sand drifts. The official Iraq tourist guide, published in 1982, claims that Hatra was equal to Rome in terms of architecture, sculpture and the 'arts of war'. The origins of the city are obscure, but it seems to have been first settled around the third century BC. Later, Christian Arab kings ruled here for some six centuries until the Sassanian king Sapor laid siege to Hatra for a year and eventually destroyed it in AD 241.

Due to its position it became a staging post and trading centre for precious commodities such as Indian spices, silk, precious stones and woodwork, and protected the two main caravan routes that connected central Mesopotamia with Syria and the rest of Asia Minor. It must have been a tremendously colourful outpost, where all manner of exotic people, speaking strange tongues, gathered to share news and do business. The two rivers, the Tigris and the Euphrates, formed the natural eastern and western boundaries of the kingdom that had Hatra as its capital. The city itself, circular in shape, was protected by great city walls and had a series of temple buildings at its heart. Its strong fortifications allowed it to withstand numerous Roman attacks on the route from Syria to Babylon, and its inhabitants were not without enterprise – they used the mangonel, a device that could propel large stones, burning oil and arrows.

For the first time in Iraq we were now confronted by a vast, deeply exhilarating expanse of golden limestone buildings: a city, in fact, that could almost be slumbering. While there has been considerable reconstruction, a lot of original details remained; and unlike at Babylon, the rebuilding had been done with a sympathetic eye – helped, no doubt, by Hatra being on the UNESCO World Heritage List. One of the most striking aspects of this mesmerizing site was the abundance of statuary: the Hatran holy trinity of gods, the enigmatically pre-Christian father, mother and son of God: Maran, Martan and Barmarin; Abbu, the Great Queen of Hatra; Shamash, the Sun God; and a wealth of unnamed deities. Perhaps most impressive, architecturally, were the huge temple of Shamash and the immense *ewans* or vaulted halls, derived from the shape of a nomad tent, which opened on to an inner courtyard. Drawing on Assyrian, Hellenistic, Roman and Parthian styles in their magnificent dimensions and engineering they were reminiscent of the arched vault at Ctesiphon. More prosaically, they offered welcome shade from the relentless sun. Here we saw the great fusion of classical and Eastern architecture, pointing to the future of Islamic architectural design, especially in the decoration and design of the honey-hued temple buildings.

One of the *ewans* was being swept by a caretaker and we asked him about the site. Saba Mohammed Zab told us that he had worked at Hatra for 15 years and in between nervously extolling the virtues of Saddam Hussein (you never know who might be listening), he was emphatic about the importance of such sites: 'This is our life and our heritage,' he told us, adding that many people used to visit, though now few made the trek. We wondered about the danger of looting, given its remote location, but he said that only once in his time had anything major been taken; this was reassuring. When pressed, he admitted to being worried about a war, though it was difficult to stand in this deserted grandeur, far from those who control such matters, and reconcile the two. But even Hatra could not be immune to the perils of war or its aftermath. In front of the temple were arrayed thousands of pieces of sculpture – figures, columns and architectural details – awaiting inspection and, presumably, reintroduction to the site. Their beauty was abstract and poignant, and in their jumbled expanse they resembled an architectural graveyard of the gods. We could only hope it would not prove prophetic for this still-proud, shimmering desert city.

As we headed south, through Kirkuk and then Tikrit, birthplace of Saladin, the scourge of the Crusaders, but also Saddam's home town and still very much a Baathist stronghold, our journey took us to perhaps the greatest architectural icon of Iraq – the spiral minaret of Samarra, known as the Malawiya. As Gavin Young adroitly points out, this lonely masterpiece resembles an old-fashioned helter-skelter, and the name Samarra itself means 'happy is he who sees it'. Built in AD 847, it stands 52 metres high as it winds its way from earth to heaven, and exemplifies the way in which Islam, in its infancy, embraced the form of the earlier religious buildings in its quest for its own distinctive architectural identity. Put simply, the minaret is an Islamic ziggurat, full of mystical symmetry, and offers a brilliant transitional fusion of old and new.

Next to it lie the ruins of the Friday Mosque, once the largest mosque in the world; now, beyond the vast outer walls, measuring approximately 240 x 160 metres, and the inner foundations, little remains. In the 1990s a start was made on restoring it to its former glory, but when we were there work seemed to have slowed, or even stopped. From AD 836 to 892 Samarra – formerly Surra Man Ra'a – was the capital of the Abbasid Empire and one of the largest cities of ancient times. It was claimed to be a spectacular feat of urban planning and decoration, with boulevards over 32 kilometres long. Today, a busy, modern town with about 200,000 inhabitants nestles beside the ancient remains, and small reproductions of the minaret are dotted all over the streets, roundabouts and shops. This was an image we had all wanted to see before beginning our trip, and, unusually for such things, it did not disappoint.

As is so often the case with Iraq's ancient sites, there is little point in visiting Samarra during the middle of the day; only in early or late light can one truly appreciate its geometric, sensual beauty, when the shadows draw out its dramatic lines. A walkway lifts the pilgrim to the base of the minaret, where the spiral, snaking ascent begins. At first the path, with its stones worn smooth, seemed reassuringly wide, and the modern handrail unnecessary. The gradient was gentle, and for three or four minutes our ascent was graceful and measured, with the fields and minor settlements on the edge of the city starting to take shape. The spiral is not an endless repetition, like a circle, nor is it like the Egyptian snake biting its own tail; rather, it represents the soul travelling upwards towards the heavens. Then suddenly, we became conscious of the path apparently narrowing, the turns getting faster and the view growing vertiginous. The drop to the next level was only a matter of feet, but the illusion was that it was sheer. At the top of the path was a short staircase inside the final stonework, which opened out on to the top plinth, less than 4 metres in diameter, where the muezzin would once have called the faithful to prayer. There we sat, legs dangling over the edge, and felt the wind on our faces as we gazed out over the Mesopotamian plains. It was a simple pleasure, but a timeless one, and Iraqis still come from miles around to enjoy it.

In theory, something of such obvious beauty as the Malawiya should never be under threat, but the region around Samarra was littered with military camps and had been suspected of harbouring facilities for the production of weapons of mass destruction. There had been growing evidence that, contrary to his professed pride in Iraq's culture, Saddam Hussein had been setting up military installations near sites of historic importance. Such actions were undoubtedly intended as a deterrent, but such provocation allows the possibility of a cultural disaster. Little can be safe from the pursuit, and consequence, of any war.

Continuing down the highway, we drove back south through Baghdad until we reached the road to Babylon. Home to the Hanging Gardens which were one of the wonders of the ancient world, the name of Babylon is duskily seductive, reeking of decadent splendour, and yet this world-famous ancient city, only 90 kilometres from Baghdad, is in many ways the most controversial archaeological site in Iraq. We had already caught sight of Saddam Hussein, or at least his image, in every public space in Iraq. He was portrayed in various guises from military hardman to religious zealot, from faithful Arab to gun-toting tyrant. However, on the outskirts of his country's richest treasure Saddam had raised the stakes to an audacious high with a roadside hoarding bearing a dazzling montage of historical scenes that showed him sitting cheek-by-jowl with King Nebuchadnezzar, watching over historical and contemporary shows of power from the chariot to the AK47 assault rifle. This, perhaps more than anything else we saw, captured the arrogance of the President and his desperate bid to take what he perceived as his rightful place alongside the great leaders from his country's past. Newspapers often talked of his ambition to emulate Saladin and to defeat the Christians; but he also desired the lasting achievement of Nebuchadnezzar in creating a city whose magical legend could withstand so powerfully the passage of time.

The first sight to greet us as we arrived in Babylon was a reproduction of the city's Ishtar Gate. Much of the original had been removed to the Pergamon Museum in Berlin in the 1880s, but its smaller-scale replacement did a reasonably faithful job. Given its name and its proximity to Baghdad, Babylon has not surprisingly been Iraq's premier tourist attraction of the last few decades, though like the others it has suffered greatly since the first Gulf War. As we got out of our vehicles we were approached by guides, and looking around we noted a small museum and a shut-down restaurant. Slightly thrown by this unusual degree of commercialism, we pushed on to the site itself – and received a real shock. Nowhere, perhaps, had Saddam realized his policy of rebuilding, consciously emulating the feats of his predecessors in order to attain immortality through architecture, so fully as at Babylon. Awed at the scale of his conceit, we turned corner after corner through historically meaningless, dreary reconstructions of the walls of Babylon's palaces, temples and courtyards which were at best an irrelevant 'Disneyfication'. Ahmed Azez Selman, a mild man in his thirties, attached himself discreetly to our party and guided us through the labyrinth. He pointed out the new bricks bearing Saddam's inscription: 'In the time of the victorious Saddam Hussein, President of the Republic of Iraq, the Guardian of the Great Iraq, here achieved the third stage of reconstruction of Babylon in 1989 like the palace when it was reconstructed by Nebuchadnezzar in 605 BC.' Even as we proceeded towards the older sections, the air was filled with the sounds of workmen busy continuing this desolate folly.

And then something magical occurred. We came to a set of sturdy metal gates, which Ahmed unlocked. Beyond lay the real Babylon, 'the beauty of the Chaldees', and a glimpse of its magical allure. We were in the original Procession Street, the main thoroughfare of the city, lined with the towering walls built in Nebuchadnezzar's time and adorned with moulded bricks depicting fantastical beasts. There was the lion, representing the goddess Ishtar; the bull, symbol of Adad, the god of storms; and the dragon, formed by parts of a snake, eagle and lion and the symbol of the patron deity Marduk, or, as he is known in the Bible, Bel. These highly intricate, skilful images were first moulded on panels of clay then cut into bricks, glazed and reassembled on the façade of the walls, their multidimensional appearance adding spectacular vitality. The floor was higher than it had originally been, reinforced by modern hands to improve drainage, but the route was the one of biblical times that the prophet Daniel would have walked along.

In Akkadian times, around 2350 BC, Babylon was but a small village, but over the following centuries it grew steadily until, in 1792 BC, King Hammurabi, a contemporary of Abraham, made it his capital. Hammurabi's greatest legacy was his code of 282 laws, displayed on 8-foot-high steles, one of which can today be seen in the Louvre in Paris, resplendent with its lines of cuneiform. Babylon's second period of power and prosperity began after the fall of Assyrian Nineveh to the Babylonians and Medes in 612 BC. Nebuchadnezzar, who reigned from 605 to 563 BC, rebuilt Babylon and restored it to its former status as the centre of the civilized world. The so-called Neo-Babylonian period lasted only 40 years or so but its achievements were vast. Nebuchadnezzar captured Jerusalem and brought thousands of its Jewish inhabitants, including the King of Judah, into captivity in Mesopotamia. As well as being active in warfare and conquest, Nebuchadnezzar encouraged the arts and architecture, and bricks stamped with his name continue to be found throughout southern Iraq. There were some still *in situ* on Procession Street. We found several examples, their inscriptions slightly worn by time but legible. It was understandable that Saddam would want to emulate the deeds of such a leader, who had literally left his stamp on history.

Beyond Procession Street, to the north, we found one of the great symbols of Babylon as seen on a million postcards. The savaging stone lion on top of a human figure is somewhat softened after centuries of caresses, but it still packs a powerful presence on its plinth. This, interestingly, was one of the few occasions on which our fixer, Khaled, became twitchy and stopped us filming. Silhouetted on the horizon behind the lion was a huge presidential palace looking down on the ancient centre of the world, and its presence set our alarm bells ringing again. If any air attacks were to pinpoint this Baathist stronghold, would Babylon escape unscathed? Media reports had stated that the US military would be given the coordinates of all significant archaeological sites in order to avoid them, but in the heat of battle anything is game. The juxtaposition of history and ego was a dangerous, possibly destructive, one.

Our guide wanted to show us the reputed site of the Tower of Babel, famous from the Bible as a symbol of man's arrogance in aspiring to be nearer to heaven. But before that particular treat Ahmed took us into some dark vaulted arches which, it is claimed, were the foundations of the legendary Hanging Gardens. The brick vaults and piers were more reminiscent of Victorian engineering and it was difficult to conjure up such a vision of beauty in the dank half-light, but the location seemed reasonably authentic. We were certainly in the bowels of what was a large structure, and the gardens were probably built on terraces on a tiered structure much like a ziggurat.

Then we drove a couple of kilometres to a series of undulating dunes, littered, unbelievably, with thousands of shards of glazed pottery. Some pieces were patterned, others the inimitable pale blue of the Neo-Babylonian era or earlier, while bigger pieces were quite clearly fragments of pots. This was incredible; never before had we stood in a place so rich in archaeological treasures – of minor value, perhaps, but of huge interest and aesthetic appeal. Ahmed told us that the sand was teeming with these shards and urged us to take some with us. It was enough to stand on these windy heights and look down on Babylon as the Tower of Babel, most likely a ziggurat, may once have done. Would Babylon fall again? Time would tell.

When we were still in Baghdad, a French photojournalist had urged us to visit his favourite site in Iraq – Borsippa. He had called it the most dramatic, unspoilt archaeological location in Iraq. It was on our route south, so we decided to go there now. The light was failing, and we were driving along an unmarked road in the middle of nowhere when we caught sight of a magnificent, blasted ziggurat on the horizon. Little is known about the history of Borsippa, or Birs Nimrud as it is sometimes known, though it is believed it was built for the worship of Nabu, son of Marduk. We clambered on to the scree mounds surrounding the ziggurat and started to pick our way carefully to its summit. In its untamed beauty, it offers an idea of how the pioneering archaeologists would have seen these Mesopotamian sites. Suddenly, we spied in the rubble a large, broken brick bearing the unmistakable stamp of Nebuchadnezzar, found where it had lain for 2600 years. The thrill was immeasurable. Back in Britain, we asked a contact at the British Museum if they would have liked one brought back, if it were possible. 'We have people every year bringing in Nebuchadnezzar bricks,' she said. 'We show them a room full of them. What we really want,' she added, 'is a Saddam brick ...'

A portion of the ziggurat's facing brickwork had been exposed, the dusty rubble blown away, and it showed quite clearly the inward incline of the ascending courses. Out of the chaos emerges architecture, the actual craftsmanship, the physical, tangible product of this ancient design. In some ways this obscure location, little known outside of archaeological circles, was a quiet highlight of the trip, particularly coming immediately after the theme-park aspect of Babylon.

That night, we broke our journey in the pilgrimage city of Najaf. Despite the importance of the place it typified the north–south, rich–poor divide in Iraq. As a simple example, the houmous that invariably arrived with other salads at the beginning of a meal had been getting steadily more watery the further south we headed. Here it was particularly thin. We slept in a modest but clean hotel catering for the pilgrim trade, and were on the road again just after dawn. Our next destination was regarded as the first-ever city-state, the world's first real example of urban civilization. Uruk, or Erech, or Warka in Arabic, was, Dan confided, for him perhaps the greatest treasure of all. We reached it by crossing the Euphrates east of the provincial capital of Samawa and driving through the lands that were at the heart of the ancient region of Sumer, and that, through irrigation, have been magically transformed into crop fields. The roads in the south, as we had been warned, were far inferior to those of the north. Single-laned and badly potholed, they made travelling a slower, more frustrating experience. A feature of them was the feral dogs that hovered at their edges. A fair number also lay dead on the road – it was as if they lived off road kill until they themselves became it, in some kind of brutally short food chain. Even now, in late autumn, the landscape was still parched and bleak, not yet recovered from months of arid, scorching conditions. This, perhaps, was our most isolated location, far from present-day civilization yet instrumental in its creation, and guarded by just one man, his family and a pack of snarling mongrels.

Uruk was the city-state of the legendary King Gilgamesh, who was the subject of what is regarded as the world's first literary work, *The Epic of Gilgamesh*. This long poem, believed to have been composed 1500 years before Homer, was originally written down on clay tablets in cuneiform, the first written language. Gilgamesh's face can be seen on many cylinder seals; he is often holding one or more lions, to suggest his indomitable strength. The epic is a wonderful story, full of adventure, and ultimately explores man's painful acceptance, or at least endurance, of mortality. The tale also contains the Sumerian legend of the Great Flood, from which the more familiar biblical version derives: the waters are sent by the supreme god Enlil to punish man's arrogance, and Uta-napishtim, the equivalent of Noah, builds a boat to escape from them. It was in about 2700 BC that Gilgamesh ruled over Uruk, famed for its fortified walls, ziggurat and tended gardens at a time when the inhabitants of the British Isles were living in crude huts. In the epic, in fact, Gilgamesh complains at one point that he has not yet achieved immortality through architecture, using words that seem astonishing in the light of Nebuchadnezzar's and Saddam's vainglorious attempts: 'I have not established my name stamped on bricks as my destiny decreed.' In death he was perceived as 'two parts god, one part man', and his extended people, the Sumerians, were perhaps the most amazing innovators of any era of history. In addition to inventing concepts such as writing, urban architecture, skyscrapers (or, at least, buildings in which height, or closeness to deities, was a conscious concept), the wheel (leading to engineering), and agriculture, they developed systems and ideas from which the modern world is still learning.

As we clambered over the low dunes, past the derelict single-rail railway track once used by archaeologists to ferry artefacts back from the far reaches of the site, it was impossible not to feel exhilaration. We were inside the world's first city, and though it was now being inexorably reclaimed by the desert we could still make out the rooms, chambers, corridors and doorways of the temples and their outbuildings. There was so much here that felt fragile and desperately vulnerable, yet Uruk had already lasted 6000 years. In a strange sense we wanted it to be reburied, to live on under the desert, perhaps to be rediscovered in future millennia and learnt from again. This was the heart of what we in the West call, almost casually, the cradle of civilization – this dusty, forgotten landscape that could be trampled once more beneath the march of armies. After the first Gulf War it would no longer be a shock to see tanks and armoured vehicles advancing across this scrubby terrain, but it would be a tragedy of unimaginable proportions if the symbolic origins of so much that we claim to hold dear, and define as 'civilized', were to be obliterated. The disdainful, tumbling ziggurat would surely survive, but the millions of smaller items, the detail of this rich history, could vanish for all time if this place were to become a battlefield. Ishtar's lament in the ancient *Epic of Gilgamesh* could just as easily refer to the country in which we found ourselves today: 'Alas, the days of old are turned to dust.'

The man at the gate, who had guarded and guided for decades, was keen to show us something before we departed. Carrying a can of water, he led us away from the main buildings and stopped by a patch of wall. Slowly we made out, under the film of dust and grit, a section of clay and stone cones, a few inches long and shaped like cartridges – we had noticed similar ones strewn amongst the ruins. These, though, were still *in situ*, fixed into the wall to protect the sun-baked bricks from rain. The guide then poured water on to the cones to remove the dust. The effect was instantaneous and miraculous. Their uniform sandy surface was transformed into a mosaic of greens and blues of varying hues, in intricate geometric patterns incorporating the chevron, spiral and lozenge. We were witnessing the decorative wall of what was probably a temple, built 6000 or so years ago – and this style of decoration was to re-emerge 5000 years later in Christian Romanesque architecture. We were entranced at this private glimpse of a world that had never died. Like the land itself, it only took water to bring it back to life.

Onwards, further south, we broke our journey at Nasiriyah. More down-at-heel and shabby than Najaf, Nasiriyah was as far as the Allied troops reached during the first Gulf War. It suffered many casualties, one bomb alone destroying a main bridge over the Euphrates and killing hundreds of people. Our drivers and fixer were keen for us to know this, displaying psychological wounds still sore from the conflict. Khaled was not happy in the south. He did not want to stay in the small hotels of Najaf and Nasiriyah, and tried instead to suggest routes that went via major cities such as Samawa and Basra. He remained helpful and polite, but warned us that it was not safe in the south as there were bandits everywhere. We had to take him seriously and were constantly watching our backs, but it was hard not to think of Khaled as a big-city dweller afraid of leaving what he knew. Our arrival certainly aroused local curiosity, even though we were here for the same reason as many Western travellers in the past – Nasiriyah had the nearest food and accommodation to the ruins of Ur.

We were up at 4 a.m. to see the sun rise behind Ur, on what a decade ago was the front line. The great ziggurat of Ur is reckoned to be the finest in Mesopotamia, its mighty brickwork emerging from the Sumerian flatlands like a work of the gods, or at least an attempt to aspire to one – indeed, some authorities have seen this structure as the original Tower of Babel. When built, Ur was located near the mouths of the Euphrates and Tigris on the Persian Gulf, and close to Eridu, the most sacred city of Sumer. Now well inland due to the rivers silting up, it is known locally as Tell el-Mukayyar and consists, besides the ziggurat, of mounded ruins in a roughly oval shape. The first occupation of Ur seems to have been during what is known as the Ubaid period, but it was then abandoned until around 2600 BC. The city was sacred to the moon god Nanna, to whom the temple on the ziggurat was dedicated. There were three dynasties at Ur, the last of which saw the rule of Ur-nammu from 2112 to 2094 BC. Ur-nammu oversaw the building of many temples, including the ziggurat, and introduced sophisticated systems and laws comparable to those at Uruk. The city then fell to the Babylonians and subsequently to the Chaldeans, giving it the name by which it is known in the Bible: Ur of the Chaldees. It is described as the birthplace of the biblical patriarch Abraham, and at that time was the major political centre of the region. There was further building there in the sixth century BC by the Neo-Babylonians under Nebuchadnezzar, but a century or so later it was again abandoned.

The principal excavations at Ur were conducted between 1922 and 1934 by the noted British archaeologist Sir Leonard Woolley. He and his team uncovered 1850 burials and 16 royal tombs which contained a host of priceless items such as a lyre with a golden bull's head, and golden helmets and head-dresses. At the time, news of the discoveries excited a public whose appetite had been whetted by Howard Carter's recent discovery of Tutankhamen's tomb in Egypt. Woolley was a charismatic character and Agatha Christie, whose husband Sir Max Mallowan had been his assistant, wrote of him: 'Leonard Woolley saw with the eye of imagination: the place was as real to him as it had been in 1500 BC, or a few thousand years earlier. Wherever he happened to be, he could make it come alive.'

The ubiquitous site guide, a job which is often passed from father to son for generations, wanted to show us something on the eastern flank, and we remembered Dr Donny's words in Baghdad about the 400 rounds of machine-gun fire which he said had been discharged from a US tank into the wall of the ziggurat. The Americans had claimed that the Iraqis were hiding fighter jets in the ruins, but this was no excuse for wanton destruction. The guide, Thaif Mohsin, claimed that his father had witnessed the US attack in 1991, and showed us impact marks – a dozen or so rather than the 400 reported by Donny George – in the brickwork 'from the aeroplanes'. As proof, he handed us what he said was part of a missile. Dan asked him why the Americans would have done this. 'I don't know why,' came the response. 'Because this is an ancient city.' Were there Iraqi planes here? Dan wondered. 'No, no aeroplanes here.' He dismissed Dan's question with a dissembling smile. Dan asked him how he felt about this building being attacked in such a way. 'I know, and anyone knows, that they made this damage on the walls of the ziggurat. When you talk about the importance of this, it is very important. Iraq thought of the important things – writing and architecture.'

Unfortunately Ur now lay within a military compound, so we had to rouse the slumbering guard to check our paperwork and allow us in. We parked close to the ziggurat and were soon joined by a patrol of soldiers, who sat in the warmth of their vehicles and watched us. They were right to stay inside; the hour before dawn is chilly everywhere, and here, with the winds whipping across the plains, conditions were bitter. The ziggurat was constructed with a core of sun-fired mud bricks covered in a layer of kiln-fired baked bricks set in bitumen, much rebuilt in the 1960s, with wide, processional flights of stairs leading up to its three levels. It is perhaps the most faithful model for Saddam's palaces, particularly the one at Babylon. Not surprisingly, in view of the hour, we had the place to ourselves, and so we clambered eagerly to the top and gazed out at the slowly brightening horizon. The view, flat as far as the eye could see, was as grand as Ur-nammu had intended. These plains had been, however, also the killing fields of the Gulf War, the terrifying terrain of battle, and could be again. We were only able to film in certain directions due to the proximity of the military base, and Dan spotted, with trepidation, what looked like reinforced bunkers for planes. Once again, this seemed unfortunate; more realistically, we felt Saddam had chosen to do this for strategic reasons – not to imperil the ziggurat but to offer maximum protection to his forces. If there was an invasion by American forces from the south, Ur would be on the axis of advance. We feared that this great city could once again be in the firing line.

We travelled on through the delta of the Tigris and Euphrates, the former marshlands of Iraq, immortalized by writers such as Wilfred Thesiger, Gavin Maxwell and Gavin Young who all came and spent time with the Ma'dan, the Shia Marsh Arabs, who had inhabited these waterways for centuries with little change. But in an act of catastrophic folly, over the last decade Saddam had drained the marshes and 90 per cent of what had once covered nearly 8000 square miles had now disappeared. Inevitably, this had resulted in the dispersal of the Marsh Arabs into other parts of Iraq, mostly Baghdad, in search of work, where they experienced a rude awakening to modern urban life. This was an appalling anthropological and ecological tragedy that could never be righted. There has been talk of reflooding the land but even if this is accomplished the people will never return from the cities.

Finally, journey's end. We reached Qurna, now a desolate, sleepy town on the delta but for centuries a scene of conflict due to its strategic position. This spot has been identified as the birthplace of mankind, the location of the Garden of Eden from the Book of Genesis. On the rivers, men and children still threw their fishing nets into the water from hand-fashioned canoes with upturned prows, while livestock grazed on the banks. Such a bucolic idyll seemed very far removed from the world of Saddam Hussein and George W. Bush. A tree in Qurna, known locally as Adam's Tree and located beside a derelict tourist hotel and a deserted children's playground, is reputed to be the biblical Tree of Knowledge. This seems unlikely since the tree in question is little more than a couple of hundred years old but, more symbolically and ominously, it is also dead.

It was a chastening conclusion to our trip, which had taken us on a journey back in time, from the modern bustle of Baghdad to the great cities of the Assyrian, Babylonian and Sumerian empires, and finally to the location of what some believe is the beginning of human existence itself, the Garden of Eden. We had visited nine lost cities, now in varying degrees of ruin but all retaining their own unique, priceless significance to the world as much as to Iraqis. Gavin Young quotes an old Iraqi adage: 'Why put a lock on a ruin?'; but the ruins we had seen were lost treasures that continue to hold the key to so much that we value in the West. Ultimately cities – architecture – are only expressions of the human spirit, and they can be just as easily destroyed by those who do not know their worth or have forgotten it. We found the Iraqi people dignified and welcoming, if poor and extremely vulnerable, yet we were left with the feeling that this could be the peace at the centre of the storm. It was the West that helped Iraq rediscover its historic past in the nineteenth and early twentieth centuries; it would be a travesty if it were now to have a hand in destroying it.

CHAPTER THREE

RETURN TO BAGHDAD

WHEN WE LEFT IRAQ at the end of November 2002 we resolved to return at the earliest possible date, so great was our attachment to the people and their imperilled cultural heritage. We were in Israel and the Occupied Territories for the first two weeks of the war, but remained painfully conscious of developments in Iraq. The aerial bombing of Baghdad made us extremely worried, our concern for the Iraqi people mixed with the knowledge that the city with which we had become so familiar was being brutally pounded. When the Coalition ground forces entered Basra in late March we knew that progress towards Baghdad would begin in earnest, and in the troops' way would be locations such as Ur, Uruk and Babylon. However, it was almost impossible to obtain accurate information about any damage to historic sites. Then, just before our return to the UK, we heard that Jane Root, Controller of BBC2, wanted us to go back to Iraq as soon as possible. The question was how quickly would it be safe, and advantageous, to return?

News started to filter through on 11 April 2003 that the Iraq Museum in Baghdad was being looted, and a conversation with the Ancient Near East department at the British Museum seemed to confirm this terrible fact. In the coming days the press picked up on the story, with cataclysmic headlines such as 'A Civilisation Torn to Pieces' (*Independent on Sunday*, 13 April); Robert Fisk, one of the first journalists in the museum, reported that 'something truly terrible has taken place: the mob has turned upon its own heritage'. On 14 April, Raeed Abdul Reda, an archaeologist at the Iraq Museum, was quoted in the *Guardian* as saying that 'Eighty per cent of what we had was stolen', and the media, including the BBC, were quoting the words of Nabhal Amin, deputy director of the Iraqi National Museum, that 'looters [had] taken or destroyed 170,000 items of antiquity dating back thousands of years'. One senior American academic, Piotr Michalowski, was moved on History News Network to make this dramatic proclamation: 'The pillaging of the Baghdad Museum is a tragedy that has no parallel in world history; it is as if the Uffizi, the Louvre, or all the museums of Washington DC had been wiped out in one fell swoop. Some compare the event to the burning of the Alexandria Library.' All of us, especially Dan, had always deeply admired the Iraqis' respect for their culture. How could such a country turn on its history in so brutal a manner? It seemed unbelievable.

Our conversations with Dr Donny George, the Iraq Museum's Director of Research, back in November 2002 had focused on the possibility of aerial attacks; at no point had he seriously contemplated that the museum might be plundered. What had happened? Why had items not been evacuated, according to the plan that Dr Donny had outlined, and what was the role in all this of the American military? The newspaper reports seemed contradictory in terms of who was actually responsible for the looting. Abdul Rehman Mugeer, described in the *Guardian* as a senior guard at the museum, said: 'Gangs of several dozen came. Some had guns. They threatened to kill us if we did not open up. The looting went on for two days.' Other media claimed that the looters were an 'uneducated' mixture of the old, women and children, implying that they were from the poor Shia neighbourhoods nearby. And some were hinting at darker thoughts. In *The Australian*, a member of the museum staff, who declined to be identified, said: 'The fact that the vaults were opened suggests employees of the museum may have been involved. To ordinary people, these are just stones. Only the educated know the value of these pieces.' There were even reports that the museum's safe storerooms had been penetrated, and that thousands of items stored there in metal trunks had been ransacked.

The Americans were bearing the brunt of the world's outrage. Museum employees said that the US military had put tanks outside the museum on 9 April, but that they had left again soon afterwards. Archaeologist Raeed Abdul Reda acknowledged that a small group of US soldiers had returned with a tank on the eleventh, but claimed that half an hour after the looters had left so did the tank – enabling the looters to return later at will. Reda said he had asked for a tank to be parked there permanently, but his request had been refused. This seemed strange and, if true, would mean that the US Army had been at least partly culpable for the looting. Jane Waldbaum, president of the Archaeological Institute of America, was among those who were appalled at the US military command's failure to safeguard the building, especially given the warnings that archaeological experts had been sending to the Pentagon since January: 'It was completely predictable, and we did predict it. We begged authorities to watch out for this in the aftermath of actual fighting. All it would have taken was a tank parked at the gate.' Dr Donny popped up on CNN, apparently furious at the way events had unfolded. He told Jim Clancy how he had tried to persuade the Americans to protect the museum. 'Three days ago, me and [the] chairman of the State Board of Antiquities [Dr Jaber Ibrahim] went to the headquarters of the Marines in the Palestine Hotel. We waited there for about four hours until we met a colonel. And that day, he promised that he will send armoured cars to protect what's left of the museum. That was three days ago. But until now, nobody came.' Meanwhile Donald Rumsfeld, the US Defense Secretary, brushed off the news with the words 'Bad things happen in life, and people do loot.' The US military were saying they did not have the manpower to protect every building in the newly liberated Baghdad, but critics pointed to their ability to protect the Ministry of Oil, thus highlighting their priorities – commerce over culture. Back in Washington, three cultural advisers to the Bush administration – Martin Sullivan, who chaired the President's Advisory Committee on Cultural Property for eight years; Richard S. Lanier, director of a New York cultural foundation; and Gary Vikan, director of Baltimore's Walters Art Museum – resigned in protest.

It was hard to know what, or whom, to believe. All that seemed clear was that in the days following the taking of Baghdad by US forces, the Iraq Museum had been pillaged to a considerable degree – a cultural catastrophe.

But was this our moment to return? In theory, we were eager to revisit the ancient sites, the nine lost cities, to ascertain what, if any, damage they had sustained during the campaign. There had been little or no news on these fronts, but that was not unexpected – it would take a specialized team to give any accurate assessment, and many parts of Iraq were still extremely dangerous. Taking all this into account, we decided that the Iraq Museum story was too important for us to delay. Then we heard that John Curtis, Keeper of the Ancient Near East department at the British Museum, was to travel there to assess the damage and report to a meeting in London on 29 April, at which Tessa Jowell, the Secretary of State for Culture, Media and Sport, would be present. We agreed to pool resources and travel together to Baghdad. The BBC would arrange transport, security, supplies and so on, while John knew both the Iraq Museum collection and the museum staff personally, in particular Dr Donny. With new director Guy Smith, an experienced BBC current affairs hand who had worked on *Panorama* and *Correspondent,* the team left Heathrow on 22 April determined to get to the truth of this story that had shaken the world.

As on the first trip we would be flying to Amman, but since Saddam International Airport was now a base for US forces we would be obliged to do the rest of the journey by the long desert road from Jordan. As was required by the BBC for travelling to what it termed Hostile Environments Category 1 countries, we had two security advisers with us, both former members of the British Army's special forces. Dale Allen, who met us in Jordan, had been in Iraq and its neighbouring countries for weeks working with various media companies, including the BBC, while we had first bumped into Gav Kerr, who flew out with us, in Afghanistan a year before. Dale had made all the arrangements from the Jordanian end, which meant that we were able to leave in the very early hours of 24 April in order to be at the border by dawn – it was too risky to travel across Iraq outside of daylight hours. Our vehicles were three GMCs, loaded to the hilt with equipment, supplies and bottled water. For personal protection we wore flak jackets which, though heavy and cumbersome, particularly in the desert heat, were prerequisites on a road notorious for bandits and in a country where fierce fighting had been taking place until a week or so previously.

The lights of Amman quickly gave way to the dark of the highway.

John Pilger once wrote that the Jordan–Baghdad road was the most dangerous he had ever driven on, mainly due to the leviathan oil tankers that used to pound its tarmac remorselessly. There were certainly fewer of these now, but in return there would be an increased threat of robbery after crossing into Iraq. A couple of hours from Amman we broke the journey at al-Safawi, a small pumping-station settlement lined with ranks of 24-hour food and supplies shops. These outlets used to buzz with trade from the trucks, taxis and buses that once thronged the route, but now it was barely worth their while opening, and between customers staff would sleep with their heads on the counter.

From al-Safawi, the Jordanian border was only about two hours away. By the time we arrived at around 5 a.m. there were already queues of traffic, mostly GMCs like ours containing aid workers and supplies. It took a while for our paperwork to be processed, so we set up the camping stove and had plates of bangers and beans, washed down with bitter coffee, as the sun rose through the hazy cloud over Iraq, beyond the barbed wire and checkpoints. An hour or so later we were heading through no-man's-land for the Iraqi border. There was a cursory vehicle inspection, and a passport check by one Iraqi soldier and a team of US soldiers (including one, curiously, from Watford), before we finally gained entry to Iraq and drove past hundreds of refugee tents as we headed for Baghdad.

It was a cool, bright morning, and at first there was little to indicate there had been a war. Suddenly, into view came a shattered bridge that had clearly taken a hit from a heavy bomb. As we moved on we filmed the scene. Then a troop of Australian SAS turned up: they had noticed that we were filming, and this presented a major problem. We were halted and questioned, and they insisted we erase the shots of them. It was our first real indication that we were entering a war zone, where the slightest misinterpreted move could have severe consequences.

At this point it was hard to predict what we would find. On the previous trip the Iraqis we had met had been courteous, kind, and warm in their welcome. But how would they view us this time? We were now the enemy: it was an unpleasant but brutal truth. People could well be angry at the death and destruction, at the lack of food, water and security, at the military humiliation of their country. It was a dangerous time to be in Iraq, but to find out what had happened at the Iraq Museum our presence was essential. John Curtis confided his fears of what we might find. He had spoken by satellite phone a few days earlier to Dr Donny, who had told him that it looked like a 'hurricane' had been through the museum's storerooms.

After the town of Ramadi we crossed the Euphrates and dropped into Mesopotamia; here the landscape softened somewhat, with groups of date palms breaking up the desert flatness. As we neared Baghdad the traffic gradually built up. The expanses of desert on either side of the highway started to reveal both the distinctive tells on the horizon that signified ancient settlements, and burnt-out Iraqi tanks and armoured vehicles. We stopped for petrol on the outskirts of the city, and felt incongruous in our bright blue flak jackets among the Iraqis in their long, flowing *dishdashas*. They watched us with inscrutable expressions, wondering no doubt who and what we were. As we entered the suburbs, the sights drove home the change since our last visit. Not least among them were the convoys of American Humvees and articulated trucks, with machine-gunners up top, poised for attack. The scenes of people walking along with their children and donkeys were immediately and reassuringly familiar, yet many of the buildings around them had been shelled, and reduced to debris. Nothing could be the same again; we had known this, but to see Baghdad so scarred and broken rendered us all silent. We crept past a former Ministry of Defence building that was completely gutted, its exposed floors littered with gnarled metal and rubble. Numerous smaller buildings were still smouldering, and mingling with the smoke was the putrid stench of a garbage-choked city. The absence of traffic lights and the previously ubiquitous traffic police had caused highway anarchy, with many major roads clogged and vehicles going in both directions on the same carriageway. Most of the people on the streets were walking around wide-eyed, apparently not sure what to do.

When we saw the familiar mock-Assyrian gatehouse of the Children's Museum, which abutted a corner of the Iraq Museum, we observed that a large shell-hole had appeared in its upper storey. This did not augur well. But as the main part of the museum came into view we could at least confirm that an Abrams tank was stationed outside and there seemed to be a swarm of US soldiers in the museum grounds. Our vehicles pulled up at the gates, which were locked. This was the first test: could we persuade the US Army to allow us into the museum compound? At first, obviously fatigued by media enquiries, they batted away our request, but we persisted; playing our trump card of John Curtis, we asked the guards if they would see whether Dr Donny would come out.

Five nervous minutes later he appeared uncertainly at the museum door, but on seeing John in our party his eyes lit up and he greeted us all with recognition. It was something of a shock to see him looking so wan and drawn. After speaking with the soldiers, he ushered us into the grounds and up to the door of the administration offices. We had hoped to spend our first night camped out in the galleries, but the museum had now been padlocked for the night and so we asked Dr Donny if we could camp outside it instead, in order to be at the scene of the crime at first light. In any case, it was already too late to tour Baghdad safely in search of hotel accommodation, which we knew to be at a premium. With his agreement we started to unpack our sleeping bags in the covered entrance to the museum. The only thing we still needed was permission from the US guards, who informed us that their colonel should be back soon. In the meantime, they kindly brought over some hot rations and let us use their shower – a garden hose – and the toilet in the museum library, where they were camped. We were at this moment in a strange position: a media team on a mission, keen to do what we could to help the Iraqi museum staff highlight the terrible events that had apparently taken place there, but indebted to the US military for their hospitality and protection.

Despite the early hour we were tired after our journey and anxious to bed down when the colonel finally returned. Army officers can often live up to our misconceptions of them, but Colonel Matthew Bogdanos defied stereotype. Slight, but lean and fit, Bogdanos was a Marine reservist who had been called up after 11 September 2001 from his day job as a homicide prosecutor in Manhattan. Formidably articulate, he spoke with a gentle lisp that suggested a soft touch, yet it was Bogdanos who in February 2001 had prosecuted rap mogul Sean Combs, aka Puff Daddy, over a charge of possession of a firearm and attempted bribery to pervert the course of justice in connection with a nightclub shooting. He was not afraid to stand up to anyone – indeed, Combs's lawyer had called him 'one tough son of a bitch'. In his mid-forties, a classical scholar and an amateur middleweight boxer to boot, Bogdanos was heading the Joint Inter-Agency Coordination Group, a special unit set up at US Central Command to investigate the looting of the museum. He had agents from the US Homeland Security Department who were offering advice on the art-smuggling aspect, and a dozen FBI agents 'in the theatre', though not at the museum, on whom he could call for assistance at any time.

Although happy to let us stay the night in the museum, Bogdanos told us not to use any lights after sundown or we would attract Iraqi snipers, and not to wander around in case we were shot by the US guards as intruders. A tank company might have secured the grounds, but that did not offer protection against incoming fire, or against someone firing a rocket-propelled grenade (RPG) into the compound. We nodded meekly, and resolved to keep our heads down.

In time we realized that Bogdanos was probably pleased at the timing of our appearance. Frustrated at the obstacles put in his way by the museum authorities, he was keen to document the efforts his team were making to assess the damage and to recover stolen items. He confirmed to Dan and John Curtis that a preliminary list of around 20 stolen objects had been drawn up, which was being circulated worldwide via the Homeland Security Department. He hoped this would start to put the dampeners on any attempts to sell looted items on the international art black market.

The night passed fitfully. Through the heat came the rattle of gunfire, a sound with which we were quickly to grow familiar – though at this stage it often sounded uncomfortably close. We were also kept awake by the pulsating wheeze of the generator used by the US military to power their computers, and were bitten by sandflies when we finally slept. But we were the fortunate ones. For the rest of Baghdad there was virtually no electricity, which meant no water; mounting piles of rotting garbage in the streets; and looting still prevalent. Up soon after daybreak to the sounds of tank manoeuvres, we were getting washed when one of the soldiers cheerfully informed us that some of the shots we had heard during the night had been fired around the museum. Welcome to the liberated city. Being inside the railings of the museum grounds made us feel ambivalent, reinforcing a sense of separation from the ordinary Iraqi people who wandered by and looked in.

Suddenly, we spotted a familiar face at the gate. Khaled, our second government minder from our first trip, was waving to us. He was one of those whom we had worried about during the war, and it was a boost to our morale to see him there. He had been in Kerbala during the fighting, but was now back at work with a media crew. Dan asked him how things had been. 'Everything is terrible,' came the short reply. He seemed glad to see us, though, and had his own theories on the looting at the museum. As we were to hear more than once in the days to come, Khaled claimed that it had been carried out by foreigners, mostly Jordanians and Syrians, who had deliberately smashed up the building and its contents after removing what they wanted. While we could understand Iraqi people stealing items of worth if they were hungry and poor, the notion of deliberate destruction of their culture and history had seemed implausible. So, could Khaled's story be true?

As the rest of Baghdad slowly stirred we awaited the arrival of Dr Jaber Ibrahim, the Director-General of the State Board of Antiquities. Dr Jaber had been the invisible power that had kept us waiting for days on our first trip before finally signing our letters of permission to leave Baghdad. At the time we had been quietly angry at his procrastination, which seemed little more than a tactic. Now he held the key – literally – to our quest. He turned up at around nine o'clock with Dr Nawala Mutiwalli, the curator of the museum, undid the padlock on the metal-barred doors and let us into the administration block. It was virtually unrecognizable. The sofas, tables and desks had all disappeared – presumably looted – and the floor was thick with rubble and trash. The way to the Director-General's office was littered with broken statues and pots, while the main corridor was blocked, presumably as a defensive measure, by a couple of steel door-frames through which we clambered to gain access. As we picked our way through the gloom – there was no electricity – we glanced into the offices on either side. Papers, file cards, irreplaceable slides and books were strewn everywhere, the history and records of the institution ruthlessly discarded in a frenzied search for, presumably, money or saleable objects. Glancing across this mess one could pick out phrases, images, pictures; order had been essential for the museum staff's work, and for their relations with the government, but now there was only this appalling jumble. We glanced into Dr Donny's office through a gaping hole smashed in its wooden door. It was where we had interviewed him the previous November; now it had been emptied – even the coffee machine had gone. As we walked down the corridor every office told the same story: anything of worth – air-conditioning units, computers, photocopiers, telephones – had been removed by the looters and anything too heavy, such as safes, had been broken into and ransacked. The degree of looting was thorough and, in the case of the safes, painstaking, involving considerable know-how.

Dr Jaber, a gaunt, slightly stooping man whose quiet voice was often lost in the building's melancholy echo, appeared to be still traumatized. We believed him to be a political appointment, despite his qualifications and expertise. He hailed from Tikrit, Saddam's home town and a Baathist stronghold; one of his predecessors had been Dr Hana Abdul Khaleq, the sister of the Information and Culture Minister. Apparently exhausted by the ordeal, he shuffled along with heavy feet. There was a small mountain of papers on the floor in the corridor, which he said had been brought from all over the building. 'To make a bonfire', he concluded sadly. 'First there is looting, then there is burning.' John Curtis, well used to the fact that what one sees in the galleries represents only a fraction of the collection and operation of a museum, shook his head disconsolately at the wanton destruction and sympathized frequently with the Director-General. We were shocked at the degree of destruction and theft, but had already turned our minds to the galleries – if this was the state of the offices, what could we expect in there? It hardly bore thinking about.

Finally, we reached the corridor that led to the museum from the administrative block. Even this short stretch was strewn with smashed pots and 2000-year-old Hatran statues, some on their sides. Now was the moment of truth. The staff had been deeply reluctant to allow any foreign media into the museum itself. We were to be the first foreign TV crew, and Dan the first journalist, to view the galleries – and, we hoped, the storerooms – since they had been secured. It was a tense moment as Dr Nawala unlocked the gates and ushered us in. Suddenly, we were filled with trepidation: what would we find after the events of the past tumultuous weeks? A carpet of shards of priceless pottery, smashed statues and empty glass cases?

The first room was a Sumerian gallery, containing artefacts between 5000 and 6000 years old, which we had seen on our previous trip. Natural light from high windows gave reasonable visibility. As we surveyed the scene, our initial impression was that the damage was not as bad as we had feared. Dan was immediately heartened by the sight of the 6000-year-old temple wall of cone pegs, rescued from Uruk, still apparently untouched and still attached to the wall. All the glass display cabinets were empty, but most had not been smashed, suggesting that their contents had been successfully evacuated before the war. The diminutive Sumerian statues with which Dan had stared eye to saucer-eye the previous autumn had presumably been hidden away by staff, as their cabinet appeared undisturbed. But a closer investigation of other exhibits revealed that they had not fared so well. An ancient skeleton we remembered from before had been disturbed, its case smashed open and the grave goods displayed with it stolen. Other smaller, precious items were still represented in their cases by colour photographs, implying their safe storage at some as yet unspecified site. A number of cases had been smashed, however, and the evidence suggested that artefacts had been hurriedly wrenched from their mountings by looters. A trail of blood and broken glass told its own story. Bigger items had not escaped the looters' attentions, either. A beautiful statue had been toppled from its plinth on to the protective foam that had been tied to it to cushion any impact, though the perceived threat had been from bombing rather than looting. The ingenious thief had intended to use the foam as a sledge on which to drag the statue away, but it would seem he had been disturbed in the act. The noble statue, whose head had itself been lost at some indeterminate point in its 4500-year history, now lay on its side on the floor, safe if undignified.

In the main Assyrian gallery there was less destruction, although some of the statues bore visible scars on their plinths where unscrupulous looters had tried to chisel them free. But in the adjoining gallery there were noticeable gaps in display cabinets where objects must have been removed. I went with Dr Donny and John Curtis to see what the former claimed was evidence that at least one of the museum's five secure storerooms had been breached. He took us to a door whose glass was smashed. Down a dark staircase we could see a walled-up doorway, with the top couple of courses of concrete blocks missing. We went down and shone a torch through, and saw that it was a storeroom. Little detail could be made out beyond some pots on the floor, not visibly damaged, and rows of shelves holding smaller pottery items. Despite my requests, Dr Donny claimed we could not film this location as Dr Jaber would not allow it. So we returned to the galleries, Dr Donny and John going on to another gallery while I returned to the rest of the team. I remembered that we had filmed in the Hatran gallery on the previous trip, so we went off in that direction, unaccompanied, to see how it had fared. It too had seen attempts to remove statues, and in one or two cases the thieves had been successful. Most striking was a delicate statue of a deity which now bore gouge marks on its neck where someone had attempted to decapitate it. The array of sandbags on the floor was yet another reminder of what the museum staff had actually been preparing for: bombing, which could topple exhibits. Sandbags were not so effective against looters. Then a strange thing happened. As we filmed the evidence we heard the sound of someone running. Suddenly Dr Nawala appeared, panting and in a state of panic. We calmed her down and asked what was wrong. She could only tell us that the museum was now closing, that we could not film any more and that we would have to leave. What had put her in such a frenzy? Was it our proximity to the one storeroom they had shown me? What did she fear us discovering? It certainly aroused our suspicions.

Overall, while pieces had obviously been taken and damage was clearly visible, the scene was not as bad as we had feared. Many of the larger items, such as the Assyrian winged bulls and reliefs, were too big for anyone to have even contemplated stealing, and so had been left intact and fundamentally unvandalized. But where had the items that had been removed before the war been stored? If they were in the storerooms, what had been their fate? And where had the stolen items been located? Had they been in the galleries? Had they been stolen from the storerooms? Or had they been elsewhere?

We were intending to talk to Dr Donny about what precautions had been taken when news came through that someone had returned some objects. In the entrance hall a young man was nervously waiting for us. Nabil Aref had with him a selection of minor pottery items; most were stamped with their museum catalogue number, which Dr Nawala duly noted down. Nabil told the staff that he had bought the pieces in a nearby market, and hoped to bring back more. Dan, sensing a cover story, asked Dr Jaber if he thought the man had stolen them himself. Dr Jaber winked as he mouthed, 'Probably'. These were the first real results since the US military had started making radio broadcasts throughout the city, offering an amnesty on artefacts returned to the museum. Nabil insisted he was not a looter himself and stuck to the market story, emphasizing that he was sure he could, and would, bring back more pieces. Perhaps the slow wheels of recovery had started to turn.

Meanwhile our security advisers had been trying to get accommodation for us. The Palestine Hotel, where most of the media had stationed themselves, was booked to the rafters, with six or seven people to a room, and had not been cleaned since the start of the war. The only other hotel open was the Sheraton, opposite. Both were protected behind barbed wire and US tanks, but each day hundreds of Shia protesters gathered outside to show their anger at the American occupation of their city. After much wrangling and a little financial persuasion we were finally given two rooms at the Sheraton, with the promise of a third when it became available. Perhaps inevitably, when we turned up at the end of the day the rooms had been given to another media crew. Thus began hours of wheeler-dealing with the hotel management, who had misplaced any earlier memory of our negotiations or the money exchanged. Finally, through a mixture of good will on the part of the other crew and sheer doggedness, we were 'found' rooms, one overlooking the Tigris and the other looking down on Fardos Square, where the statue of Saddam had been toppled in front of viewing billions. To celebrate, we cracked open some military self-heating rations (MREs – meals ready to eat) and a bottle of whisky.

Next morning we finally got to sit down with Dr Donny, outside the museum in the now burning sun. On our last visit he had stated that there was an evacuation plan for the collection. So what had happened? What immediately became clear was that, as the appearance of the galleries suggested, the museum staff had put up their defences against the wrong kind of enemy. Donny admitted that the looting 'was a big surprise for us. I never thought it would happen, because this is a very important building, as everybody knows, whether Iraqi or American. We never thought it would be looted in this way.' The most valuable items, such as jewellery and gold, had been taken away to a location about which Dr Donny felt confident: 'We've seen that it's an area secured by American forces, so they are safe.' Other items from the galleries, such as the Sumerian statues, were also safe, according to Dr Donny, but in the museum's storerooms. Dan then asked Dr Donny if it was known how many things in storage had survived; he said he was not sure. 'We know they went into the storage rooms in the cellar of the museum, but we do not know accurately what has been taken. We have to check thing by thing, box by box, and then go to our inventory to know exactly what is missing.' Yet it was apparent that Dr Donny *did* seem to know that some pieces had gone. As he went through the 1975 museum catalogue, he was able to point to items such as the 5000-year-old Sacred Vase of Warka, the Lady of Warka stone sculpture, a bronze Akkadian statue, a 4600-year-old headless statue of a Sumerian king and some ivories, and say that these had definitely been taken. It was odd that on the one hand he refused to estimate the losses in the storerooms, and that on the other he could identify high-value items that he said were definitely missing.

Whatever the truth, his pledge the previous November to safeguard all the museum's treasures had not been kept and key items, such as the famous lyre from Ur, had gone missing or had been badly damaged. The lyre's gold head was in secure storage, Dr Donny said, but its wooden frame had been smashed. How could it have been left so vulnerable to attack, even if they were expecting bombs rather than looters? Once more, the answer to so many of these questions seemed to be behind the storerooms' doors – and still no one was producing the keys, despite the requests of both Colonel Bogdanos and ourselves. In the meantime, the staff were returning to work for the first time since the war, but could not get in as Dr Jaber had not turned up that morning.

Keen to share his vexation, Colonel Bogdanos took a few minutes to brief us from his perspective. 'Eight days into our investigation,' he began, 'we are still struggling to get an accurate inventory of what was in the museum prior to the war, so that we can determine what is missing. We don't yet have complete inventories from the museum itself, and that's been a challenge for us. I've asked for an inventory of items on the gallery floor prior to the war, and we still haven't received that. Nor have we received any inventory of items that were alleged to have been removed to the Central Bank of Iraq, nor an inventory of items in storage in the basement of the museum.' His frustration was palpable, but, at least officially, he was reluctant to respond to Dan's suggestion that the staff might be obstructing his investigation. 'I really can't comment on individuals or the staff at the museum. That isn't the focus of our investigation, which is, and remains, the recovery of artefacts.'

There were two different mentalities at work here. The American attitude was that you find a list of what you had, check it against what you now have, the difference being the things that have gone missing. The Iraqis' approach was far more circumspect and, with the exception of certain high-value items, seemed to involve waiting to see what was returned, and then confirming whether it had been stolen. Whether haplessness or something more sinister was guiding this, it was impossible yet to tell.

Then Bogdanos and his team had their first real break. A member of staff had informed them of a secret location in Baghdad where storage crates from the museum had been taken before the war. Sensing a scoop, Bogdanos agreed to let us accompany his team on their visit. We had to follow their Humvees through the nightmare Baghdad traffic, which proved even harder than it sounds. In a bid to keep up with the

Americans, at one point our driver, Whaled, mounted the pavement and drove at about 30 mph through the crowds. I shall never forget the look on one man's face when he saw us bearing down on him and threw himself into a bush. We could hardly approve of such tactics, but at the same time we could not afford to lose the Americans. I would like to think that Whaled would have swerved. Eventually.

We pulled up behind the Humvees in a smart suburb. Bogdanos ordered his troops to seal off the street, then marched into a squat, modern air-raid shelter, having first dramatically instructed his men, 'Safety off!' We descended a flight of stairs and entered a bunker full of hundreds of metal trunks. Bogdanos signalled for one of the local men to open a trunk. The man lifted the lid on the one nearest him, to reveal a hoard of what looked to be old books and manuscripts. After a few more conversations and a couple more cursory inspections, it became clear that all the trunks contained the same kind of material: more than 40,000 items, moved three or four months previously from the Museum Library. It was an important find of valuable and rare manuscripts, but it was not what we were looking for. And curiously, when a US lorry was sent the next day to pick up the trunks, the local people persuaded the would-be collectors to leave them. This seemed remarkable: the Iraqis felt the books and manuscripts were safer under their control than in the hands of those they considered still associated with the old Baathist regime, even though the museum building had now been secured by the Americans. Bogdanos accepted their argument, and the local people vowed to maintain a 24-hour watch over their hoard.

Then we were told of another lead. Bogdanos knew that sealed cases from the museum, possibly containing as many as 7000 objects, had been taken to the Central Bank of Iraq. Surely these would be the high-value items, the jewellery and gold? He was going to find out, and we could join him. We jumped into the car and again followed the American convoy. The Central Bank had reportedly been visited a couple of days before the war began by Qusay Hussein, Saddam's younger son, who had left with over $1 billion in cash. Locals claimed he had made a second visit just before Baghdad was taken. Did he know about the museum items stored there? If he did, then suspicions about the involvement of those close to Saddam's regime in the theft of museum artefacts might be proved true.

The bank, on al-Rashid Street, was heavily protected by tanks and a barbed-wire no-go zone. We could see that the building had been heavily pulverized by US missiles, leaving only a mass of twisted girders and smoke-blackened stone. As we descended to the vaults, deep in the bowels of the building, the floor was thick with rubble and fragments of banknotes – crumpled portraits of Saddam still keeping an eye on us. We had got as far as the heavy-duty steel doors, which appeared unviolated, before we were informed that the man with the keys was not to be found. More frustration, but it did feel as though we were getting closer, and it was confirmed that before the war Dr Donny had come to the bank on three occasions with up to 20 sealed chests. So there were museum treasures there – if they had not been plundered.

Colonel Bogdanos was upbeat about the two missions. 'The best word I can use is "thrilling", to have come across the priceless manuscripts, parchments and vellum at the bunker. As for the bank, we knew we wouldn't get into the bank today – the purpose was to ascertain which is the bank in question, whereabouts in the bank, and to question the bank representative further as to what exactly had been brought there.' Bogdanos also acknowledged that, while they could ask these questions, what happened next was a matter more for diplomacy than for the law. 'We're here at the invitation of the museum officials, and I'm not sure we have the legal authority to breach these safes if we are unable to get the keys.' This was a tricky line to walk, but if anyone had the skills to manage it, it was the colonel. Turning to the question of the museum storerooms, he acknowledged that his team were hampered by not being able to gain access, and that they would not know exactly what had gone until they could – though he confirmed that, as far as he had been able to ascertain, the rooms had been partially looted. But, as he was to reiterate throughout the investigation, 'Until I open each of those individual cases, we won't know.' Did he not hold a set of keys, as head of the investigation? Dan wondered. A smile flickered across Bogdanos's usually inscrutable features. 'Caesar's wife should be above reproach,' muttered the erstwhile classical scholar.

John Curtis was due to return to England with Dr Donny for a press conference at the British Museum to give his assessment of the damage. John had been making his own record while we had been following the colonel: 'One hundred and twenty rooms trashed – it's a terrible mess, and for any museum that would be a disaster.' But was he more or less optimistic than before the trip? Dan wondered. 'About the same,' John replied. He thought the condition of the galleries wasn't as bad as it might have been, 'the storerooms we don't yet know about, and the offices are much worse than I imagined'. Back in London, he would have meetings with top museum officials from Europe and America in order to formulate a programme to assist the Iraqis in their conservation and repair work. Dr Donny was to explain events from the point of view of the museum, and would be praised as a hero by his international colleagues and the British government.

Before they left, however, we were keen to try to make some sense of what had happened during the battle for the museum. This was the one area in which almost all the world's press had been critical of the US Army, because of its failure to provide immediate security for the museum and its contents. Dr Donny took us to the corner of the compound by the Children's Museum which had been hit by a shell, and explained what had taken place: 'It was Tuesday morning, 8 April, between ten and eleven. All night there had been a big battle over the local area, and that morning it was getting closer. There were American tanks approaching from that area,' he gestured to the rear of the museum, 'and again from here', gesturing again to another corner. 'At that moment, we noticed some militiamen with RPGs. They jumped into our garden', Dr Donny pointed to a spot a few feet away, 'and you can still see some grenades there. They were firing on the tanks from here. It was at that moment that Dr Jaber decided it was too dangerous, we were in the crossfire, and we had to leave by the back door.' One of the reasons the fighting had been so fierce around the museum was that there were so many government buildings in the locality.

Dr Donny continued. 'I feel so sorry they used this building for firing, because then this building became a military point.' This was indeed so, from both sides of the fence. But something was puzzling Dan. Pointing to the three or four bunkers and shallow trenches in the museum garden, he asked Dr Donny when they were dug and why. 'Actually, we dug them because we were afraid of the missiles …' So they were in fact air-raid shelters? 'That's right. I had all the staff come to these shelters to protect themselves from any kind of shelling.' Much as we wanted to believe Dr Donny's explanation, the pits, roofed as they were with palm trees and asbestos sheeting, would have been little use against missiles raining in. In November we had visited the Amariyah bomb shelter, where 408 civilians had died when it was hit by American bombs. We had seen what a bomb can do even to reinforced concrete. In our opinion, endorsed by our security advisers, these dug-outs were almost certainly fighting positions. At this point, Dr Donny told us, he and Dr Jaber left the compound. 'There were a few militiamen here and there, but by now the tanks were here, so we thought we'd leave for a while – they would watch the building, and it would be safe. I was very confident of that. We did not return until Sunday [13 April]. As far as we know, the looting took place on the Thursday, Friday and Saturday [10–12 April].' So, according to Dr Donny, for three days the museum was open to anybody.

Suddenly, while we were talking, there was an explosion of gunfire close to the museum. Dr Donny was unperturbed – 'I think they are celebrating the return of the electricity,' he joked. This explanation was to be offered ever more sardonically during the next week. As far as he was concerned, then, the looting had come as a total surprise. He saw it as the work of two groups. The first were, in his view, organized, professional gangs, and he had evidence of this in the form of diamond glass-cutters which he had found discarded in the museum. Such tools were easy to come by in Baghdad, and to him were a sign of premeditated action. These gangs also passed by various gypsum copies in the galleries, picking out only original pieces, which suggested expert knowledge. The second category of looters he saw as those who went in and turned everything upside down, particularly in the administration block.

So this was the view that had been presented to the outside world. Dr Donny and Dr Jaber had locked up the museum and departed on the

Wednesday morning, confident that the presence of the American tanks would deter any would-be intruders. They did not return until the Sunday, by which time the museum and its offices had been ransacked. It would appear that the tanks had been withdrawn soon after their departure, and, according to reports, were not properly deployed there again until 16 April, a week after their first appearance. Dr Donny was claiming that the museum had been virtually undefended, and that only 'a few' militiamen had jumped over the wall to find shelter in the grounds during the heat of battle. This account confirmed criticism of the US troops' failure to act, so we decided to seek out the officers involved in the battle for Baghdad.

Jason Conroy, a young captain and tank commander in the 3rd Platoon, C Company, 3rd Infantry Division, had been a company commander in the force that fought its way through Baghdad to the museum. Standing with us on the street outside the museum compound, he told a different story from Dr Donny. On 9 April his unit had seized the nearby intersection, and for three or four days had engaged with the Special Republican Guard, Saddam Fedayeen and militiamen holed up in the surrounding ministries and streets. It was a tank in his company that had fired the shell that killed an Iraqi gunman shooting from the Children's Museum in the compound, but Conroy confirmed that his men had taken a lot of RPG and small-arms fire, especially from the rear of the museum where the militiamen were running into the street and launching grenades at the American tanks. 'When we first came up here to the museum,' said Conroy, 'it looked like a military compound. There were bunkers on the outside, and probably 150 troops at the rear of the museum building. Some were Special Republican Guard, others were in civilian clothes, but all had an RPG or an AK47.'

This version of events contradicted what we had already been told, and was disturbing. Captain Conroy was depicting a scenario that involved more than 'a few' militiamen, which could explain the reluctance of the Americans to move swiftly into the vicinity of the museum. And Conroy was in no doubt regarding the bunkers in the museum garden. 'They were clearly fighting positions. When we came in here, we found RPGs, AK47s and hand grenades right by them. It was definitely a prepared position, a strong point, and the whole area was heavily fortified, with close to 300 troops we had to fight through. To us, the museum had been turned into a military complex, a headquarters for a military operation.' Conroy then took us to the rear of the main building, to a small office complex now completely derelict with its windows shattered, its walls and doors shot out or burnt out, and a jumble of papers, pictures of Saddam and human excrement on the floor. This, he claimed, had been the headquarters for the force occupying the museum grounds, with a map of Baghdad on the wall on which they plotted the American advance. He then walked us to a gate through which he claimed the militia would run into the street to take aim at his unit. As we talked there was still considerable gunfire in the vicinity. The captain was almost apologetic: 'We still receive a lot of sniper fire.'

We were not sure what to think. Dr Donny's account had appeared plausible, but in the face of the captain's testimony it seemed sparing of the truth. Feeling we had to delve further and corroborate Conroy's story, we drove to our old abode, the Al Rasheed Hotel, formerly a hotbed of Iraqi intelligence. The US forces had taken the building on 10 April after a fierce battle, shown by the pattern of machine-gun hits on the outer wall. The hotel had not been hit by any missiles, though at one point the military commanders were considering dropping a 2000 lb bomb, which would have flattened it. The Americans were now using the building as a headquarters for operations and to billet troops. By luck we came upon Lieutenant-Colonel Eric Schwartz, who had been in charge of the troops fighting in the area of the museum. A wiry man who spoke with a cheery forthrightness, he was even more emphatic than Captain Conroy.

'On 11 April,' he told us 'my commander started taking intense fire from the museum. This removed it from the protected sites list,' which, added Schwartz, meant that within US military regulations it could have been specifically bombed – a thought too awful to contemplate. Schwartz then repeated something we had read before we came: that Dr Donny had put together a 'Dad's Army' of vigilantes. 'They said their job was to defend against looting, so if anyone wants to know who failed, it was

Donny George and his defence force. I can only presume the looting started when the museum security staff left.' But what of claims by staff that they had begged US soldiers to bring in a tank to protect the museum? Schwartz confirmed that a man had approached one of his soldiers, but added that at the same time another appeared, said that the first man was Fedayeen, and told the soldier to shoot him. Both then ran away.

According to Schwartz, once the museum lost its protected site status he had turned to other priorities within the area. He had no regrets: 'In hindsight, I wouldn't do a thing differently. If I'd raced up from south Baghdad to the museum, I'd have had a lot of dead soldiers outside the museum. It wasn't a museum any more – it was a fighting position. I think it was a pretty quick response from us – a pretty good success story.' While this might be stretching a point, Schwartz seemed confident of his company's role in the sequence of events. And with the best will in the world, the American version had fewer holes in it than Dr Donny's. Why did he downplay so severely the number of Iraqi militiamen who entered the museum compound? His explanation of the bunker in front of the museum seemed disingenuous, at best, and he had failed to mention to us dressing up his archaeologists in military fatigues and issuing them with AK47s, as claimed by Schwartz, to defend the museum. If the compound was as dangerous to American forces as both officers had explained, it would account for their reluctance to station troops there until they knew it was safe to do so. We were keen to get Dr Donny's reactions to these new allegations, but for the moment he was on his way to London to attend the British Museum press conference.

While at the Al Rasheed hotel, we could not resist sneaking a look at our old rooms. Also high on our list was to discover what had happened to the notorious mosaic of George Bush senior set in the floor at the entrance to the hotel. We found that the face, and the slogan 'Bush is Criminal', had been chiselled up, though you could still just about make out the features. Lieutenant-Colonel Schwartz explained, slightly awkwardly, what had happened. 'The Iraqis had tried to cover it up with a carpet, but we pulled it back, dusted off old George senior, and decided to rip it out. It took 30 men one hour to chip it up – it took a lot

Left: Al-Rashid Street, one of Baghdad's major thoroughfares, in November 2002. A cart of fish can be seen, being sold for *mazguf*, a Baghdad speciality we were to sample during our stay. Though it was delicious, a look at the Tigris the next day persuaded us not to repeat the experience. Below: The breathtaking vaulted arch at Ctesiphon, on the outskirts of Baghdad, dates from the third or fourth century AD. This remains the widest unreinforced brick-built vault in the world, and is a potent symbol for the vulnerability of the country's historic sites.

Top: The 3200-year-old ziggurat at Ashur is the greatest surviving feature in this ancient Assyrian city.

Left: The leaning minaret of Mosul. Beautifully made and curiously formed, it dates from the twelfth century.

Above: An empty fairground on the banks of the Tigris in Mosul. This is where Micky Mouse met Saddam Hussein.

Left: Two Assyrian winged bulls dating from about 850 BC guard the ancient site of Nineveh, on the edge of Mosul. Further examples of these wonderful beasts can be found in the Iraq Museum in Baghdad and the British Museum in London.

Centre: A group of Bedouins camped in the shadow of the ziggurat at Nimrud. They venerate cars, sheep and women – in that order.

Below: The monastery of St Matthew in the Mountain, or Mar Matta, spectacularly sited on the Maqluub mountain north of Mosul. In November 2002, the dwindling Christian community here was under threat from mounting anti-Western sentiment among Muslims.

Top left: A Yazidi shrine at Ain Sifni, near the Kurdish Autonomous Region.
Far left: The dazzling desert city of Hatra, which grew up around 2000 years ago as a great commercial centre at one of the trade crossroads of the ancient world.
Left: A carved stone head at Hatra.
Above: The Malawiya, or spiral minaret, at Samarra – an abstract and elemental Muslim stairway to the heavens, created in the mid-ninth century.

Above: The bland reconstruction of the biblical city of Babylon, ordered by Saddam Hussein.
Left: A fantastical brick-made beast, representing the god Marduk, adorning the Processional Way in Babylon.
Below: A billboard on the outskirts of Babylon in November 2002 showing Saddam Hussein alongside Nebuchadnezzar. This typical piece of propaganda was intended to associate Saddam and his regime with Iraq's great history.

Left: A section of a 6000-year-old temple wall at Uruk, made up of a mosaic of decorative cones in burnt clay and stone, forming chevron and spiral patterns.
Below: The mighty ziggurat at Ur, the lower stages of which were rebuilt in the 1960s.
Bottom: The Tree of Knowledge, dead, at Qurna on the delta of the Tigris and Euphrates rivers – supposedly the site of the Garden of Eden.

Left: The Iraq Museum in Baghdad, shortly after the US capture of the city in April 2003. One of the bunkers in the garden can be seen in the foreground.
Below left: The museum's trashed conservation room.
Bottom left: Dr Nawala Mutiwalli and Dr Donny George examine some returned museum items with Colonel Matthew Bogdanos.
Below: Bogdanos approaches the Central Bank of Iraq on bomb-damaged al-Rashid Street.

of hard work. Then we put a portrait of Saddam over it, and allowed each of our soldiers to walk over it, and wipe their feet on Saddam.' Schwartz paused, almost apologetically. 'We've been here in Kuwait and Iraq eight months, so that was a bit of stress release for us.'

The marble lobby felt cold and empty, shorn of its decoration and staff. Khaki camp beds and boxes of rations sat where portraits of Saddam had stood, and the leather sofas, so beloved of the surveillance agents, had gone to new homes. With no lifts due to the absence of power, we took a dark emergency staircase to the second floor and picked our way through the rubble with torches until Dan found his old room. The television, inevitably, had gone, as had the mattress but otherwise the disturbance was relatively minor. A soldier informed us that most of the looting had been done by the ex-staff, who nevertheless kept asking when they could return to work. Had the room been bugged, as we had feared back in November? It was hard to tell.

The soldier mentioned discovering a series of bunkers and rooms in the basement when they took the building. Aware at the time that the Al Rasheed was not what it appeared – 'It is more than a hotel', as its slogan dubiously proclaimed – we asked to be taken there. Amazingly, no other journalists had yet done so. As we suspected, there were two worlds at the Al Rasheed: upstairs for media and other guests, downstairs for government officials and people who listened in on our phone calls. Corridor after corridor led to a variety of offices containing technical or administrative equipment. On a whim, we opened one door and found a tiny closet with what appeared to be a switchboard and monitoring equipment. It was odd to think that someone had sat in this claustrophobic space and listened to our conversations with London. Further down we came across a shelter with a secure door, which was set up as an office with books such as *Petroleum Refining for the Non-Technical Person* lying around. There was a strange sense of sudden abandonment that was to reach its zenith in the last bunker, where we chanced upon an astonishingly familiar set-up. Two tables in a T-shape, covered in green baize, surrounded by cheap white plastic chairs, with one at the head … it struck us all that we had seen this recently on television. Could this be one of the last locations used by Saddam and his generals to hold their televised meetings before the Americans took Baghdad? It was a strange thought, like being in Hitler's bunker in Berlin in 1945. Certainly whoever was last here had departed hastily – food was still sitting in an adjacent room, slowly rotting. Whether or not we were correct in our hunch, no one, not even the US soldiers, had done more than glance in here.

It was time to return to the museum, to speak with one of the more mysterious figures in this increasingly perplexing saga: the Tikrit-born, probably politically appointed Dr Jaber. The Director-General had been polite with us, but lacked the charm of Dr Donny and seemed unsure how to proceed with the recovery of the museum. However, if we were to gain access to the storerooms, now the focus of our attentions, we would need his permission. After a series of abortive attempts to speak with him – and Bogdanos was also having little success – Dan managed to corner him in the museum foyer.

Dr Jaber wanted to know the questions in advance, and appeared edgy. Speaking in staccato sentences, he called those who had looted the museum 'very bad people'. He confirmed that the storage rooms had been looted, and though he could not say how badly as he had only seen them once and it had been very dark, 'a large number' of things had gone. Everything Dan asked him seemed to be 'difficult', and he answered 'difficult' questions with mumbled, confused replies. A request to see the storerooms for ourselves was brushed off with, 'At the moment, I think it is so difficult.' Dan persisted, saying that if the world was to be denied sight of the storerooms rumours of the museum staff's complicity in the looting would arise. This proved too much for Dr Jaber, who terminated the discussion with a shake of his head and pursed lips. We were left feeling incredibly frustrated. Here we were, enticed by the museum's own early hysterical declarations that 170,000 artefacts had been stolen or destroyed, anxious to help assess what had been looted and to show the world the tragedy that had occurred – and yet at every step we were being stonewalled or evaded. We were being made to feel less and less welcome in the museum, and it now felt beyond doubt that something was being hidden.

Baghdad was an increasingly dangerous place to be. A couple of days earlier there had been an incident in Falluja, 50 kilometres west of the city, in which the US Army had fired into an Iraqi crowd, killing 13 and injuring dozens more. Self-defence, said the Americans. Unprovoked, said the local people. Whichever, the mood was ugly, and getting tenser by the day. It was not a good time, or place, to be British. Then, that morning, a huge arms dump had blown up in southern Baghdad, killing at least 12 civilians and injuring scores more. The initial explosion rocked the hotel while we ate breakfast, and for the next couple of hours we continued to feel further huge explosions wherever we were in the city. We were left feeling incredibly vulnerable, like every other resident of Baghdad.

Resolved to take the initiative in our hunt for missing artefacts, we asked one of our drivers – a friendly, unflappable man, but also something of a wheeler-dealer – to see what he could discover for sale on the streets. We equipped Munther with $200, described the distinctive 'IM' serial numbers on genuine items to him, and told him to come back that evening. In the meantime we would do the same in the more obvious areas of the city. First, we went to Saddam City. A poor, crime-ridden suburb even when Saddam was in power, starved of resources because of its mainly Shia population, it had become synonymous with looters and disorder in the days since the taking of Baghdad. Our minders had sought local advice, which was that it would only be safe for us to visit early in the morning, and even then we should be as quick as possible. Clad once more in our flak jackets, we clambered into our vehicles and headed northeast. The atmosphere in Saddam City was calm, but not friendly. Market pitches were being set up, but little of consequence was being sold; most of the merchandise – second-hand shoes, old telephones, antiquated computers – was of pitiful quality, but undoubtedly looted. As for museum items, we found no evidence whatsoever. We moved on to the area around al-Rashid Street, where on our previous trip we had found shop after shop selling antique silver, carpets and precious stones. Now we found everything boarded up, with no one in the streets except stray dogs. As we returned to our vehicles, a local man came up and advised us to leave quickly, as there was a drunk with an AK47 who was looking to shoot any foreigners. We did not need to be told twice.

At the hotel, there was shocking news. John Curtis and Dr Donny had been robbed at gunpoint on the road from Baghdad to Jordan. A car had forced them off the highway and into the desert, where they were stripped and had all their money stolen. The one stroke of luck was that Dr Donny had managed to persuade the robbers to leave them their passports and the vehicle, so at least they had managed to reach Amman. The road to Jordan had been getting increasingly dangerous, with frequent attacks on media-crew vehicles. With each day it seemed more likely that someone would be killed on that road as the bandits became more and more audacious. John and Dr Donny had been fortunate to escape physically unharmed.

That evening, Munther returned with his booty. To our delight he had managed to buy a bag full of items, all of which were alleged to be from the museum. Only a few bore the characteristic 'IM' number – though that might only mean that the others had not yet been catalogued. In his hoard were many small red and pale green beads, an amber ring, a beautiful, broken spiral piece of pottery, much like the minaret at Samarra, and several other small but seemingly authentic objects. The next morning we took them along to Dr Jaber and Dr Nawala, who, after examining them carefully, pronounced them as indeed coming from the Iraq Museum. Dr Jaber was a little unconvincing in his thanks to the BBC for returning the objects, but perhaps our deed had persuaded them to look on us with a little more kindness. Our ability to buy these items had proved that there were museum artefacts for sale on the streets of Baghdad, if you knew where to ask. The harder bit was getting people to return things without payment, by appealing to their consciences.

Nevertheless, stolen artefacts were still trickling back, and one man said he had been persuaded to return items by the imam at his local mosque. The involvement of religious leaders seemed an encouraging sign, perhaps indicative of a gradual return to normality in Baghdad. The looter gave us directions to find the imam. When we did, he was walking down the street flanked by grim-faced men carrying AK47s. Our timing was unfortunate: a handful of locals had recently been killed in a fierce explosion at a petrol station. The Americans said the cause was a cigarette; the Iraqis accused the soldiers of sabotage. Either way, feelings were running high. In the mosque, the atmosphere was similarly edgy. People were polite but no more, and we left our security adviser Dale on the door. At Friday prayers, the imam once again asked his people to consider their actions if they had taken things from the museum. He told them that it was *haram* (forbidden) to steal, according to Muhammad, and that the pieces did not belong to Saddam but were the heritage of Iraq. If you took pieces, you were stealing not from Saddam but from Iraq, and the only reason the Americans were here was because Saddam had brought them here. His words were ingeniously designed to appeal to his Shia congregation, who were anti-Saddam, anti-American, yet pro-Islam.

In an interview with us, via an interpreter, the Imam Kamal al-Mosul was initially keen to blame the Americans for the looting, claiming that they had stood by and 'opened the doors of the museum' to let the people enter. As had many observers, he pointed out that they had managed to secure the Ministry of Oil quickly enough. This was not unexpected, but just a question of which party the imam blamed more – Saddam or the Americans. He moved on to an intriguing rumour, which we had heard before from several sources. 'There were two white lorries,' he explained, 'that stopped in front of the museum and collected what was in there, and then left. It was after that, the looting started.' This mysterious twist lent credence to theories of either organized crime or the last throes of the Baathist regime grabbing what assets it could. When Dan asked the imam who he believed was driving the vans, he admitted to not knowing – although in his congregational address he had been happy to attribute this action to the Americans.

Even if one agreed that the Americans were to blame for leaving the museum unguarded, there could be no denying that subsequently it had been looted and vandalized. This had been a key point for us: to try to understand how the Iraqi people could turn on their own culture. To steal through poverty and hunger would be explicable, but how did the imam explain the wanton destruction? 'There were,' he told us, 'in Saddam's prisons thieves that he released [earlier in the year]. Then, when the war started and the regime lost its power, they started to steal.'

Once again, so it seemed, it was not the 'ordinary' Iraqis who had participated in the rampage. Yet it was 'ordinary' Iraqis who were bringing pieces back to the mosque. The imam expanded his theory. 'Those who robbed the museum fell into two groups: the thieves, and those seeking revenge on Saddam's regime. But the museum is not the museum of Saddam Hussein; it is of the Iraqis, and an ancient civilization known all over the world. As Iraqis, we are pleased Saddam's regime has fallen.' This felt like perhaps a chink of light, an acknowledgement that at least some Iraqis had felt stirred into a destructive frenzy against a public building run by, and for, the Baath Party – a Saddam stronghold. This perception, even if erroneous, might start to explain why the mob had trashed the administrative offices.

Back at the museum, Colonel Bogdanos's team had been delivered a trunkload of treasures. His men brought out an aluminium case that had been seized from smugglers on their way to the Iranian border. It was surely from a storeroom as the trunk lid bore red-painted words in Arabic that stated its contents to be Babylonian. The objects were of very high quality – cuneiform tablets, a delicate carved head the size of Dan's thumb, and intricate cylinder seals – and to know they were safe was a morale-boost for us all. Bogdanos then took us to examine the rest of the cache, which had been digitally photographed and catalogued by his team. Laid out on a long table, the booty contained some exquisite items including a series of further cuneiform tablets, lovely Sumerian figures over 4000 years old, bowls, and a Hatran female figure with wonderfully curvaceous hips. Bogdanos seemed genuinely moved by these artefacts, not least by the fact that one of the cuneiform tablets had been fractured during the looting – as he lamented, after thousands of years intact, to then fall victim to one moment of greed. Once again, the uncertainty in the country meant that the smugglers had been released, with neither the Americans nor the Iraqi National Congress sure of what legal basis there would be for detaining them; so perhaps valuable witnesses who could provide details of the looting had slipped through the investigators' fingers.

However, on the positive side, a reasonable number of high-value items had been recovered, which established one important fact, as objects such as these had almost certainly been on display in the museum's galleries prior to the war. That they had been recovered in this condition, each carefully stored in a brown protective envelope and then placed in a marked aluminium box, meant that they had been stored in a museum storeroom and, more worryingly, that this storeroom had been looted. And Bogdanos had something interesting to say when asked whether he was happy with the number of looted items being returned from the local community. 'The amnesty programme is working quite well. We've had approximately 200 items returned, each time with no questions asked. However,' he continued, 'almost uniformly we've been told that they only wanted to return items to US forces rather than the museum officials, who in their minds were identified too closely with the Baath Party regime.'

Was this a message that we too should heed? In the anarchic chaos of post-war Baghdad, was no one to be trusted, even museum staff? Before we could ponder this too deeply we suddenly heard, after days of waiting, that we were to be shown the storerooms. We could scarcely believe our luck, and hurried inside with the museum curator, Dr Nawala. We had so far had little interaction with Dr Nawala, though she had often been at Dr Jaber's side when we had seen him, and had always been on hand to note down any looted items returned. She frequently seemed more stressed than her colleagues and had always rebuffed our attempts to make conversation with a stern stare or a terse reply. Now here she was, leading us to what we hoped was the missing link, the museum's own storage rooms. But it quickly became apparent that relations had not improved.

We picked our way down a dark, paper-strewn corridor in the main administration block until we reached a door which read 'Temporary Store'. The room was in a terrible state, with drawers pulled from filing cabinets, their contents spread all over the work surfaces and some of the cabinets themselves pulled over. The floor was ankle-deep in broken pottery, glass and papers and would take days, if not weeks, to sort. It was shocking – yet this was not one of the main storerooms, we were sure. With its workbenches and the kind of materials we could see, it looked like a conservation room. Why were we being fobbed off? There followed a remarkable exchange between Dan and Dr Nawala, as the frustrations of both sides bubbled to the surface.

DAN: This is a conservation room. Was this one of the storerooms?

DR NAWALA: You wanted to see this room. As Dr Donny told you.

DAN: I didn't want to see any particular room –

DR NAWALA: You wanted to see this room. Dr Donny said. All the computers were looted from here. Pieces were also looted from here, or damaged.

DAN: I don't know why you're so angry. You must tell me what I'm being shown. You brought me here.

DR NAWALA: You asked to see this room.

DAN: I did not. I said, 'Can I see the storerooms where the objects from the glass cases were put into store before the looting?'

DR NAWALA: No, this is not the matter. You asked about this room. You asked Dr Donny about this room.

DAN: No, I did not. I asked to see the storerooms.

DR NAWALA: (Pause) This is one of the storerooms.

DAN: Thank you. Please, can we be courteous, I'm not here to do anything but see what you have suffered. I'm not here to offend anyone. I seem to be treated in a rather strange manner. This is one of the storerooms?

DR NAWALA: Yes.

DAN: Where items were looted?

DR NAWALA: Yes.

DAN: And these are the cases that were broken into?

DR NAWALA: Some of them.

DAN: How many storerooms are there?

DR NAWALA: We are starting to make our list.

DAN: How many storerooms are there?

DR NAWALA: This is our job.

DAN: How many storerooms are there?

(Dr Nawala repeats her previous answer in Arabic to our driver)

DAN: You can't tell me how many storerooms there are?

DR NAWALA: No, I cannot tell you.

DAN: I find it very strange, this approach. I need to be told what I'm looking at, otherwise it's without meaning.

DR NAWALA: This room is as you see. All the showcases were damaged, pieces were damaged, documents, papers, were thrown here and there.

DAN: There were other storerooms that were not looted?

DR NAWALA: That is our job. If there is any other storage. You wanted to see this room and what happened here.

(Dan asks our driver to ask the same question in Arabic. Dr Nawala responds in Arabic with the same answer)

DAN: How many storerooms are there?

DR NAWALA: I won't answer that question.

DAN: Won't answer that? Why?

DR NAWALA: It's our job.

DAN: Our job not to answer questions, is that what you mean?

(Dr Nawala inclines her head)

DR NAWALA: If you want, you can ask Dr Jaber.

DAN: Can we look round this storeroom?

DR NAWALA: Look around, but be careful because of pieces.

At this point, Dan made an absolutely shocking discovery. Amidst the carnage he spied the base of the lyre from the royal tombs of Ur. One of the most significant pieces in the Iraq Museum collection, it dated from about 2450 BC. It had featured a gold bull's head with shell-encrusted eyes, and the body of the lyre was also inlaid with gold. There are other examples of such lyres – the British Museum has one – but the one in the Iraq Museum was a unique, wonderful piece of craftsmanship, and its loss was a tragedy, though Dr Donny had informed us that the golden head was safe. It beggared belief how the lyre had come to be in this room, and not in the secure storerooms or even the bank. By the end of our trip, neither we nor the Americans had received any explanation for this.

DAN: Donny George said he thought the bull's head was safe.

DR NAWALA: (Bows her head) No.

DAN: Gone. Absolutely tragic. But why was it stored in this room? (Dr Nawala bows her head again) Don't know. I do not understand. We're being treated as though we are … responsible. How many storerooms are there?

DR NAWALA: We have other storerooms. I cannot tell you how many.

DAN: Were inventories lost?

(Dr Nawala waves her hand and starts to walk out)

This was deeply perplexing and unsettling. We had come to the Iraq Museum simply to report on what had occurred during the days following the so-called Battle of Baghdad. Dan's repeated questioning of Dr Nawala was not an attempt to be hard-nosed or belligerent, but rather the result of the museum officials trying to palm us off with a room that self-evidently was not a main storeroom. Whether this arose from a misunderstanding between Dr Donny and Dr Nawala, or whether our requests had been unclear (though we felt certain they had not), such evasive responses and confusing behaviour could only arouse suspicions that things were not as they seemed. Even more importantly, we had found the shattered remains of the lyre, which had clearly not been put in safe storage. The more questions we asked, the more murky the picture became.

The following day the staff were crowding back to the museum to receive their first pay for several weeks. We, on the other hand, were awaiting Dr Donny's return from London so we could put to him some further questions that had come to the fore in the light of our discussions with the Americans. It was a long, draining wait in the increasingly burning Iraqi sun, with the unrelenting soundtrack of gunfire. Other journalists were starting to circle, so it was essential that we spoke to him before he became swamped. Then, unexpectedly, in a quiet corner of the grounds Dan came across a pile of burning identity cards. Were the staff embarrassed at their Baath Party membership and obliterating all evidence? Or were they finally able to register their displeasure at the party without fear of punishment? Whichever it was, it seemed a remarkable act, indicative of feelings bubbling away under the surface.

While we sat in the shade, a man who had worked at the museum for over 30 years surreptitiously passed to Dan a home-made whip, which he said came from the security office and had been used to beat staff. What on earth was such a barbaric instrument doing there? And why, indeed, would the museum have a security department? There was certainly more to the staff dynamics than we had yet been able to penetrate.

Eventually Dr Donny appeared, looking tired after his travels. He had received a message at the airport that we were keen to talk to him again as soon as we could, and so he came directly to us and promised that he would find time once he had been into the museum offices and caught up with business. But he did have one point he wanted to communicate immediately: 'The Jordanians on the border are capturing antiquities and documents being smuggled by journalists. As of last Saturday, they had 12 cases, all from European and American journalists.' It was uncertain what he meant by telling us this. We had heard rumours of documents being smuggled out, as the biggest scoop for any media at that time would be proof of a banned weapons programme; but even this, obviously, was to be condemned. All it served to do was add another category of people to the culpable list: us.

It was then, as we idled in the sun, that we heard vital news. Bogdanos and his team had gained agreement from Dr Jaber and Dr Nawala to enter the museum's storerooms for the first time. Mohsin, the man with the keys, had been located and the visit was imminent. The only problem, as Bogdanos explained, was that Dr Nawala was refusing to let Dan or Guy join the party – catastrophic news for us. Throughout the trip I had attempted to play the so-called 'grey man' and keep our contacts with everyone as cordial as possible, while Dan and Guy had asked the hard questions. Perhaps I would be able to join unobtrusively on the end of the party, without disturbing the equilibrium. At any rate, I volunteered to go in and shoot the footage without Dan. Bogdanos was sceptical, but Steve Mocsary, a senior special agent with Homeland Security, persuaded the colonel to give it a go. If Dr Nawala insisted I leave, I would do so. Mocsary would then take the camera and film what he could.

And so about a dozen people – American soldiers with crowbars ('Just in case the keys don't work,' quipped one), Homeland Security agents, Iraqi museum officials and an oddly furtive cameraman with a borrowed desert hat pulled down over his eyes – entered the museum and made their way to the first storeroom. We passed through immense foot-thick steel doors to reach a high-ceilinged inner chamber and a set of padlocked green metal doors. Dr Nawala fiddled with a fat bunch of keys, half-heartedly trying different ones but without success. After waiting patiently for a few minutes, during which he beckoned the camera forward to document the attempt, Colonel Bogdanos called for a soldier with a crowbar, and while he gallantly shielded Dr Nawala from any flying debris the lock was carefully broken. Bogdanos pushed open the doors, and we crowded in for the first sight of the storerooms by anyone other than the museum staff. The immediate impression in the torch-lit gloom was of chaos, and my heart sank. Rows of tall shelving units lined a passageway strewn with pottery fragments, screwed-up paper and boxes. But the shelves themselves seemed reasonably undisturbed, stacked with bowls, jugs, pots and fragments from various digs – 'old excavations', according to Dr Nawala. The few metal boxes on the ground, amongst the empty cement bags and cardboard boxes, were confirmed as relating to digs from the last few years, and most of these had been gone through, if hurriedly. The difficult task, for the uninformed eye, was to work out how much of what we could see had occurred after 6 April, when Dr Nawala had left the building for the last time prior to the looting. In other words, though the storeroom looked a mess and was full of broken pots, to what extent did it just *look* like it had been looted? After all, many of the fragmented pieces would have been discovered in that very state. It seemed a ridiculous thought, but could this have been how the museum stored its artefacts? The picture became a little clearer at the end of the room, which seemed to have attracted the greatest share of jumbled artefacts, foam padding, paper and discarded boxes. The mess included steel-framed doors on their sides and statues on their backs and, when asked by Bogdanos if this was how it had always been, Dr Nawala amazingly confirmed it: 'As it is.' Then, as if to make a mockery of the scene, she picked up an item, examined it and moved it a couple of metres. So nothing had been looted from this storeroom. The colonel, one of life's more organized people, did well to stay poker-faced.

We then went to a storeroom on the first floor, which was twice as long as the one downstairs. The door was open and the lock undamaged – a great surprise. The contents of the shelves here seemed in even better order than downstairs, and the way through was much clearer as we moved towards the daylight streaming in through slit windows at the far end. Beyond the shelving units we saw dozens of ancient Torah scrolls and parchments rolled up and standing on their ends, like small rockets. Dr Nawala pointed out a pile of bagged Islamic artefacts amid a flurry of beige file cards, which she believed had been emptied from one of the aluminium boxes, but she did not know where the box was.

Suddenly there came a shout from the other side of the room: 'Colonel, grenade!' We scurried to one side as Bogdanos marched across, ordering: 'Back, back, back.' After quickly examining it with Steve Mocsary, he pronounced it a discarded dud. Then another soldier came upon a wooden box for RPGs, with some of their springs still in it and Russian writing on the casing. The evidence of military activity was consolidated with the discovery of the stock and magazine from a Sten gun, a broken rifle stock and what appeared to be a defensive firing position at one of the windows – boxes had been pushed to the wall to stand on, and the long, vertical window was ajar. Close by in the outside wall was an entry point from a 50-calibre round fired from a US tank: this would seem to indicate that someone had been firing on US forces in the street, who responded. Dr Nawala, who seemed quietly shocked by these discoveries, confirmed that none of these things was in the storeroom when she had left, and then said, 'But this grenade is surely American?'

'No,' replied Bogdanos. 'It's Soviet, so probably the Iraqi Army came in here.'

This disquieted Dr Nawala, who countered, 'Iraqi Army? Iraqi Army? There was no Iraq Army in here.'

Bogdanos immediately sensed the need to keep her calm, and employed his considerable charm to persuade her that he was not accusing anybody, only stating a possibility. Luckily, this stubborn, taciturn woman, with whom we had managed to achieve little or no rapport, was much taken with Bogdanos. Having recovered her poise, Dr Nawala was now explaining each section of shelving to the colonel – here were old items confiscated from the public, here were other items bought by the museum without excavation numbers, here were rows of fakes, and so on. Further signs of some military presence kept cropping up. A soldier spotted an AK47 and a grenade ammunition pouch on the floor, and Steve Mocsary identified what he thought might be a booby trap in the form of a rolled-up scroll, about 2 feet tall, with a thin piece of metal sticking out at right angles from the top of it, like a trip wire. If looters or militia had been through this storeroom, he reckoned, it was unlikely that such a delicate object would still be standing. Happy to be cautious, we gave it a wide berth.

Dr Nawala was still prattling happily away, but I could sense that Bogdanos was readying himself. As the two of them looked at an aluminium case on the floor, apparently unlooted, he said gently, 'Will we be able to tell if any boxes are missing? If someone took this box, would you know? I don't see a number on it.'

Dr Nawala paused, and asked what he meant.

Bogdanos persisted carefully. 'OK. If I take this, how do you know? How do you know it's gone?'

Dr Nawala looked down sheepishly and shrugged.

'Is there a list?' Bogdanos asked.

'No, there is no list for the boxes,' Dr Nawala admitted.

Bogdanos pressed on. 'Can anyone tell me if there's 75 in here –'

'Seventy-five?'

'Or a hundred –'

'A hundred?'

'Can somebody give me …' Bogdanos took a moment to compose himself. 'Can somebody give me a number of the boxes that were here on 6 April?'

Dr Nawala could stall no longer. She replied quietly, 'It's difficult.'

A smile flickered across Bogdanos' features. 'Difficult … or impossible? … It's possible?' He gave her an imploring look.

'It's not impossible, but it's difficult, it's very difficult. If any boxes come back, we will know if they're our boxes,' suggested Dr Nawala brightly, neatly encapsulating the clash of approaches in one comment.

Even a man of Bogdanos's composure could not restrain a chuckle. 'I know you can tell me if a box is back,' he replied, 'but I want to know if you can tell me if a box is *missing*.'

Dr Nawala paused. 'Yes.' Pause. 'From downstairs,' she added, with a neat sidestep.

Bogdanos, enjoying this verbal shadow-boxing, laughed again. 'From up here, can you tell if a box is missing?' he qualified.

Dr Nawala could hold out no longer. 'At least the ladies, when they prepare the lists, maybe they can have an idea. Approximately.'

'Approximately is OK,' Bogdanos reasoned. 'Maybe we can have that list tomorrow?' he joked, with a broad smile.

'Wow!' said Dr Nawala and laughed.

'Inshallah,' was Bogdanos's hopeful reply.

It was an exchange that summed up so much of the previous ten days or so. Bogdanos would not give up his good humour and diplomacy or, equally, his leads. Whoever had thought he was the man for the job had judged the situation well.

Just as the mood relaxed, though, one of the entourage walked straight into the 'booby trap', knocking it over. We froze … and then carried on breathing, deeply. 'Holy shit!' exclaimed the colonel. 'Do you have a death wish?' The culprit looked shamefaced, but if anything brought home the stark reality of poking around locations previously occupied by a defeated enemy, that moment was it.

Shortly afterwards we reached another storeroom door, locked and with no keys available. This time, as there was a metal grille in the door, Bogdanos left it unbreached – we could see it was in reasonable order, especially by the standards of the previous rooms. Back downstairs Mohsin, the 'key' man, opened more security doors to reveal a familiar-looking corridor that led to the conservation room in which Dan had found the remains of the lyre. On this occasion the mood was less acrimonious, as Bogdanos and his team noted the damage. Through another door, and this time we descended some very dark, narrow steps to an imposing-looking steel door. Each member of the US team had a turn at opening it, without success – and when Dr Nawala stepped forward to try, the colonel quipped, 'If you get it open after I couldn't, I'll die.' So we retraced our steps to a long, twisting, filthy slipway – on which we found an Iraqi army belt – which led down to yet another storeroom. This one was again secured but, viewed through its metal grille, could be seen to contain hundreds of locked and stacked aluminium boxes. Dr Nawala was happy to accept that this one also had not been broken into, so Bogdanos asked if we could see the final storeroom, the one that had originally been sealed up but which now had several courses of concrete blocks missing, suggesting that someone had indeed got inside. This was the room Dr Donny had shown to John Curtis and me at the beginning of our trip.

So we returned to ground level and walked through the galleries, with their empty cases and statues padded with foam mattresses. When, at the end of the Hatran gallery, we reached the staircase down to the blocked-up doorway the US soldiers went down with their sledge-hammers to make a hole large enough for us all to clamber through.

Inside were four large rooms. At the entrance the floor was lined with stacked-up pots, but none seemed to have been disturbed. In that first room none of the shelves appeared violated, and Dr Nawala seemed quite perky. So we moved into the second room, which initially seemed in a similarly clear state. But then disaster struck. In the far corner we found hundreds of small boxes that had been systematically emptied; their contents were later confirmed to have been items such as cylinder seals, amulets and pendants. At this sight, Dr Nawala collapsed with her hands on her head, sobbing. A paramedic was sent for, along with Dr Jaber and Dr Donny, and the scale of the looting was assessed. The other rooms appeared untouched, but this particular section was precious to Dr Nawala as she had been involved with the excavation of the pieces. Dr Donny once told us that 'losing an important piece is like losing a child,' and Dr Nawala's reaction brought that home graphically. Despite this setback, the examination of the stores had achieved a great deal, and for the first time in the investigation we now possessed a more detailed picture of the looting. Three out of the five storage areas had suffered a degree of looting, and perhaps thousands of pieces had been taken of which a few hundred had already been returned; it would, however, take months of thorough checking to produce a precise figure. In the final, new, storeroom some of its most valuable and portable treasures had been looted, although the rest of its vast resources seemed to have escaped untouched. This appeared to be incontrovertible evidence of an inside job. There were also the issues of the alleged fighting position in the upper storeroom and the general lack of order in the museum, but for the moment the looting from the storerooms seemed less severe than we had feared.

As we emerged from the basement, with Dr Nawala being comforted by colleagues, I passed the camera back to Guy as Dr Donny had appeared at the door. Now that we were finally able to snatch a few minutes with him he confided that when he and John were ambushed they felt they were very close to being shot, as the hijackers had been so nervous. Having just come from the storerooms himself he claimed to feel depressed, but, despite the evidence, absolutely refuted the suggestion that militia had been permitted to use the interior of the museum as a defensive military position. He and Dan went outside to discuss the discrepancies between Dr Donny's account of the events of 9–16 April and the Americans' version. We had been in Baghdad for more than ten days, Dan began, and while he felt emotionally connected with the museum and its losses he still felt very confused over what exactly had happened. In particular, he found it hard to reconcile the Americans' declaration that the museum was a prepared and fortified military position with Dr Donny's categorical denial.

'I'll tell you something very important,' said Dr Donny. 'These bunkers, we dug them for our people, because of the bombing. They were not weapons stores [as the Americans had alleged]. I helped dig them with my own hands – and look, there are no holes to fire from. If you were here when they bombed the telecommunications centre [opposite the museum], it was hit by four cruise missiles. And on the Thursday [10 April], one of our men went and asked the tank to come, as there was nobody here. There was no firing, and the battle had finished. Then the looting started, with hundreds of people here – how could that be if there was fighting?' But the Americans were reluctant to approach the museum as it had been a hostile place, Dan countered. 'It was just a matter of moving the tank position there to here,' said Dr Donny, pointing to two spots a few metres apart.

With the benefit of hindsight it was hard not to have sympathy with this analysis, and of course the distance between the two points seemed ridiculously short now that the museum was secure. But then there was the issue of Donny's staff carrying guns and wearing military fatigues. Might this not have proved confusing to the advancing Americans? Dr Donny was emphatic, if a little confusing, in his denial. 'I told everyone, even the Americans, that we had guns for our boys. They had specific instructions, if anything happened. If the American tanks were here, they should not fight, because it's suicide to fight a tank with a machine gun. They were to be against looters if it happened during the bombing.' These subtleties of instruction were perhaps difficult for the American soldiers to read. And there seemed an inherent contradiction between Dr Donny's earlier assertion that the looting was unexpected, and arming his staff, mostly archaeologists and academics, against that eventuality.

We wanted to ask Dr Donny about the political affiliations of the museum staff, especially in light of the remarks by the custodians of the book bunker that they thought the books were safer with them, and the repeated statements from locals that they would not return looted pieces to museum staff, only to the US forces. What role did the Baath Party have in the running of the museum? Dan asked. 'Nothing,' was Dr Donny's emphatic reply. 'It's just we were supported so much by the President, he liked so much to support our work.' Did Baath Party officials take any objects prior to the war? 'Absolutely not.'

Time was running out, as Dr Donny had to be somewhere else and did not know when he would return, and we ourselves had deadlines. Dan asked him if he could confirm the status of various key objects. The wonderful Lady of Warka? 'The original is gone.' The ivory of the lion devouring the Nubian? 'Gone.' The golden bull's head from the lyre of Ur? At last some good news, even if it did contradict Dr Nawala's information. 'For a long time now it has been safe, and a copy was on display before the war. I don't know where it is stored, but I know it is safe.' If it transpired that it was in the boxes delivered to the Central Bank of Iraq before the war, we had been told that it was Dr Donny who had handed them over. Perhaps, even now, evasion was the order of the day.

Finally, in a bid to understand all the obfuscation, obstruction and misinformation we had experienced during our stay, Dan asked how this attitude could be felt to be beneficial to the staff, and the museum itself. Dr Donny looked abashed, but spoke with a quiet assurance. 'You must excuse the people in the museum and Department of Antiquities. We have had journalists even before the war asking where we hide our objects, and are they safe. So we are always suspicious when people ask about numbers and places. We do not want to lose any more.' As for the Americans, he praised their 'thorough' investigation team, but pointed out the clash of approaches that we had ourselves witnessed throughout our stay. 'The Americans want, in one or two days, 300 items that have been lost, with their pictures and information, so they can go searching for them. But we have to check everything. A museum is not a shop.'

There seemed little to be gained by pushing Dr Donny further. His and the US interpretations of events could not be fully reconciled. He was a warm, charming man who had graciously made time for us on more than one occasion, and whatever his involvement with the fortification of the museum he continued to work long and hard, in dangerous conditions, to safeguard a collection he had worked with for over 25 years. It was time to discover what the Americans had made of the storerooms.

Steve Mocsary, who had been so instrumental in helping us gain access, had little doubt that, in the last storeroom, 'someone had to know – they went straight to the location, and other bits were not touched'. Colonel Bogdanos concurred. 'The obvious conclusion – it doesn't even bear mentioning – is that whoever did that knew exactly what he or she was doing, exactly where to go. I don't know how that could have been effected without inside knowledge. There's no other explanation.' He believed that the corner in question had been looted 'systematically', even though other shelves and storage vessels had been left untouched.

In fact, later investigation revealed that the thieves had keys to storage cabinets, adjacent to these looted boxes, that contained many thousands of Greek, Roman and Islamic gold and silver coins. However, in an incredible stroke of misfortune for them and luck for the rest of the world, they appeared to have dropped the keys in the dark and not been able to find them. But where, and how, the thieves had obtained the keys was not clear.

Bogdanos was also left in little doubt that the upper storeroom had been 'opened by, or for the purpose of, someone firing out at US forces'. Mocsary claimed that Dr Donny had initially told the investigation that Fedayeen forces had come in and prepared positions there, contradicting the story he had told us; whatever the truth, Mocsary took the same view as the colonel: 'I have to think that in the haste of battle, somebody got in there and perhaps the door was left unlocked, and perhaps some military people had access to the room for defensive fire.' He was at pains to emphasize that this 'hasty firing position' was the only evidence of military action within the museum, and inclined towards generosity in his assessment. 'I think if Saddam's forces came and said, "We need your museum," I don't think many people would have had the right to say no.'

From Bogdanos's point of view, the episode had answered some questions but raised a host of new ones. He remained upbeat, though cautious. 'The loss of a single piece is a tragedy' had become something of a mantra for him, but it obviously rang true. 'Having said that,' he continued on this occasion, 'when we first came here we read of 170,000 missing pieces. Well, having exhaustively and comprehensively gone through the galleries, we are confident, with the museum staff, that only 38 pieces are missing or stolen from the galleries. The other thing is the level of damage. We have identified throughout the museum about 20 items that were damaged, many of which were restored pieces. Of the hundreds of display cases, only 18 were smashed for wanton destruction. The level of destruction in the museum, compared to the level of destruction in the administration offices, bears no resemblance. You may draw whatever conclusions you may wish from that …'

The following day we left at dawn in a convoy, and six or so hours later reached the Jordanian border. Our trip was nearly over, though the story would run and run. On 19 May Koichiro Matsuura, Director-General of UNESCO, admitted that, in total, only hundreds of items had been stolen from the Baghdad museum during the war rather than the tens of thousands that had first been thought. It was a move in the right direction. When Colonel Bogdanos delivered his assessment to US Central Command it followed the same lines as his final briefing to us. For him and his team, the focus would gradually open out to the rest of the world in a bid to intercept stolen Iraq Museum items circulating on the black market. But his work in Iraq was not yet finished. On 26 May Bogdanos and his team finally gained entry to one of the vaults of the old Central Bank of Iraq, and after picking their way past the bodies of looters, found 16 boxes of treasures deposited there before the war. Foremost among the 6744 items were heritage pieces and jewellery from the royal tombs at Ur. On 1 June, they were able to access a previously flooded underground vault in a new building of the bank, where they located five more boxes. When the boxes were opened they were found to contain the 616 pieces of the golden treasure of Nimrud. One of the smaller boxes also held the original bull's head from the golden lyre of Ur. At around the same time, the team entered a 'secret' storage location in Baghdad and found 179 boxes containing 8366 priceless antiquities from the gallery display cases, confirming the number claimed to have been moved there by the staff.

Pieces were still coming back through the amnesty programme, and the team received its biggest boost through this avenue on 11 June when the Sacred Vase of Warka, dating from 3000 BC and representing for the first time the relationship between the gods, humans, animals, plants and water, was returned along with 70 other items, by three Iraqi men. The vase had been damaged in the course of the theft, but museum officials thought it could be successfully restored. This was fantastic news, particularly for the museum and the Iraqi people, who now had one of the most important pieces of their cultural heritage restored to them. Still missing, though, were pieces such as the Lady of Warka, the Akkadian Basitki statue, and the ivory of the lion savaging a Nubian.

As of June 2003 Bogdanos's investigation had recovered 2027 pieces, approximately two-thirds through the amnesty programme and the rest through raids and seizures. From the public galleries which displayed the most significant items, 32 exhibits remained absent. The greatest number of missing items, 4800 cylinder seals from the new storeroom, were, according to Bogdanos, clearly the result of an inside job. The remaining 1581 missing items were primarily excavation site and Islamic pieces, and appeared to have been stolen by indiscriminate looters. By agreement with the museum officials, the Americans arranged a grand opening for part of the museum on 3 July. A single gallery, the Assyrian, in which the golden treasures of Nimrud were also displayed, was opened for two hours for the media and selected dignitaries. If not exactly business as usual, it demonstrated that the long, slow process of restoring the museum to at least a degree of its former magnificence had begun.

For the museum officials, the repercussions continued. While their colleagues in the international community stood by them, their own staff had different ideas. On 10 May, 50 staff members staged a protest outside the museum, waving placards accusing Dr Jaber of being a 'dictator' and a 'thief'. Next day's *Sunday Times* reported that Dr Donny had called the allegations 'stupid', though he now admitted that the looting of the cylinder seals from the new storeroom showed 'a certain knowledge'. He was also keen to add his voice to those dismissing the figure of 170,000 items stolen, saying that 'somehow' the total figure for the collection had ended up being quoted as the amount stolen. 'It is nothing like that,' he added.

Dr Donny himself was not immune from the fallout. On 17 June, the *Guardian* reported that at least 130 of the 185 staff of the State Board of Antiquities had signed a petition calling for the resignation of the museum directors: 'Staff said they believed that some of the thefts from the museum were an inside job. They also accused Donny George, the board's head of research, of arming them and ordering them to fight US forces.' One unnamed employee recalled that soon after the war started Dr Donny had held a staff meeting at which he had 'ordered them to fight US troops or face the sack'. He had instructed them, the source continued, that '"If the Americans come you have to fight." They never mentioned thieves once.' When questioned, Dr Donny admitted to distributing guns to his staff, as he had told us and indeed the Americans, but claimed he told these people only to guard the museum against looters. And so it goes on, and is likely to for months, if not years, to come.

There are few hard conclusions to be drawn from the fate of the Iraq Museum. The following, however, seem to be the few facts on which there is general consensus amidst the rumour and scandal-mongering. Some time between 8 April, when Dr Donny and Dr Jaber left the museum for the last time, and 16 April, looting occurred at the museum. Most likely it took place over three days, probably 10–12 April, before museum staff started to return, and the Americans finally posted a guard on the compound on 16 April. The administrative offices, as many as 120 rooms, were comprehensively and frenziedly ransacked in what appear to have been spontaneous acts of wanton vandalism, but were possibly acts of revenge on the part of ordinary Iraqis against the Baathist regime. The museum galleries, which before the war had been almost completely emptied of exhibits that were not too heavy or too fragile to move, had suffered looting of the smaller items that remained, as well as damage, predominantly to their statuary. Of the couple of hundred display cases, only 18 had been smashed, and these would seem to have been acts of vandalism rather than looting, as they contained no exhibits.

The vast majority of what are termed 'high-value' items were removed from the museum premises by officials before the war, and placed in secure storage off-site. These items included ancient books and manuscripts, which were kept in the shelter we visited on the edge of town and found unharmed, and gold and jewellery items, including the golden head from the lyre of Ur and the treasures of Nimrud, which were put into storage at the Central Bank of Iraq and recovered safely in June 2003. In terms of the museum's own storerooms, three were partially looted, and a detailed inventory will in time reveal what was taken; but the number of items is likely to run only to the low thousands, and the commercial value of these pieces is undetermined. It would appear that the thieves acted in a hurried manner, and were not guided here by specialist knowledge or direction. In the new storeroom underneath the museum, nearly 5000 cylinder seals were stolen from one section in what most parties agree could only have been a pre-meditated act, with precise knowledge of what the boxes contained. A second disaster was only averted when the thieves appeared to have dropped and lost the keys to cabinets containing ancient gold and silver coins. Thirty-two significant items remain unaccounted for, and the search for these is likely to be a long and painstaking one that will fall to international law-enforcement agencies, which will try to intercept the pieces as they move through the world's art black market. Exactly where these 32 items were on 6 April remains uncertain. The museum staff claim they were in the galleries. Some perhaps were; others could have been in the storerooms; while yet others could conceivably have been removed by Baath Party officials long before the war.

What is there to draw from this affair, which saw an alleged cultural catastrophe of international proportions turn into a very human drama? Firstly, there is now little dispute that the initial reports of 170,000 items having been looted were grossly exaggerated. Dr Donny accuses the media of seizing on the figure and misapplying it, yet some of the earliest reports attribute a quotation, giving this figure, to one of his museum staff. Newspapers won't necessarily temper a sensational headline for the sake of accuracy, but the fact remains that the figure of 170,000 objects lost was the one that stuck in the public imagination and contributed greatly to the outpouring of public grief and outrage. It took a couple of weeks for the press to start qualifying their reports, and by then the subject was off most of the front pages. During this period the museum officials made little effort to correct the error unless specifically prompted, though it could be argued that publicizing such a large figure may have had the beneficial effect of deterring any would-be looters. A source close to the US investigation, who was suspicious of the museum directors' role in the affair, used a familiar analogy: man kills wife, appears on television news that night appealing tearfully for help in finding her killer, and then a few days later is arrested for her murder. This was his perception of how the media might have been manipulated with regard to the looting. Was the sensational claim of 170,000 items stolen or destroyed a smokescreen to conceal what really happened?

The question of whether the US Army was culpable for not posting a guard on the museum before 16 April is a difficult one to answer. Despite the protestations of Dr Donny, it would seem to be true, from the accounts of the soldiers involved, that when they approached the museum on 9 April they came under heavy fire, including some from Iraqi gunmen within the museum compound itself – 'a few militiamen', according to Dr Donny, several hundred according to Captain Conroy – and, in line with US Army regulations, at that point the museum lost its protected site status. Dr Donny claims that by the next day the fighting had finished, and that the Americans could safely have posted a tank at the museum. He also described the bunkers dug in the front lawns as bomb shelters. However, both Conroy and his commander, Lieutenant-Colonel Schwartz, claim they were fighting positions beside which they found supplies of hand grenades, rifles and RPGs. This interpretation was corroborated by our own ex-special forces security advisers. The Americans also claim to have found many Iraqi Army uniforms inside the museum. As far as Schwartz was concerned, as soon as his men were fired upon from the museum he legitimately regarded the site as a military position, and was not willing to run the risk of his men being shot by acting too hastily in posting a guard. He talks of it being beyond his 'zone of responsibility', and mentions having been given other priorities in the area by his command. This seems unacceptable: a week went by between the US military arriving at the museum and finally securing it, which seems an inordinately long period even given its limited use as a fighting position. When questioned, Schwartz was given to blaming Dr Donny for the failure of his security force to defend the museum against looting. The question of responsibility in times of war is a contentious one, yet it does seem evasive to blame the looting on the failed efforts of a group of archaeologists with guns.

There is perhaps a more damning truth to be drawn from Dr Donny's group of vigilantes, his staff 'coerced' into defending the museum. If, as claimed, they were ordered to shoot at American forces attacking the museum, then they were unwittingly endangering it. Fedayeen and militiamen did in fact fire on the Americans – whether with any complicity on the part of the museum staff is still a highly contentious issue, though it is not impossible that the sight of Dr Donny's armed men encouraged the militia – and, as Schwartz spelt out, as a result he was within his military rights to drop a 2000 lb bomb on the museum to flatten it. Such an act would have been absolutely indefensible in reality, as Schwartz well knew, but he was keen to make plain that the museum had been grossly compromised by its use as a military position. He did not blame Dr Donny – 'If I was the curator at the National Museum in Washington, I would defend it as well' – but he obviously felt aggrieved that he was being blamed for not getting there fast enough, when he believed that throughout the affair he had acted with restraint and good judgement. With hindsight, too much restraint, perhaps, but as he saw it he was responsible for the lives of his soldiers even above priceless items of Iraqi – and world – heritage.

Perhaps the biggest area of debate surrounds the relations between the former regime and the museum. It would be naïve to think that those working there were not members of the Baath Party – in Saddam's Iraq, to refuse to join was likely to have had both professional and personal ramifications. And perhaps some of the lack of cooperation that we and the American investigation team experienced could be attributed to a fear that while Saddam remained at large he continued to wield a degree of covert power. Also, after decades of enforced loyalty to the Baath Party, old habits must die hard. But to what extent did party officials have access to exhibits before the war, and were they involved in any way in removing items? Dr Donny, Dr Jaber and Dr Nawala all denied this strenuously, but others said different. Both Steve Mocsary and Colonel Bogdanos reported that individuals bringing back items had insisted that during the previous regime, objects were taken by officials who had *carte blanche* to pick what they liked. Indeed, on 14 April, even before the museum was secured by the Americans, a journalist named Kanan Makiya, who was writing an online diary from Iraq for *The New Republic*, reported that a friend in Baghdad had told him that the looting of the museum was 'the work of newly deposed Baathist officials, who had been selling off our patrimony as they saw their days were numbered … one final crime perpetuated by Saddam's thugs'. This, of course, is hearsay, but it reflects local thinking at the time of the looting.

There is also the question of the white vans turning up to collect items immediately prior to the looting. We heard this from the imam, who had been told the tale frequently, he claimed, by members of his congregation. It was something the US investigators had heard from local residents, and Abbas Saeed, a respected Baghdad fixer, told me emphatically that he had seen it with his own eyes. There are always more rumours than soldiers in any war zone, but this story kept returning to our attention. Organized art thieves? Former Baath Party officials? A combination? It would make sense that someone with specialist knowledge had picked through the higher-value items, while the less valuable pieces – including fakes and copies, which are coming back in equal proportion to authentic items – were taken by mere opportunists. Certainly, all agree that a number of heavy objects, including the Akkadian statue base, were stolen from the galleries, and this would have taken time, organization and transport. In late May Dr John Russell, Dean of the Massachusetts College for Arts and an expert in looted Iraqi antiquities, made a detailed inspection at the museum for UNESCO. His opinion was that most of the returned objects 'were forgeries and reproductions'. If this is true, and there is no reason to doubt Dr Russell's word, then this proportion might be reasonably applied to the total non-'high-value' items stolen. In other words, it is possible that much of what was looted from the storerooms consisted of copies and fakes, which the museum kept alongside its originals. It now seems accepted that some of the looting, particularly of the last storeroom we visited, was facilitated by inside knowledge. Whether that was provided by a director or a cleaner it is impossible at this stage to say, but a set of keys which were kept in the director's office has never been found, and several of the storeroom doors bore no signs of forced entry. There is also the issue of the firing position in the upper storeroom, which again seems to have been attained either by, or with the assistance of, someone with keys.

And then there is Dr Donny. The most vociferous of the museum directors, in the main because of his excellent English and personable character, he has denied any Baath Party involvement in the museum, though he did acknowledge that Saddam Hussein 'liked so much to support our work'. Indeed, we had seen earlier the extent of Saddam's interest in Iraq's history at sites such as Babylon and Hatra, where he ordered rebuilding programmes that reflected his 'glory'. But an interview with Dr Donny by Rose George that had appeared in the *Financial Times* on 4 August 2001 shed a different light on his connection with the government. He revealed that Saddam would send his reports back to him with careful notes in the margin. What these reports contained was not revealed, but whatever their contents this demonstrates a closer relationship between not just the government, but the President himself, and those in charge at the Iraq Museum. It would explain Dr Donny's passionate defence of the reconstruction policy, and why, on our first trip, he came close to justifying government plans to flood parts of the ancient city of Ashur by damming the Tigris. Saddam's regime dished out harsh punishments to anyone found looting historic sites. In a well-known case from 1998, ten wealthy Mosul businessmen were executed for cutting up the head of an Assyrian winged bull from Khorsabad in order to smuggle it out of the country more easily. It was an appalling thing to do, but many would question if it warranted the death penalty. The actions of the executed men were termed 'the crime of the twentieth century' – by Dr Donny George.

Another event perhaps worthy of mention is the looting of the Kuwait National Museum in 1991 by the Iraqis: almost its entire collection was packed up and taken by lorry to Iraq. After the war ended, the UN arranged for what was at the Iraq Museum to be returned, but Kuwaiti museum staff estimate that they still ended up losing 20–30 per cent of their collection. It is believed that certain major items had not even made it to the Iraq Museum, but had remained in the hands of senior Iraqi government officials. Other pieces were said to have been badly damaged in transit. There is no implication that the Iraq Museum staff did anything other than act under orders, but it does illustrate how war – and fear – can influence behaviour.

In the course of our trip, we heard many groups of people blamed for the looting of the museum. Initially it was US soldiers who were accused of plundering the collection and then not posting a guard on the gates in time. We were told by others that, though the Iraqis had been in the museum during the looting, it was Kuwaitis and Jordanians who had done the actual stealing. The imam, who accused the Americans, also blamed the thieves released by Saddam from prisons before the war. Indirectly he also blamed Saddam, as well as those wishing to show their anger at his regime. Dr Donny told us of European and American journalists being stopped at the Jordanian border with antiquities, while he and the other museum staff were keen to extol the theory of organized crime. It is little wonder that any notion of truth has become buried beneath these accusations.

The recovery of the stolen artefacts will rumble on for years, possibly decades, but there is a more pressing matter. The 10,000 recorded ancient sites that enrich Iraq's vast landscape, holding treasures potentially as impressive as anything in the Iraq Museum, are being systematically looted with more intensity than ever before. This has always been a problem for Iraq, mainly due to its size, the remoteness of many sites, and the relatively high cost of providing security. But for every Babylon, there are hundreds of less well-known sites, where the only visitors come armed with bulldozers, trucks and guns. This is the flood that needs damming; and, as dramatic as the Iraq Museum looting story has appeared to be, that is the true, ongoing cultural tragedy, draining Iraq of its riches.

Whatever the consequences of this latest episode in the history of the Iraq Museum, one thing that seems clear is that the Baghdad people, and perhaps a proportion of the staff of the museum and Board of Antiquities, associate the museum, rightly or wrongly, with Saddam's regime. Perhaps, as Imam Kamal al-Mosul suggested, the trashing of the administration offices was only partly about crime, and just as much about an outpouring of bitterness and resentment against a perceived symbol of the Baath Party. Whether this is correct is beside the point: the perception seems widely held. Even if wrong, such an opinion is likely to engender further feelings of mistrust and suspicion that may hinder attempts to reconstruct the museum. Those in authority there may need to consider whether remaining in their posts serves the best interests of the museum, or whether their departure might help win back the trust of the Iraqi public. Ultimately, to draw on Kamal al-Mosul's views once more, the Iraq Museum's unique collection is not the property of any egomaniacal leader, or even of its hard-working, experienced staff, but rather belongs to the people of Iraq, whose ancient, enduring culture and civilization it so brilliantly celebrates.

THE SITES SINCE OUR FIRST VISIT

NINEVEH

One week into the trip, I took advantage of a lull in fighting in the north of the country to travel to Mosul with an Iraqi driver and one of our security advisers, to see how the sites around the city had fared during the war. We visited several of the gates to the ancient city of Nineveh, and found little damage. But it remained hopelessly under-protected, as it had done for years. These once-great cities, built on strong fortifications, now rarely have even a fence.

NIMRUD

We were shown around Sennacherib's palace at Nimrud by two employees, who assured me that the only item stolen was one object from the small museum. The wonderful Assyrian reliefs we had so enjoyed seeing on our first trip seemed intact and in place. However, the National Geographic Society investigative party for the north of Iraq, which included representatives from the Oriental Institute of the University of Chicago and Manhal Jabr, director of the Mosul Museum of Civilization, later found two reliefs missing and another damaged by attempted looting.

While there, we were 'buzzed' for much of the time by an American Black Hawk helicopter, and local guards were in evidence. However, Nimrud did not feel very secure and, given its remote position, it is essential that it receives a 24-hour security presence.

MOSUL MUSEUM OF CIVILIZATION

Our visit to this museum had been one of the highlights of our first trip, and the words of curator Saba al-Omari, who had vowed to fight to the last drop of her blood to save the collection, stayed with us. On arrival, from the outside the museum seemed well fortified with sandbags and defensive walls. I found the director, Manhal Jabr, wandering through its looted administrative offices, which seemed as comprehensively damaged as those in Baghdad. Unfortunately the keys to the galleries were with Bernadette Hannah Mety, the senior curator, who was away for several days. Saba, too, was staying with friends elsewhere. Manhal was able to confirm that the building had not been hit by a bomb, as some newspaper reports had suggested, though windows had been shattered when missiles hit nearby buildings. As for the collection, he claimed that some of the Assyrian reliefs had been damaged by looters, but not stolen. The National Geographic Society team, who visited several weeks later, managed to see the galleries briefly, and confirmed that a total of six items had been taken from the Assyrian gallery, including a cuneiform-inscribed brick and decorated bronze strips from the Balawat gates display. The Hatran gallery had suffered damage to statues, though none had been taken. It will take months to make a full assessment of the damage, especially as some of the museum's exhibits had been removed from the galleries and taken to Baghdad for safe keeping.

HATRA

Thankfully, this ancient desert city seems to have survived almost intact. The head of a figure from an *ewan* arch had been shot off by looters, and a small camel relief taken, though the latter has since been recovered by Department of Antiquities staff. The US military were providing a round-the-clock watch on the site, which it is hoped will continue.

ASHUR

According to the National Geographic Society team, the security guards had been effective in preventing looting, and continued to watch over the property.

SAMARRA

On our way to Mosul we turned off the highway to check on the spiral minaret at Samarra. In the early morning light it looked outrageously resplendent and in good shape, something confirmed by the local guards. It remains in an area of great sensitivity, near the Baathist heartland, but would appear reasonably secure as the main threat was from bombs rather than looters. Inshallah.

CTESIPHON

The National Geographic Society team for the south of Iraq included McGuire Gibson from the University of Chicago, Elizabeth Stone from Stony Brook University in New York, and Iraqi archaeologist Dr Riad Abdul Rahman. They found that the famous vaulted arch had been covered in graffiti, but otherwise remained intact, though Ctesiphon's small museum had been looted. They saw no evidence of any guard on the site. The arch remains a potent symbol of Iraqi achievement, matched only by its vulnerability.

BABYLON

We visited Babylon as a team in the final days of our trip. The small museum had been thoroughly looted and was boarded up, as was the gift shop. The historic remains, however, appeared in very good shape, even if they were now being trampled over by escorted parties of US Marines on sightseeing tours, which at least gave the local guides work. Children were selling Saddam-stamped bricks, three for $5 when we were there, and, if pushed, were promising rarer artefacts. Saddam's huge palace on the hill behind the site, which our government minder had not allowed us to film on the last trip, could still not be visited, as it was now a US military base. The National Geographic Society team reported that any would-be looters were warded off very effectively by a guard wielding a sickle!

BORSIPPA

There is little or no information about the condition of Borsippa, mainly due to its remote location and relatively low profile. When we were there in November 2002 there was no evidence of local guards, and this is likely still to be the case. It therefore remains vulnerable to looters, who are believed to be still roaming the expanse of Iraq's southern archaeological sites.

URUK

On 7 June 2003 the *Washington Post* reported widespread rumours that looting had intensified at remote sites in the south of Iraq such as Uruk. Such reports remain unsubstantiated but are deeply troubling.

UR

Newspaper reports in the UK had suggested that the great Sumerian ziggurat of Ur had suffered a rash of graffiti from American soldiers after the area was taken in the march on Baghdad. The National Geographic Society team saw no evidence of this, nor of the reported removal of kiln-baked bricks as souvenirs. The area now has a huge US military presence on the former Iraqi airbase, and the security level remains high.

CHAPTER FOUR

ISRAEL: THE ROAD TO ARMAGEDDON

THE TERMINAL CONCOURSE WAS SWARMING with armed police, bulked out in bulletproof vests and cradling machine guns. There was little friendly interaction with the public, no bonhomie; you took your reassurance, if you needed any, from their sheer presence. The outnumbered customers milled around in a daze, wondering perhaps if the men with guns knew something they did not, and whether today really was a good day to be flying into the eye of what could be a most deadly storm.

We knew of the high-security measures at Israel's Ben Gurion airport in Tel Aviv, our destination, but this was Heathrow, bristling with unparalleled levels of armed vigilance. In the early hours of that morning, 20 March 2003, the first shots in the war against Iraq had been fired, with a series of cruise missiles launched at Baghdad by the Coalition of US and British forces. The strategy seemed to be early, decisive 'surgical strikes' with the aim of pinpointing and 'decapitating' the Iraqi leadership by killing leading members of the military and the ruling Baath Party – including Saddam Hussein. However, the very real risk remained that the Iraqi leadership could retaliate by launching missile strikes at Israel as it had done during the first Gulf War in 1991 when 39 Scud missiles, fired on the orders of Saddam Hussein, fell on the country.

There was only one airline still flying to Tel Aviv – El Al, the Israeli national carrier, renowned for having the toughest security force of any civil airline. As we queued for our security grilling at Terminal 1 the apprehension among the team was palpable. If any of us 'failed' in our answers the entire project could collapse. On the way to the airport, we had anticipated the questions and discussed the need to coordinate our replies. We had agreed that, though our answers should follow a general course, we should not worry about minor discrepancies. On this trip Nick Reeks was, as ever, our sound recordist and second cameraman. Well versed in filming in foreign locations and keeping the technical side running smoothly, he had a sense of humour and steadiness that were essential to team morale. Filming and directing this programme was a newcomer to the team, Heidi Perry, who had made a film in Israel and the Occupied Territories only six months previously, and was knowledgeable and passionate about the region and its people.

Suddenly Dan was selected by the security man, the first of us to be questioned alone. We knew there was only one question that really mattered: why on earth would we wish to make such an apparently harmless and untopical film, about Israel's cultural heritage and historic sites, at this potentially dangerous – indeed possibly catastrophic – moment? Dan agreed that the timing appeared odd, but explained that we had been preparing the programme for many months and the BBC saw no reason to shelve its plans and give in to Iraqi threats of terror and missiles. It worked. Dan was through, and we were all to follow with relative ease.

For millennia, the region of the Middle East now called Israel has been at the crossroads of world trade and has acted as the threshold between the Eastern and Western worlds. Traders from Mesopotamia passed through here on their way to Europe and to Egypt, as did traders from Rome travelling to the eastern outposts of its vast empire. The term 'Palestine' was first used in the time of the Emperor Hadrian in the second century AD. He imposed it on what had been the Roman province of Judea after putting down what was, in modern terms, an attempted coup against the local governor. Palestine then encompassed areas of Jordan, Egypt and what is now modern Israel, and its boundaries remained much the same, despite the land being conquered by various invaders, for many centuries. After World War I, however, the British 'Palestine Mandate' covered the whole of what is now Israel and the whole of what is now Jordan. Although plans had been drawn up for the creation of separate Arab and Jewish states, after the Arab–Israeli war of 1948 following the declaration of the state of Israel, Palestine ceased to exist as a political entity, and was split up among Israel, Egypt (which received the Gaza Strip) and Jordan (which took the West Bank). Subsequent wars and other military activity resulted in some of this territory being occupied by Israel, but in the early 1990s the administration of the Gaza Strip and parts of the West Bank were handed over to a new Palestinian National Authority. There have been numerous peace initiatives over the years, most of them externally brokered, none ultimately successful. The Oslo Accords, begun in 1992, broke down, and the current attempt, the so-called roadmap, has only just been embarked upon. Today the cycle of Palestinian suicide bombings, and Israeli incursions into Palestinian areas, continues inexorably.

The Israeli security people were quite right, of course: it *was* a curious time to be visiting Israel, and we knew this very well. Throughout the television series our brief had been to examine the threat to art and architecture on the front line of conflict, and to report on the way history could become tragically embroiled in modern-day political or ideological struggles. In Israel and the Occupied Territories, perhaps more than any other country in the world, these issues were strikingly relevant. In his book *Return to the Desert*, David Praill has estimated that over the last 4000 years Palestine 'has suffered an invasion or undesired incursion on average once every 40 years'. For centuries it has been intensely holy to Jews, Christians and Muslims. And yet it occupies a relatively tiny area: 120 kilometres wide by 415 kilometres long, about the same size as Belgium. Mark Twain, who arrived on a steamship on the first American pleasure trip to Palestine in 1867, marvelled that it was not the size of the United States of America: 'I suppose it was because I could not conceive of a small country having so large a history.'

The moral justification for the state of Israel's acquisition and continuing possession of the old land of Palestine, mainly Arab and Islamic for over 1300 years, is based on history. More specifically, archaeology determines who has the legal and moral right to the land; along with traditions and ancient texts, it is being used by both Palestinians and Israelis – by Muslims and Jews – to support their claims to nationhood and possession of the region. Israelis can dig for the ancient sites of the long-lost Jewish kingdoms of Israel and Judah, of kings Saul, David and Solomon, to legitimize their presence. The Palestinians point to the ancient sites of Islam, of Arab kingdoms, to make their case. Nowhere in the world does history, and in particular archaeology, carry such a heavy load of religious and political responsibilities and implications. Is the fact that the Israelis can claim that their ethnic ancestors occupied the land perhaps 3400 years ago, and then lost control or largely left it between 2500 and 1800 years ago, more significant than the more recent Arab/Islamic occupation of the land? It is an impossible judgement to make, one that would have probably defeated even the mighty Solomon, yet it is one that Israelis and Palestinians are being forced to ponder every day of their lives.

One of the paradoxes in this struggle, in which each side seeks moral justification, is that the first victim is morality itself. Historic buildings and sites have become the tangible media through which historic precedence is expressed. History is alive here like nowhere else on earth – and it is threatened like nowhere else on earth. Not just by internal turmoil but also, at the time of our trip, by external events such as war with Iraq, when Scud missiles could once again rain down on Israel. And, in terms of timing, perhaps our trip was not so inappropriate. On 16 February 2003, President George W. Bush had used an address to the American Enterprise Institute in Washington DC to link the impending war to peace in the Middle East: 'Success in Iraq could also begin a new stage for Middle Eastern peace, and set in motion progress towards a truly democratic Palestinian state … America will seize every opportunity in pursuit of peace. And the end of the present regime in Iraq would create such an opportunity.' Was he right? Or was American involvement in Iraq more likely to bring the conflict in the Middle East once again to the boil? We would be there to find out.

Our flight took off at 2.30 p.m., and an hour or so later the sustained air assault on Iraq commenced. By the time we landed, dropping abruptly into the dusk of Tel Aviv without tail lights, the state of Israel was on full alert, bracing itself for the worst. The smart arrivals hall of Ben Gurion airport was virtually deserted, with large posters directing to a variety of 'shelters' those brave enough or foolish enough to come to Israel at such a time.

After a detour to acquire press accreditation, we moved on to what we hoped were the safer environs of Arab East Jerusalem, an hour or so east of Tel Aviv. After speeding along the fast highway until we saw the lights of Jerusalem twinkling in a clear sky we arrived at the American Colony Hotel – a charmingly old-fashioned establishment that had long been in the ownership of an English family called Vester. It was a Jerusalem institution, built in the nineteenth century as a Turkish pasha's palace, and its roll-call of distinguished guests included T.E. Lawrence, Marc Chagall, Lauren Bacall and Graham Greene. Housed in a collection of old stone buildings within gardens and around courtyards, it was a comforting place at such a troubled time. But even here we could not escape the shadow of war. As we were handed our keys we were also issued with respirators and told how to reach the hotel's 'safe area', sealed against chemical and biological weapons. Here in the Holy Land the consequences of this latest conflict – in which, emotionally at least, Jews and Muslims supported opposing sides – had the potential to be dramatic in the extreme.

Next day, the planned first stop on our trip was also perhaps the most controversial: the West Bank town of Hebron. Hebron was the first town in the West Bank that Jewish settlers moved into after the territory was captured by Israel in the 1967 Six-Day War, and it was the last one evacuated by Israeli troops following the Oslo Accords. The Torah (Numbers 13:22) states that Hebron, or al-Khalil in Arabic, was founded seven years before Zoan in Egypt, which would make it 3725 years old, while in *The Jewish War*, written in about AD 70, the historian Josephus described Hebron as 'more ancient than any town in the country – older even than Memphis in Egypt; its age is reckoned as 2330 years'; this would mean it was built about 4300 BC, putting it on a par with the Sumerian city of Ur, now in southern Iraq. As the home of the patriarch Abraham after his migration from Mesopotamia it was one of the most important of the ancient Jewish cities, and so retains huge symbolic importance for present-day Jews, while being holy to all three great monotheistic religions. This, of course, is what has always made it so contentious a location. In AD 70, following the Jewish Revolt against the Roman occupiers, Hebron was destroyed; when it was resettled a ban was placed on Jews living there. This was the start of what was to become a pattern in the city's history. Although Jews were allowed to return to the city when it came under Muslim control in the seventh century, their stay was relatively brief: the Crusader conquest in 1100 saw them once again ejected – only to be allowed back by the new Mamluk rulers in about 1250. In the early twentieth century, tensions rose again under the British Mandate after nearly 800 years of Jews and Arabs coexisting in relative peace. Following the massacre of 67 Jews by rioting Arabs in August 1929, and the plundering and burning of synagogues and Jewish homes, the survivors were relocated to Jerusalem and Hebron was left entirely Arab. Between the declaration of the state of Israel in 1948 and the Six-Day War in 1967 Jews were not allowed to live in the city, or to visit and worship at its holy sites. Since 1967, Hebron has stood as a symbol in the West Bank of Jewish settlers' determination to maintain a presence in its ancient and sacred sites. The following year, radical Zionist Rabbi Moshe Levinger led a group of Orthodox Jewish families posing as tourists to the town, stayed at a small Palestinian hotel and refused to move out. Eventually the then Defence Minister, Moshe Dayan, gave them permission to stay in an abandoned military camp on the outskirts of Hebron, and in 1971 they were given the right to establish a Jewish settlement there called Kiryat Arba – the Old Testament name for Hebron. From here, in 1979, they entered and occupied a building in the city centre, where a settlement of about 450 people has remained ever since, guarded by thousands of Israeli soldiers.

Our destination was the Tomb of the Patriarchs, the Haram al-Khalil, reputed to be the resting place of the Old Testament patriarchs and matriarchs – Abraham and Sarah, Isaac and Rebecca, Jacob and Leah, and, incredibly, Adam and Eve – and sacred to both Jews and Muslims. In 1980, six Jewish rabbinical students were killed as they left prayer at the Tomb, and in response the Israeli government officially recognized the Beit Hadassah settlement in the centre of town. Then, in February 1994, tragedy struck again, this time for the Muslims, when Baruch Goldstein, a resident of Kiryat Arba dressed in the uniform of the Israel Defence Forces (IDF), opened fire on Muslim worshippers in the Tomb, killing 29 and wounding 125 others. Israeli troops inadvertently compounded the disaster by shooting at fleeing crowds, thinking they were rioting. Goldstein, who was killed by the congregation, was buried in the Judean hills on the outskirts of Kiryat Arba, his grave bearing the chilling inscription: 'Here is buried the martyr, the doctor. May the Lord avenge his blood.'

Goldstein's terrible act led to the Hebron Agreement, signed by Israeli Prime Minister Binyamin Netanyahu and Palestinian leader Yasser Arafat in 1997. This accord divided Hebron: H1, which represented 80 per cent of the town, was put under Palestinian National Authority control, while H2, the remaining 20 per cent, fell under Israeli jurisdiction. Approximately 120,000 Arabs live in the town, with 6000 Jews in Kiryat Arba, and three Christians who are the custodians of the town's Russian Orthodox church. We had heard of threats to historic buildings as a result of this apartheid. For instance, early in 2003 the Israeli Supreme Court ruled against an IDF decree which had ordered the destruction of 22 Mamluk and Ottoman houses dating from the fifteenth and sixteenth centuries, which were situated on a road used by Jewish settlers to reach their place of worship. Hebron is seen as a touchstone of current Israeli policies, but is also the place that divides Jewish thinking most: there are those who admire the pioneering spirit of the settlers in validating Israel's right to the land, while others see their aggressive stance as causing too much trouble, putting the lives of young Israeli soldiers at risk and costing too much money. And so one of the most significant and impressive buildings in the Holy Land finds itself marooned amidst hatred and murder. This was where we were now headed.

Because of the political climate most Israelis consider it unsafe to travel in the West Bank, and so Ruthy, the Israeli fixer responsible for the logistics of our trip, had arranged for a Palestinian counterpart to meet us at the checkpoint on the Green Line – the border between Israel and the West Bank – with Palestinian vans in which we would then travel the 32 kilometres south from Jerusalem. IDF checkpoints, we quickly came to learn, are an unavoidable element of moving around the West Bank.

How long it takes to pass through them varies from a couple of minutes to hours, depending on the mood of the soldiers or on recent events such as suicide bombings or riots. Palestinians resident in the West Bank or in Gaza, the other Occupied Territory, are not normally permitted to enter Israel, while entry into the Palestinian territories from Israel is strictly controlled and can be a long, complex and sometimes dangerous procedure. So we approached the checkpoint with caution, Ruthy having telephoned ahead every couple of minutes to make sure our West Bank fixer was ready and not being harassed by the IDF.

Dan scribbled down in his diary how he felt at this first tangible demonstration of Israeli military control:

> The checkpoint is guarded in depth. Tiers of concrete blocks and barricades, wire on each side of the road which is flanked by towers draped with camouflage netting – observation posts and the nests of Israeli snipers. As we drive up we pass long queues of patient Palestinians waiting to enter the West Bank. It is evident they will have to wait hours for access. The Israeli soldiers are – in a slow and methodical manner – questioning each person. I'm not sure if the process is intended to be humiliating but it is clearly dehumanizing. Each Palestinian waits in line then – eventually – is called forward. They have to walk 50 yards or so to the Israeli questioner – the space no doubt being a buffer to protect the soldier from suicide bombers – and then they are interrogated, searched and told to justify their visit. It struck me that this scene has much in common with the attitude and methods used by the British army here, in the 1930s and 1940s – when it was holding down a violent and independence-minded Jewish population. Our turn comes. Soldiers approach our vehicle – Rob, our security adviser, warns Heidi to stop filming – Israeli soldiers, like most soldiers around the world, take a very dim view of their official actions being recorded. We decide to go on filming until told to stop. We – like most journalists – perhaps don't really appreciate the dangerous game we are playing. This time we are lucky.

A female soldier approaches, ignores or doesn't see the camera,
looks at our papers, looks at us, and waves us through.

Ali Shafout, our new fixer, was well turned out and in his mid-thirties,
and we quickly discovered him to be a kind, well-informed man with a
passion for his country that, like most Palestinians, he was eager to
communicate. Off we set for Hebron, eager to put as much distance as
possible between us and the checkpoint. But it was a wretched day, with
a slate-grey sky and blustery wind more reminiscent of winter in Britain,
as we bumped over the Judean hills on uneven Palestinian back roads in
order to avoid further checkpoints.

For much of the time, Hebron is under a virtual 24-hour curfew,
with its Palestinian inhabitants allowed out to shop for only a few hours
a week. This has the understandable effect of rendering much of it like
a ghost town, a feeling not helped that day by the desolate weather. After
a coffee at a baker's on the outskirts of town, with the al-Jazeera network
blaring from the television, we drove as close to the Old City as we dared
and then went on foot down a steep road lined with burnt-out, derelict
buildings. On the way we encountered an old Muslim, Minwer Id'eis,
with whom we exchanged a few words about life under curfew. It had
been almost a week since he had last been able to pray at the mosque in
the Tomb of the Patriarchs. Even then, it was a brief window. 'They
only lifted the curfew between 9 a.m. and 1 p.m., so we were able to say
just one prayer and then they told us to go home.'And he was not
optimistic for the future. 'The situation is deteriorating. There are no
signs that things are getting better.'

We continued cautiously down the road, aware that the IDF soldiers
manning the checkpoint at the bottom were training their guns on us.
We could understand their twitchiness: they had watched our Palestinian
drivers return up the hill after carrying our cases down, and now we
were advancing towards them with ominous-looking bags and a small
contraption perched on Heidi's shoulder. Rob strode ahead to announce
us, and after radioing through to their command they let us approach –
just as a patrol of half a dozen soldiers appeared at our rear, equally
suspicious of our presence. The men relaxed visibly once they had seen

our press cards, but were not optimistic about our chances of getting to the Tomb of the Patriarchs. They told us we were likely to be stoned or shot at – either by Jewish settlers or by Palestinians. It did not sound hopeful but we had not come all this way to be defeated by conjecture, and Dan somehow managed to persuade an armed patrol to accompany us the short distance to the Tomb. Tentatively we set off, with three soldiers either side of us looking in doorways and down alleys, and checking possible sniper points. Even if they were rather theatrically going through routine manoeuvres, it felt genuinely tense as we walked down this deserted old street with muffled voices reaching us from within the houses. It was a desperate way to have to live. Since there were no signs of aggression the patrol left us a little way from the Tomb, where we were due to meet a rabbi from the settlement who had agreed to speak with us. We went for some coffee – a scalding, muddy instant brew – in a drab and eerily empty Jewish café below the Tomb, and after a few minutes our rabbi appeared.

While much of the present building dates from around AD 1130, the outer walls of the imposing, fortress-like structure overlooking the Old City date from the time of King Herod, about 30 BC, though the Arabs believe the huge stones were magically laid by Solomon. According to legend, decreeing that such a holy burial site should not be exposed to the elements in an open cave he ordered the building to be put up to cover it. The Cave of Makhpela, on which the Tomb was built, was bought by Abraham, along with the neighbouring field, from the sons of Heth when his wife Sarah died nearby (Genesis 23). It is this purchase that lies at the heart of Jewish claims to Hebron and the Tomb of the Patriarchs – the holiest site for Jews after the Wailing Wall, and the holiest in Palestine for Muslims after the Dome of the Rock. Since the 1994 massacre the building's interior has been divided into a synagogue and a mosque, policed by the IDF and united only by a glimpse of Abraham's tomb.

Rabbi Simha Hochbaum, in his thirties with an East Coast American accent, explained how his community saw the Tomb. He began by emphasizing that it was only the Jewish religion that, since 1967, had given access to members of all three relevant religions in order to pray. This was obviously contentious, given the curfew on Hebron's Muslims, but in theory it was true, and certainly before 1967 Jews had been unable to gain access for many years. The rabbi pointed out to us the blackened stone at the base of one of the walls, which he said was the result of people lighting candles. For 800 years or more that had been the closest to the Tomb that Jews were allowed to pray, since they were not allowed to pass beyond the seventh step to the mosque. This was a poignant image, starkly laying bare the physicality of separation over such a long period. We then passed with him to the security point near the entrance to the Tomb, where we put our kit through metal detectors and had our bags searched. It had been immensely difficult to obtain permission from the IDF to get even this far, and we had secured approval only seconds before we reached the soldiers. After going through a lobby where young off-duty conscripts were lazing around we came to a corridor leading to the Jewish section, the synagogue, which until 1967 had been the Djaouliya mosque, with its soaring minarets still visible from the outside. It felt amazing to have got this far, given the situation.

Despite the vast, perfectly hewn Herodian blocks of the outer wall the space itself was fairly drab, with plastic chairs and a canopy to keep the rain off. Inside the tiny, ancient part of the synagogue that dates back to the twelfth century, a rabbi chanted while a few young settlers sat around. Rabbi Hochbaum pointed out the olive-green screen that separates Jews from Muslims, representing the sad state of affairs that has prevailed since 1994: only for ten days a year, on significant holy days, could either religion enter the other's space. He explained this as a state of being 'separate but equal'. Dan asked him if he could envisage harmony ever being achieved between the two warring factions. The rabbi smiled. 'The dream is always one day that the whole world will get together and the power of prayer is a universal language that really unites all hearts. However, at this point it hasn't worked out that way yet ...' After he had left for another appointment a burly, sweat-shirted Jew with a pistol tucked into his belt asked us casually, 'Are you BBC News?' We said no. 'That's good, 'he replied lightly, 'otherwise I'd have to shoot you.'

We had two problems. Firstly, we had been strongly advised to be back at the checkpoint before dusk to pick up the vehicle that would take us back to Jerusalem. Most incidents happen at first light and dusk, when the soldiers on guard are likely to be at their most short-tempered and jumpy. Secondly, we had just been told by one of the soldiers that we could not now go into the locked-up Muslim side of the Tomb. So frustrated was Dan that he refused to take no for an answer and asked the soldier to check again with his commanding officer, explaining how important it was for us to see the whole building. There was a pause, ten vital minutes lost, and then we were reluctantly given the OK.

It was a very odd feeling: a group of Christians allowed into the mosque while any Muslims wishing to pray there were kept well away. But the sight that greeted us was breathtaking. Here, though draughty and gloomy, was a beautiful mosque, known as the al-Is'haqiyya, its floor covered with kilims. We removed our shoes in respect and padded through the hall, which was quiet but for the flap of the wings of some trapped pigeons. Beneath the carpets we found where a staircase led down into the Cave of Makhpelah, the burial place of Adam and Eve according to Abraham's vision. Muslims never descend into the cave as they believe they will be struck dead if they commit such a sacrilegious act. It was an evocative moment to be here in this religious spot, with no one for company except a couple of Israeli soldiers and some birds. We had already seen Abraham's vast tomb from the Jewish part of the building, and now we moved across the floor to view it from the Muslim side. Here too it was behind protective bars. It bore Arabic inscriptions from the Koran, which indicated that it had been constructed in Islamic times, and the marriage of this with the sound of the rabbi chanting in the synagogue somehow exemplified an ideal, unlikely harmony. Both the Hebrew name, Hebron, and the Arabic, al-Khalil, may derive from those languages' words for 'friend', but there was little amity in evidence and little prospect of it.

Conscious of the time, we reluctantly left. The walk back to the checkpoint passed without incident until a coachload of Jewish settlers approached, returning from an outing. The driver opened his door and yelled: 'What are you doing here? Go away!', displaying the fraught passions aroused by this sterile, drained environment. Our drivers and Ali offered a friendly greeting, but we could not get back to the checkpoint, and then Jerusalem, quickly enough.

The aim the next day was to visit another contested site, the holiest one in Christendom – the Church of the Holy Sepulchre in Jerusalem. The holiest, perhaps the noisiest, and certainly the most fractious in atmosphere. To reach it we walked through the Arab Quarter of the Old City, down its alleys and cobbled steps worn smooth by centuries of merchants and crowds. Little was open early in the morning, yet the few shops that were, on streets which had once bustled with pilgrims and travellers, were now desperate to do business with the few foreigners who wandered past. Since the intifada (uprising) of September 2000, tourism has dropped off to a barely discernible level. Add to this the war in Iraq, and perhaps it is no wonder that the Arab Quarter was so empty and a little intimidating. Dan noted down his impressions:

We went into the Old City of Jerusalem. In the Arab Quarter – in the narrow and nearly deserted shopping streets – there was a tense atmosphere. We were met with steely, cold stares. This was a shock. I have travelled in many Arab countries and have never found anything but hospitality and a warm welcome. But in the streets of the Arab Quarter in Jerusalem, on the morning British and US troops were invading Iraq, killing Arabs and Muslims, being British was very definitely a problem. There was no direct threat – just anger and dismay. An Arab Islamic country being invaded and humiliated, its people killed, could only be bad for the Palestinian cause and good for Israel. I stopped to stare in a shop window – to avoid the glares – but this didn't work. The shopkeeper – a young man – asked me where I came from. I murmured something; instantly he guessed I was British. He remained polite but his excitement increased as he spoke, reaching a pitch of near hysteria. 'Why is Blair doing this? Britain was a good nation. Why is it killing innocent Iraqis?' I agreed that the death of innocent Iraqis is terrible. But this wasn't enough. He saw I was with a film crew, a member of the media. 'You have a responsibility – you must speak out against this – stop it happening.' We had entered a world where no one could be neutral.

The church, typically in this crammed, contested land, nestles among the chaos of buildings that have sprung up around it. A few police officers and guides mingled easily, their presence not merely symbolic. In order to film inside the church we had needed permission from the six denominations that worship there: the Greek Orthodox, the Armenians, the Syrian Orthodox, the Franciscans, the Egyptian Copts and the Ethiopians. Their respective movements have been set in stone since the *status quo* of 1757, when strictly regulated times and locations were laid down for each to worship. Amazingly, this arrangement still holds, with all parties terrified of losing even an inch of space or a second of time to another. Indeed, the church is still locked up every night by a representative of one of two Muslim families that were given the keys by Caliph Omar ibn al-Khattab in the seventh century, as the Christians could not decide amongst themselves who would do it. It sounds hilarious – though we discovered that its appeal quickly wore thin amid the human pettiness. But we were here to observe the morning services, hoping to feel something of the church's unique atmosphere and even, if we were lucky, some of its holiness.

The first Church of the Holy Sepulchre was built here on the hill of Golgotha, the site of the crucifixion, burial and resurrection of Christ, in AD 66, but demolished by the Roman Emperor Hadrian who replaced it with a temple to Aphrodite. In the fourth century AD the Empress Helena identified it as the site of Christ's crucifixion – indeed, she claimed to have discovered the cross in a cave under the site – and her son, the Emperor Constantine, had built a new church by AD 348. After being destroyed by the Persians and one of the Fatimid caliphs of Egypt, al-Hakim, and rebuilt by the Greeks and Byzantines, the present structure, largely the work of the Crusaders in the Middle Ages but incorporating the surviving elements of Constantine's church, evolved.

An aedicule, a column-framed niche, stood over the reputed site of Christ's tomb, and at its rear was what seemed to be a small, shadowy shrine – but was, in fact, perhaps the most discreet shop in the world. A few years previously it would have been necessary to queue for over an hour to reach the tomb; that day it was possible to wander around it at will, almost alone, such was the dearth of tourists. The dark interior of the church, an architectural jumble of chapels, shrines, recesses, courtyards and offices, was quiet when we entered, but people were starting to arrive for services. Steadily the various congregations started to build up in their own corners, with an intricate choreography that had developed over the centuries to avoid any confrontation. As we wandered among the Byzantine wall-paintings and ancient graffiti, sounds of organized worship began to fill the cavernous gloom. The chanted prayer of the Copts in their maroon fezzes, insistent and strong, started to lift and pass through the air, only to collide with the familiar organ-led hymns of the Franciscans, whose sturdy verses were punctuated by the harsh thump of the Syrians' staffs as they entered the church in procession, followed by a solitary Ethiopian monk. Meanwhile the Greek Orthodox monks carried out their daily tasks in the Katholikon, the main body of the Crusader church and the lion's share of the space, as if they were the only people there. This was as true a cacophony as you could get, and it felt like delirious madness, but after a few minutes it also felt very human. Behind the aural chaos was an order, a definite pattern, by which these monks and worshippers lived their lives, and if at times it was fractious it only served to represent the greater scheme of life. And once we had entered the tomb itself we found respite from the noise – until, that is, the drone of a jet overhead returned us to more earthly matters such as the war being waged in Iraq, whose border lay just over 300 kilometres away. It only remained to explore what was perhaps the strangest element of all in this rich tapestry of worship.

It seems astonishing, but the Ethiopians have reportedly resided on the roof since the sixteenth century, after being expelled from the main body of the church following one of many interdenominational squabbles. We climbed a stone staircase off the entrance square and emerged, after passing through their small chapel, on the flat roof. Waiting for us was Father Salomon, a small monk with an inquisitive, open face. In his faltering English, for over five minutes he read out a hand-written statement on the history of the Ethiopian presence at the Church of the Holy Sepulchre. When he had finished Dan asked him some questions about their world, perched high above the holy site. Although all the Churches defend their spaces downstairs inside the main building, the Ethiopians' main opponents are the Egyptian Copts who, as Father Salomon put it, 'don't want us in this area'. The Egyptians claim the roof area for themselves, and have even forbidden Egyptian pilgrims to visit Jerusalem until this is achieved. When Dan ventured that this was not very Christian, Father Salomon flashed a bright smile and shrugged: 'What can we do?' He said they felt like the outsiders they literally were, and wanted the Israeli authorities to help them – even if it meant they had to stay on the roof. 'During the winter the monastery is extremely cold, while during the summer it is extremely hot. We don't have enough electricity, and the toilets and kitchens, if you could see them – well, no one could live here, except the Ethiopians. It is only for the love of Christ that we remain here. It is a miserable life.' He admitted that the Ethiopian monks no longer even dreamt of regaining their original chapel in the main body of the church, now occupied by the Armenians, such was the disdain that the other Churches felt towards them. All the Ethiopians wanted was the Israeli authorities' help in renovating their monastery on the roof, which was in urgent need of repair. Father Salomon then took us on a tour of this ramshackle roof-top village, among Crusader ruins and mud-hut cells which were home to 20 monks and 3 nuns. Father Salomon claimed, with touching pride, that they were 'the chosen people' because of their position – an admirable attempt at triumph over adversity.

In recent years the enmity between the Egyptian Coptic and Ethiopian Churches had escalated and violent clashes had taken place. When asked, Father Salomon at first refused to be drawn – 'They have done a lot of crimes but we don't speak about it' – but he later admitted that the Egyptians had what he termed 'street police', who beat up the Ethiopians: 'They beat our heads and so most of the monks were completely unconscious.' Iron bars and chains were allegedly used, but again Father Salomon's refrain was 'What can we do?' We were shocked by this account of fraternal brutality. Later, a professional fixer at the church, who had helped us obtain our permissions, covertly produced some photographs he had taken immediately after an incident in July 2002. He would not allow us to film them or make copies, as his job required him to walk a diplomatic tightrope, but in the photographs we could clearly see an Ethiopian monk lying unconscious on the ground, with blood pouring from head wounds. Egyptian monks, too, had been injured in the mêlée. The argument was apparently the culmination of a feud that had been running for days, initiated by an Egyptian monk who had put a chair on the Ethiopians' roof, challenging the centuries-old demarcation of lines. He had been moving his chair around each day, to claim more and more of the roof, before the Ethiopians realized what he was doing and objected. The final straw was when an Ethiopian woman allegedly pinched the intruder. It was appalling that interdenominational squabbling should come to this, but we were quickly learning the brutality, physical and doctrinal, of these ancient Churches.

Father Salomon was showing us their small chapel, and a wonderful ancient Bible cut in the shape of a cross, when an Israeli policeman appeared at the head of the staircase leading to the street. Apparently the Egyptian Copts had caught wind of our interview and had objected, claiming we had not asked their permission to go on the roof – something we were unaware we had to do. The policeman advised us to leave as soon as possible or there might be a major incident and possibly violence. Although frustrated at having our visit cut short, we had no choice but to agree. Down in the front square we asked Ibrahim Zaki, our contact at the church, what had happened. With a swarthy Egyptian Coptic monk breathing down his neck, Ibrahim explained that the Copts had become 'nervous' at our talking to the Ethiopians and wanted the interview to stop, as they were sure that Father Salomon was criticizing them. A debate, an intellectual tussle over doctrine, we could tolerate, but going at it hammer and tongs over property seemed completely incongruous in this most holy of Christian sites. The only conclusion we could draw was the sad one that there was something wrong with this Holy Land; in Dan's words, 'This is the most unholy land I've ever been to.'

The city of Jerusalem was at the very heart of the battle for history, and one sacred site often sat quite literally on top of another. The Church of the Holy Sepulchre was the centre of the Christian world, but even its domestic wrangling seemed tame when compared to the dispute over the Temple Mount in East Jerusalem. Generally accepted as the site of the First and Second Temples – the First built by Solomon to house the Ark of the Covenant and razed by Nebuchadnezzar's Neo-Babylonians in 586 BC, the Second built soon after and then rebuilt (some call it the Third Temple) by Herod in 20 BC and destroyed after the first Jewish Revolt in AD 70 – this vast esplanade was now home to the third most holy site in Islam, the magnificently ornate Dome of the Rock. Also in the al-Haram al-Sharif complex (as it is known to the Muslims), with its 35 acres of gardens, avenues and assorted examples of Islamic architecture, is the sacred al-Aqsa mosque, the earliest example in Palestine. To pressurize the situation still further, defining the western edge of the Temple Mount is the Western (or Wailing) Wall, the main remnant of Herod's Temple. And for Christians, too, the site is intensely sacred, since this is where Jesus walked and preached. The situation could hardly be more dramatic and, unsurprisingly, the area has witnessed many violent confrontations. Indeed, Muslim leaders claim that the intifada of September 2000 was triggered by Ariel Sharon walking on the Temple Mount, though in response the Jews claim that the campaign of violence had already been planned. Either way, it has been a focal point for hatred and violence for decades, and it is hard to see a solution. And since the intifada, access to the Temple Mount has been confined to Muslims.

More in hope than expectation we tried to enter the complex, but were politely turned away by the Israeli police on duty. Frustrated to be so close and yet so far, we hit on a ruse: we asked Labeeb, a Palestinian cameraman we had met, if he would film the Dome of the Rock for us. As a Muslim, he should have no problem gaining entry. He agreed and, equipped with a pocket-sized digital video camera, set off for the gate.

Within a couple of hours Dan was finally able to get a closer impression of the Dome of the Rock, a structure he had first visited some 15 years before. Built between AD 687 and 691 by the ninth caliph,

Abd al-Malik, the triumphant structure encloses the great rock from which the Prophet Muhammad is said to have ascended through seven heavens to meet Allah, and which Jews see as the symbolic Foundation Stone of the world and the site where Abraham nearly sacrificed his son Isaac. Often referred to as a mosque, the building was in fact intended as a shrine for pilgrims; the nearby al-Aqsa mosque was built in AD 715 to receive their prayers. Quite apart from its associations with Muhammad, it remains a significant site geographically and politically. The octagonal building is perhaps the only one that can be seen from almost anywhere in Jerusalem's packed Old City, the sun glinting off its perfect golden dome. Designed by Byzantine architects, its immaculately detailed tiled exterior of brilliant blue and green is decorated, according to the requirements of Islam, without any representations of living beings: flowers, texts from the Koran and abstract patterns, constantly revitalized over the centuries, express spiritual reverence through sacred geometry. The crowning glory, the dome, is 20 metres high and 10 metres in diameter, and is supported by a double system of pillars and columns. Originally covered in pure gold, the dome was recoated in more recent times with anodized aluminium, the gold having been sold off a long time ago, allegedly to pay the caliph's debts. Architecturally it derives much from the Romano-Byzantine legacy in its shape, vaulting, columns and arches; however, it is clearly Islamic in its mosaic decorations, clarity of ideas and refusal to subjugate decoration to architecture, allowing the former an integral, rather than a merely superficial, role.

Unfortunately, even Labeeb had been prevented from filming inside the shrine, so the marvellous juxtaposition of raw stone with immaculate mosaic work and marble remained off-limits. It seemed a tragic state that visitors of other faiths and denominations could not derive pleasure from one of the wonders of the modern world. Once again, art and culture were being held hostage to political ends. Indeed, there had long been fears that Jewish extremists intended to blow up the Dome of the Rock in their quest to reclaim the Temple Mount; Rabbi Shlomo Goren, the army's chief rabbi at the time of the Six-Day War, reportedly urged that this terrible act should be carried out only hours after Israeli troops had captured Jerusalem from the Jordanians in June 1967. Since then there have been dozens of incidents: various extremist groups have plotted the Dome's destruction, or tried to invade the compound, and many riots and gun battles have taken place on its sacred ground. In 1969 a demented Australian tourist started a fire that destroyed a magnificent carved wood pulpit, in the belief that the Messiah would not come until such abominations had been cleared from the Temple Mount. In fact, many pious Jews will not set foot on the Temple Mount for fear of inadvertently treading on the Holy of Holies. In July 2003, however, there were press reports that the Israeli police had resumed escorting groups of tourists on to the Temple Mount, despite failing to come to an agreement with the Waqf, the Muslim administrators in Jerusalem, and Islamic leaders warned that a bloodbath could easily ensue. Against this background, the Dome remains at serious risk.

Keen to learn more about the Muslim perspective on this holiest and most controversial of historic locations, we went to talk to Adnan Husseini, head of the Waqf. After the Six-Day War, Israeli commander Moshe Dayan promised the Muslim leaders that they would retain control over the Islamic sites, including the Temple Mount. Although they did not acknowledge Israeli control of Jerusalem until a few years ago, the Waqf had in general cooperated with the authorities. In his bright office overlooking the al-Haram al-Sharif, with a picture of Yasser Arafat above his desk, Husseini responded to Dan's question about the Jewish belief that Solomon's temples lay below the site of the al-Aqsa mosque, which, they asserted, enabled them to lay claim to earlier occupation of the site. The Waqf leader was adamant: 'If you to go the Dome of the Rock, there is no place underneath it to be a building because it's natural rock. The buildings were built to protect the rock from weathering and people pray around it. So, under this shrine, it's difficult to say that there is a building.' Denial of any historical Jewish connection with the site was the official Arab line, patently propagandist and absurd. Husseini patiently explained that Muslims were forbidden to build on any site that had previously been sacred to another religion, and cited the well-known example of the caliph Omar ibn al-Khattab, who, when he accepted the surrender of Jerusalem in AD 638, declined to pray in the Church of the Holy Sepulchre on the grounds that it might encourage his followers to turn the church into a mosque. Husseini went on to deny that the Waqf had been responsible for any archaeological digging of their own. Yet there have been reports of them 'renovating' the site, building a new mosque in the southeast corner, and then cutting additional exits through the Temple Mount walls. Some Jewish groups even claim that spoil from the digging, dumped in the Kidron valley, contained valuable archaeological material from the First Temple period, 960–586 BC.

The Muslim authorities have not been the only ones to dig on, or in, the Temple Mount. In September 1996, when the Israeli authorities opened up the Western Wall tunnel by the Temple Mount, a riot was sparked in which 80 Palestinians and 24 Israeli soldiers died. The Israelis claimed that they were assisting not only historical research but also the tourism infrastructure of the Old City. The Palestinians, on the other hand, believed, or had been led to believe, that the Israelis had been undermining the Temple Mount in order to weaken it. In addition, a new section from the ancient tunnel was opened into the Via Dolorosa in the Arab Quarter of the Old City, and they feared that it would be used as a route to get Jews into the Quarter. Whatever the truth of these allegations – and certainly the first would appear unfounded – it was a provocative act on the part of the Israeli authorities to open the tunnel without consulting the Waqf, and tragedy ensued

The tunnel is still open, and we visited it to follow its course into the Arab Quarter and to view the lower portion of the Western Wall in its entirety. Entering on the prayer plaza of the Wailing Wall, we passed through a series of medieval vaulted chambers into a large cruciform hall built in the Mamluk era (AD 1252–1517), on the east side of which could be seen the Western Wall. Israeli archaeologists had dug a tunnel against the wall heading north, exposing around 300 metres of the wall in pristine condition. We passed along the tunnel and saw individuals and small groups praying to its vast blocks at a synagogue positioned, it was believed, close to the Foundation Stone and the Holy of Holies, the innermost sanctum of the Temple. Mostly women, the faithful rocked gently while praying, and the crevices of the tightly packed stones were crammed with scribbled prayers. Below the foundations of old Arab houses we inched along the tunnel, its tight dimensions emphasizing the solidity and expanse of the wall itself. At the end we entered the Hasmonean water channel, the extension of the tunnel that had been rediscovered at the north end of the wall in 1987. Then, a newly cut section of the tunnel, approximately 20 metres long, led to stairs that rose to street level via a heavy turnstile. We came out as expected on the Via Dolorosa, by the First Station of the Cross and beneath an Islamic school, at a doorway guarded by two casually dressed young Jewish men with conspicuous machine guns. Layers of history were once more being used in this political war, with different histories being dug through to find the one that fitted the appropriate religious or political agenda.

Unlike the stretch exposed by the tunnelling, the lower part of the Western Wall, known as the Wailing Wall or Kotel ha-Ma'aravi, has been exposed for nearly 2000 years. Between 1948 and 1967, however, when Jerusalem was under Jordanian control, it was impossible for Jews to gain access to it. In addition, during this black period in Jerusalem's Jewish history many ancient synagogues and artefacts were destroyed in a callous bid to reduce Jewish claims to the Old City. Yet the Wailing Wall is the most sacred site in Judaism, and Jews now come from all over the world to pray here. They pray to a memory, the loss of the Second Temple in AD 70, and the place has a heavy air of grieving about it. Visually, the scene can be read as a worship of architecture, such is the intimacy of each worshipper with the stones, their prayers intoned with rhythmic rocking or whispered into the crevices. According to Jewish lore, the Third Temple had to be built in order to welcome in the Messianic era at the end of time. However, all except Ultra-Orthodox Jews took this metaphorically – as indeed the wall itself should be taken to a certain extent, as it was most likely a retaining wall rather than intrinsic to the Temple itself. There is also a thriving industry here, showing that the faithful are in touch with the modern as well as the ancient world: the prayers and petitions wedged between the mighty stones on behalf of the sick or needy can be paid for by phone or email.

The wall is divided into men's and women's sections – when we were there the women's section, though smaller, was far busier – and it seemed extraordinary that a piece of masonry could provoke such intense religiosity and awe. In the past the presence of women was fiercely opposed by the Ultra-Orthodox, who had even thrown objects at them as they prayed. While today the Wall itself may not seem under threat it remains technically owned by the Waqf; the explosion of violence when the tunnel was opened in 1996, and the rows over archaeological digging, suggest that even this most holy of places could become a battleground with little provocation or reason.

The war of the archaeologists has always been very much a theme in the Holy Land. Sir Mortimer Wheeler famously remarked that archaeology was not a science but a vendetta; and in Israel it could be more than personal. On the Western Wall plaza we met up with Joe Zias, a sprightly, articulate man in his fifties who worked as a paleopathologist at the Hebrew University and had a fund of horror stories about the harassment endured by archaeologists: 'Our jeeps have been burned, obscene phone calls in the middle of the night, and a lot of vandalism. Archaeological sites in Israel have been destroyed, trashed, because of religious fanaticism. Statues have been tarred, mosaics tarred; sadly this is part and parcel of working in the field here in Israel.' When Dan asked who was responsible for this bullying and wanton destruction, Joe, although Jewish, did not blink. 'The Ultra-Orthodox. It's a combination of a little bit of theology and an awful lot of politics.' Ultra-Orthodox Jews take the view that any potential burial site is sacred and thus should not be disturbed for any reason, even, or especially, historical research.

On the question of layers of history, and respecting other religions' archaeology, Joe Zias was emphatic. 'There are a lot of accusations that we run through one level of civilization to get down to something else. Perhaps this was happening back in the 1950s or 1960s, but I've been working in this field since 1965 and this really hasn't been true. We treat with equal respect all cultures. Fifty years ago, a lot of archaeologists felt that their job was to prove or disprove the Bible, but that is the archaeology of the past. Today, our job is not to prove or disprove, but simply to show what was happening back in antiquity. Left- or right-wing, let the rabbis and the priests and the rest of them go and deal with it.' Strong words, but there is probably nowhere else in the world where layers of rock and stone can provoke such strong emotions. He went on, 'Someone once said of the American pilgrims, "These are people who love God with all their heart and hate their neighbour with all their soul." I think that's the story of much of the history of the Middle East.' It was a damning analysis, which felt uncomfortably accurate.

It was time to return to the West Bank, to the magical, holy town of Bethlehem – not so little any more, but still all too often the centre of the world's attentions. We wanted to see the Church of the Nativity, one of the earliest churches in the world and formerly a major centre of Christian pilgrimage. However, for 39 days in 2002 it had grabbed the world's attention for a very different reason. On 2 April a group of local Palestinians, including known militants, took refuge in the church from Israeli forces who were conducting raids throughout the West Bank. The IDF laid siege to the building, one of the most sacred in Christendom, while those on both sides attempted to negotiate a surrender. Claims and counterclaims flew back and forth, and international diplomacy was stretched to its limits in an attempt to find a solution. Finally, on 10 May, everyone came out, including 39 Palestinian militants. It was an ugly, tense incident, and to many observers the relative apathy of the Christian world seemed astonishing.

Bethlehem is only 8 kilometres from Jerusalem and their suburbs seem to reach into each other, separated only by an IDF checkpoint. Our timing was not good: the previous day, four Palestinians had been killed by the IDF, and emotions were running high. Whole rows of tourist shops, offering every variation of religious iconography, had been boarded up since the intifada of September 2000. Before that date, over 5000 tourists and pilgrims a day visited Bethlehem; now, barely a handful of intrepid souls braved the journey. Christianity is on the wane throughout Israel and the West Bank, and in Bethlehem the churches have taken to tolling their bells as a sign of mourning when a Christian girl marries a Muslim. In Jerusalem, the numbers of Christians have declined from about 29,000 under British rule in 1944, to 15,000 under Jordanian rule in 1966, to about 10,000 today under Israeli rule.

We turned into Manger Square which, despite its evocative name, was no more than a car park and meeting place. The Church of the Nativity looked more fortified than glorified, wearing the scars of its turbulent history. For centuries it had been one of the most fought-over holy places, seized and defended by a succession of armies including Muslim and Crusader forces. Today it is controlled jointly by three Christian denominations – the Armenians, the Roman Catholics and the Greek Orthodox – who sustain a fragile harmony through a complicated schedule of worship and presence, not unlike the system adopted in the Church of the Holy Sepulchre in Jerusalem.

As we approached the entrance we were struck by its proportions: the main door, known as the Door of Humility, had been deliberately lowered so that adults of average heights or above were forced to bow their heads, in an involuntary act of supplication, before entering. The door had been built in this way within the Crusaders' gothic door, itself lower than the original, reputedly to prevent visitors from riding their horses into the church. Having tied our steeds outside, what greeted us in the main body of the basilica was a breathtaking vision, one of the oldest working churches in the world, presently occupied by a couple of elderly women with brooms, and a handful of wandering monks; in essence we had the place to ourselves. Light poured in through the windows, its rays darting between the wonderful double rows of red limestone columns that define the nave. The Empress Helena conceived the original building, but much of what one sees today has survived from its enlargement in approximately AD 530 by the Emperor Justinian. In fact, given the way its space is organized, it is like walking into a Roman pagan temple. Over the centuries various monasteries and chapels have been added, including an Armenian convent, but the basic church is still simply a shrine over the grotto where the Virgin Mary is said to have given birth to Jesus. A local guide, Adel Thweib, showed us the wooden slats that, when lifted, reveal a section of the original mosaic floor from the fourth century, discovered in 1936 and humbling in its beauty. The walls still bear traces of the mosaics with which the Crusaders decorated the church, and at the tops of certain columns we could pick out ghostly, faded images of saints and kings. As with the Church of the Holy Sepulchre, the trinity of denominations that administer the Church of the Nativity cannot discuss any changes to the building's fabric without an unholy row; as a result much of the decoration is falling into disrepair, with rain reportedly seeping through the roof on wet days. Adel saw little future for the town as it stands now. 'Bethlehem is definitely destroyed. We have no business at all now, as tourists are too scared to come to a trouble area,' he concluded sadly.

Our fixer Ali took us to a school just below the church to introduce us to Father Ibrahim Faltas, who gained international prominence during the siege for his efforts, as one of those trapped inside the church, to help the injured and feed the hungry. A swarthy man in his late thirties with close-cropped black hair, wire-rimmed spectacles and a goatee beard, he took us back to the church to talk about his experiences the year before. We stood in the Crusader cloisters, where the impact marks from bullets at the time of the siege were in plain view. Father Ibrahim was at pains to relate the uneasy status quo that he and the other monks had tried to maintain. 'We tried to stop there being heavy clashes between the Palestinians and the Israelis, and we did our best to stop the Palestinians from opening fire from within the church. Conditions were very bad and, as priests, we had never envisaged that the church might be under siege for 39 days.'

Despite the enormous importance of the site, Father Ibrahim claimed to have been more concerned for the people hiding inside, and he had risked his own life by helping the wounded from the church and carrying out dead bodies. 'All of us could have been victims, but our presence there, our prayers and our thoughts, were aimed only at saving people, both Palestinian and Israeli.' There were casualties, even so, but Father Ibrahim was keen to see the episode in terms of mediation and survival. 'Seven people were killed inside the church and one at the door, and in addition 25 were injured, but all the 240 people who were inside could have been martyred. Yet thanks to God and to our steadfastness we were able to arrive at a peaceful solution.' And he saw the bigger picture as one of political, rather than religious, divide. 'The conflict we have here is not between Islam and Judaism, but between Israel and Palestine. We hope that the day will come in this Holy Land when people – the Palestinians and the Israelis – can live together in peace.'

Throughout our trip we were to hear individuals from all sides pay lip service to a peaceful future; but Father Ibrahim's idealism felt sincere, won as it was through hard experience. Inside the main body of the church he showed us where people had lived and slept during the siege, but within minutes of our entering a burly Greek Orthodox monk approached and swiftly terminated the interview, banishing Father Ibrahim from the building. As a Catholic, his presence was not welcome. Even this dignified, gentle man was prey to such pettiness.

A service was starting in the nineteenth-century Church of St Catherine that adjoined the main church, and we followed the procession of priests and nuns down into the Grotto of the Nativity, lit atmospherically by long, flickering tapers. The site of the birth itself is marked by a 14-pointed star on a marble slab, and the crowded sub-terranean space contains other small altars such as the Altar of the Adoration of the Magi and the one in the Chapel of the Manger. Simply to stand and observe rituals that have been repeated at this spot for centuries momentarily strips away the bickering and back-stabbing, and reveals something of the original spiritual quality of the church.

Before leaving the Church of the Nativity we climbed the bell tower and were rewarded with a superb view of this ancient town. Beyond it sat a Jewish settlement overlooking the scene, while in front of that we could just make out the controversial West Bank security fence and trench under construction. Three times the length and twice the height of the Berlin Wall, this 360-kilometre barrier is designed to encircle and divide the West Bank and will cut Bethlehem in half, separating it from Jerusalem. It seemed like an act of madness on the part of the Israelis, aimed at preventing the movement of Palestinians, protecting the settlements and grabbing as much as 10 per cent of the West Bank.

We were reluctant to leave, but had one more destination to visit in Bethlehem before we returned to Jerusalem. Rachel's Tomb has been situated inside the town for centuries – but not for much longer. On 11 September 2002 the Israeli security cabinet approved plans to annex the traditional burial site of the biblical matriarch, absorbing it into the city of Jerusalem. The site has long been associated with fertility and safe birth, and Jewish women enter through their own separate entrance in order to pray to be blessed in these ways; it was also sacred to Muslims because the cemetery of the Bedouin Ta'amre tribe is in its grounds. Between 1948 and 1967 the tomb was under the control of the Waqf and not open to Israelis, but since the Oslo Accords it has been in Israeli-controlled territory. We drove across town to its deserted, ghostly location. What was once a small, simple stone building has been, since 1997, a heavily fortified and defended position with watchtowers, barbed wire and mounted security cameras. We pulled up by the three main doors on the street, opposite a boarded-up row of shops, and approached nervously, trying not to glance up at the soldiers monitoring our every move. All three doors were locked. We waited, but nobody appeared. Someone was watching us, that was for sure, but their lack of communication was unnerving.

Directed via a series of back streets to the other side of the compound, we again approached under the watchful eye of armed guards. As with so many of these locations, obtaining permission to visit had been a lengthy process; yet the latest advice we had had from the IDF was just to knock on the door and ask. It was amazing how one of the most organized and resourceful states in the world so often operated in this arbitrary fashion. Not expecting much, Dan knocked on a huge metal door and announced our presence. A disembodied voice enquired whether we were BBC News. Dan explained that we were making an arts documentary on the cultural heritage of Israel, and after a few seconds of fumbling the door was opened by two fresh-faced, embarrassed-looking IDF soldiers. One of them, Eitan Ben David, seemed delighted to show us around on what we guessed was a very boring afternoon for them. At the end of a long corridor we entered the vaulted section of the seventeenth-century Ottoman building, restored in 1860 by Sir Moses Montefiore to mark the site. The tomb itself was a little disappointing: when Dan lifted its white covering all we could see was the whitewashed stone underneath. Eitan was almost apologetic about the heightened security at the site and interrupted himself to ask a question: 'How did you get here?' When we told him, his disquieting reply was 'But you usually need a bulletproof bus'.

It was hard to know what to make of Eitan. Charming and open to the point of naïvety, some of the things he said came out with a casual brutality: 'Even here, you have kids who from the age of one or two already know how to use a Kalashnikov, and they know they want to be suicide bombers. I don't want to generalize but there is so much rage and hatred. I can't expect them to love the Israelis but ...' He seemed genuinely frustrated, but then went on. 'I have friends in the army, and in the last three years they've stopped about 300 suicide bombers who have wanted to go to Jerusalem and blow up mothers and children.' He abhorred physical destruction in the course of an operation, but said there had to be exceptions: 'Sometimes the army will ruin homes, but I know that the Israeli army really tries not to target worshipping areas, and we really try to just fight those people who are creating terror, and leave the other ones alone.'

As his accent revealed, Eitan was an immigrant from New Jersey. 'This is my country – we've been waiting to come back here for 2000 years.' He had given up his studies and left his parents in America, though he had many cousins in Israel. While he had grown up in a very religious community, he expressed an interest in Middle East studies and regretted that there was so little contact with Palestinians due to fear. Yet in the next breath he recited a Zionist mantra: 'How I look at it, there are 23 Arab countries in the world and there is one Jewish country. Who else has been willing to give up half their country, their capital city and their Temple Mount? All we get is this rage of Palestinian terrorism. I don't want to kick them out, but if you're going to create terrorism, then you have no right to be here.' We wished him well, this likeable young man in a difficult position. Yet as we drove away from Bethlehem we could only feel pessimistic about the future when religious sites, Christian, Jewish or Muslim, resembled fortresses, and people either could not get to them, or, as we had heard, had to travel there in bulletproof buses.

While major Christian sites such as the Church of the Holy Sepulchre and the Church of the Nativity were situated in the towns, there was also evidence of an abundance of Christian life in the Judean desert between Bethlehem and the Dead Sea. From about the fifth century, believers from regions such as Turkey and Armenia had come to the desert to live a harsh and unforgiving life in the caves that litter the hills. Thousands of monks had lived in this way, yet their scholarship was astonishingly progressive. In time they built a network of monasteries across the unforgiving landscape, a few of which survive today. Though it meant further checkpoints, we wanted to see some of these last outposts of Christianity in the desert where Jesus wandered for 40 days and nights, tempted by the devil. And in William Dalrymple's book *From the Holy Mountain* we had read of the Mar Saba monastery, high above the Kidron Valley.

As we wove our way along the narrow Palestinian roads the desert was touched with a smattering of green, soon to be burnt off as the summer sun became more intense. We had stopped to brew coffee when one of our drivers heard a radio report that the Iraqis had used chemical weapons against the US forces. It was unconfirmed, and subsequently proved to be false, but in the quiet expanse of the Judean desert it felt even more sinister and unsettling. A series of hairpins descended to the back of the monastery. A brilliant blue, sunken door was the only access, so we pulled the rope that clanged the bell. Eventually, the door swung open and a young Greek Orthodox monk with a black beard welcomed us, but said we should return in two hours as the monks were at prayer; it was Lent and so in addition to fasting, most of their day was spent in prayer or contemplation.

We clambered over the rocks to view the Kidron valley, through which the monks believed a river of blood would flow on Judgement Day and the legions of the damned would troop with the Pope at their head. The landscape was certainly dramatic enough, though all we could see in the water was sewage from Jerusalem. On the opposite side we could make out dozens of small caves which had been monks' cells over 1500 years before. We returned to the monastery at 2 p.m. but certain conditions were placed on our admittance: due to a ban on women, Heidi would not be allowed in, and we could not take cameras as the monks had had a 'bad experience' with a film crew.

St Saba, the founder of the monastery, came from Cappadocia in central Turkey accompanied by 70 hermits, with whom he established the first church here in AD 482. The fraternity grew, and Mar Saba soon administered another half-dozen monasteries around the valley. The community suffered repeated attacks and persecution: in 614 the first Sabbaite holy martyrs were created when the invading Persians slew 44 fathers. But Mar Saba always recovered to re-establish itself as a centre for study and contemplation. Today, its 110 cells are home to 15 or so monks – they were reluctant to confirm the exact number – and the community clings to existence as the monastery itself clings to the side of the ravine. Father Rafael, a reserved but quietly warm man, showed us round.

In the impressive church is a shrine containing what is claimed to be the uncorrupted body of St Saba, dressed in elaborate burial robes and a dark hat. He did not look completely uncorrupted, it had to be said, but Father Rafael admitted there had been a fire, which accounted for his slightly charred look. The walls of the church are adorned with icons, most notably a depiction of Judgement Day. On the river side of the monastery a large modern terrace gives splendid views of the whole valley; it was not difficult to imagine spending one's life gazing at such natural beauty. Back in the monastery complex, Father Rafael led us into the rock-hewn Chapel of Saint Nicholas with its whitewashed walls, in which, displayed in glass cases, were the skulls of the monks slain in the Persian invasion almost 1400 years ago. We could make out cracks in some of the craniums, visible evidence of the attackers' brutality and a reminder of mortality. Before we left, Father Rafael showed us a grate in the yard floor where they buried their dead, who through the miraculous powers of St Saba did not suffer rigor mortis and did not smell when decomposing.

On that edifying note, he took us into a building and offered us impeccable Greek coffee and gelatinous Greek Delight. Here Dan tried with great delicacy to persuade him to let us film inside the monastery, but Father Rafael was not a man for turning. He told us that the monks felt safe there, whatever was happening in the world outside. It was frustrating, but we had at least been afforded a glimpse of what was perhaps a vanishing world. Mar Saba had survived countless assaults and tragedies. We could only hope that its indomitable spirit would survive the pitfalls of the future, and not just fade away unremarked.

We remained eager to hear other accounts of monastic life. Keeping to Palestinian roads, we made our way to St George's monastery, or Mar Jiryis, in the Wadi Qelt valley near Jericho. Just before its arched gateway the road was barred with concrete blocks. On the other side of the blocks, in contrast to the potholed dirt-track that led down to Jericho, was newly laid gleaming tarmac – an Israeli road that led eventually to Jerusalem. The disparity was painful. We continued on foot until we came to a viewing point opposite the monastery, which clung spectacularly to the cliffface, its turquoise-domed roofs a splash of brilliant colour in the rock. It was founded in the late fifth century by St George of Koziba on the site of an earlier oratory, and as at Mar Saba its monks were put to the sword by the invading Persians; though the Crusaders revived it for a while in the Middle Ages, it lay in ruins for many centuries before being restored at the end of the nineteenth century to it present magnificent state

As we gazed at the timeless images of men on donkeys traversing the narrow ravine paths, we saw, worryingly, that our vehicle had been surrounded by a group of about 20 men. Our Palestinian fixer came and told us that they were a mixture of IDF soldiers and Jewish settlers, and that they had told our driver to leave. We made our way down to the scene, where an IDF officer, tall and humourless, informed us that we could stay but our Palestinian driver had to leave. As he well knew, that meant we too had to go. Dan defused the tension somewhat by explaining that we were making an arts film, but, although the soldiers were not unfriendly, the settlers, who wielded the largest firearms, remained silently glaring at us. What was going on? A bulldozer was positioned by the blocks, and started to shift them to clear the road. Our driver was apparently told that if he did not move our van it would be tipped into the valley. We had little choice but to leave. It was an odd moment. Had we by coincidence arrived at the same time as the IDF unit, or had they reacted to our presence? Why were they shifting the blocks? The only explanation we could think of was that they were moving them further down the Palestinian road to enable the settlers to claim more land. This was how it appeared to work in this country – possession was at the very least nine-tenths of the law, whether in an ancient church or a remote valley. It felt primitive and tribal. But it was crudely effective.

There was one last monastery to see in this region, and its location could hardly be more evocative. High above the sunken town of Jericho, perched on a mountain known as Jabal Quruntul or Mountain of the Forty, is the Monastery of the Temptation. A Greek Orthodox outpost, the building dates from 1895, replacing a twelfth-century Crusader church; both were constructed around the cave identified by the enterprising Empress Helena in the fourth century as the place where Jesus sat when he was tempted by the devil. The 30 to 40 caves on the eastern slopes of the mountain had been inhabited by monks and hermits since the early days of Christianity. The site, which has magnificent views over Jericho and the Jordan valley beyond, was certainly an enticing one.

We had been warned that only one monk lived there now and that he preferred us not to film. As we arrived a throng of chattering Palestinian schoolchildren were about to enter the monastery, so we decided to leave the solitary monk to his charges. Instead, we descended into Jericho, one of the oldest continuously inhabited cities in the world, and certainly the lowest, set 250 metres below sea level. This situation, combined with numerous springs, makes Jericho the bread basket of the West Bank, though in summer temperatures can reach in excess of 55°C. Famed in the Bible as the first city captured from the Canaanites by Joshua and subsequently destroyed by dint of trumpet-blowing and yelling, it was to be destroyed and rebuilt several times despite Joshua's warning: 'Cursed be the man before the Lord, that riseth up and buildeth this city Jericho.' The site was first settled by nomads as early as 8000 BC – there is evidence for a walled Neolithic settlement from that time – and ancient Jericho, known today as Tel al-Sultan, was prospering by about 3000 BC before the arrival of Joshua and the Israelites. The city was later to have a string of illustrious rulers, including Alexander the Great, Mark Antony (who gave it to Cleopatra) and Herod, who rebuilt it to his own design. It was during the Byzantine era that the city was moved from Tel al-Sultan to its present location, and it continued to flourish under the Ummayads in the eighth and ninth centuries and the Crusaders in the Middle Ages. After World War I, during the British Mandate over Palestine, Jericho flourished as a fruit-producing region before being flooded with Arab refugees after the creation of the state of Israel in 1948. In modern times Jericho was the first West Bank city handed over to the the Palestinian National Authority (PNA), in May 1994 as a result of the Oslo Accords. Today the City of Peace, as it is known, is a likeable, relaxed town, though sadly – and disastrously for its tourism infrastructure – little visited.

As we approached Jericho, flanked by cropfields, a notable White Elephant reared up on our right. The large, lavish Oasis Casino, the PNA's most lucrative business venture, was controversially opened in the late 1990s to attract wealthy Jewish patrons, in a bid to revitalize a city that had always experienced less trouble than elsewhere in the West Bank. However, following the September 2000 intifada and rioting, the gamblers thought the stakes too high and stopped coming. After the casino was closed down Israeli tanks fired rockets at it, and its walls are now riddled with shell- and bullet-holes. As a symbol of lost hope it could hardly be more striking.

In Jericho itself, there were few signs of visitors. We popped into the tourism office, just one or two bare rooms with a handful of friendly, helpful, slightly desperate staff who directed us to the remains of ancient Jericho, a couple of kilometres away. In a car park built for several thousand cars we left our solitary vehicle and headed for the gates. The guard looked up, surprised to see us. A few years ago, a state-of-the-art cable-car system had opened to transport visitors to the Monastery of the Temptation. As its steel cables glistened in the sun the guard showed us the cherry-red cars in their little port. He would turn the power on if we wanted, he said, but they kept it off as a rule these days. Two huge restaurants were impeccably laid for dinner, and a gift shop was piled high with Palestinian hand-painted pottery. Jericho's time for visitors will surely come again, and it will be ready.

The Tel al-Sultan archaeological park illustrates, perhaps better than anywhere else in Israel and the Occupied Territories, the layering of civilizations that characterizes the region's rich and difficult history. It was extensively excavated from 1952 by Dame Kathleen Kenyon, who in the course of her work found evidence of a remarkable 23 cities. As we looked down into the excavation pit, we could scarcely imagine how so many millennia of existence and achievement could be compacted into this very man-made hill, itself a tangible reminder of the human race's earliest attempts to abandon its nomadic lifestyle and fortify a permanent presence. We clambered down the dusty slopes into the ravine, now returning to nature after the archaeologists' endeavours. Rising from the pit was a Neolithic tower with what has been described as the earliest staircase in the world, its 22 steps still solid and imposing. A Bedouin shepherd had allowed his sheep to graze amongst the ruins – much to the chagrin of the site guide, who tried to chase them off. The shepherd angrily retorted that this was his land as a Palestinian, and he could graze his sheep where he liked. This minor exchange perfectly encapsulated the fundamental questions of occupation and possession that remain today as topical as ever.

Our final destination in Jericho was an ancient synagogue a little way out of town. We drove through fields of orange, lemon and papaya trees to reach a low modern structure, in the basement of which we found what we had come to see. Rediscovered in 1936, all that remained of the venerable synagogue, dating from the late sixth century AD – the late Roman–Byzantine period just before the arrival of Islam – was its superb mosaic floor. When sprinkled with water its rich colours and geometric designs were revealed to be immaculately preserved. Its most distinguishing feature lies at its centre: a brilliant round tableau containing the traditional Jewish motifs of a candelabrum, a palm leaf and a trumpet, with emblazoned beneath them in Hebrew, the words 'Shalom Al Yisrael' – 'Peace Upon Israel'. Despite its seemingly harmless beauty, the site was attacked and vandalized by local Palestinians in October 2000, when they broke into the *yeshiva*, the rabbinical school, above the mosaic, destroyed prayer books and furniture, and burnt much of the second floor (in response, the IDF reportedly fired eight missiles at a Palestinian police-training centre). Luckily the mosaic itself remained undamaged, but the PNA, who control the site, were deeply ashamed; they rebuilt the main structure and posted guards, who now lolled outside on the porch. It will be a long time before this is a synagogue again. Once more the enmeshed histories of this land, and their vulnerability to spiteful destruction, had been laid bare. The grim irony with which the mosaic's message is read at present might one day fade into history itself.

In need of a change of scene we headed north, to the region known as the Golan Heights. Bordering Syria, Lebanon and Jordan, this finger of land at the top of the country is of immense strategic value. Israel captured the area during the Six-Day War and formally annexed it in 1981. Nowhere in Israel has been fought over as much as this region – in the past it stood at a great trading crossroads of the ancient world, with goods coming from India and China to the east, from Constantinople to the north and from Egypt to the south. Today, while the Syrians still covet the territory, it remains stable, though pockmarked by minefields, areas of no-man's-land, demilitarized zones and general military debris. And nowhere has been dug quite so much by archaeologists in order to prove its 'Jewishness'; finds include the early Talmudic synagogue at Qazrin and the ancient stronghold from the First Jewish Revolt of AD 66 at Gamla. At the city of Kaztrin, archaeologists have restored an ancient synagogue and, in doing so, removed a later Mamluk mosque. Archaeology can be a destructive art, and he who holds the trowel wields the power.

We drove alongside the Sea of Galilee, with its line of cafeterias serving fried St Peter's fish, a species of tilapia unique to its waters. The further we travelled up-country, the greener the landscape became, like rural Wales or Scotland. The arid lands of the south, on the edge of the Negev desert, were long forgotten despite being only a few hours' drive away. At Mount Hermon, on the border with Lebanon, there is skiing in winter and we stayed the night at a ski lodge, in replica Swiss chalets that could hardly be more different from either West Bank accommodation or the American Colony Hotel. The next morning we got up early to catch the dawn over what is perhaps the region's most spectacular site – Castle Nimrod rose on a rocky outcrop like a fairytale vision with mists chasing around its foundations. Although it takes its name from the biblical hunter who, according to legend, built it, the castle owes its construction more to the Arabs and Crusaders. Abandoned in the sixteenth century, in the twentieth it was used by the Syrians as an observation post and mortar position in the Six-Day War. What remains is a series of towers and the outer wall, looking out over the lush landscape – calm on the day we visited, until a volley of gunshots echoed over the plains. Even in this apparent idyll, menace still lurked. Driving on, we quickly found ourselves surrounded by cordoned-off minefields with yellow signs warning us they had yet to be cleared – a sinister reminder of the area's violent recent past. When we came to a ridge with extensive views we discovered networked trenches and shelters left intact after the war, with several abandoned tanks overlooking the scene. This martial theme park was a show of strength, a display of how the peace had been won – and a reminder of how easily these killing fields could become so again. Castle Nimrod could once more be called out of retirement. But now it was time to move on to a place where the conflict was still all too real.

Nowhere in the West Bank has such a reputation for militancy and trouble as the ancient town of Nablus. Formerly known as Shechem, a name by which some Israelis still refer to it, Nablus is also the West Bank's largest town. The region's secret treasure when it was settled in AD 72 as the Roman colony of Flavia Neapolis, there had already been a settlement there for thousands of years. In order to reach Nablus we needed another fixer. Ruthy, as an Israeli, was not available, and Ali could not travel between Bethlehem and Nablus due to IDF restrictions on Palestinians moving around the West Bank. Our new contact was Sawsan, a likeable young woman who worked for a Palestinian television production company based in Ramallah. We met Sawsan and her driver at the sprawling, desolate Kalandia checkpoint on a wet and stormy day and headed off towards Nablus, 63 kilometres north of Jerusalem. Of all our destinations in the Holy Land, none looked as devastated as this town. While Hebron was kept in a curfew vice, life abounded in Nablus – but the evidence of damage by Israeli military incursions was everywhere. Most of the kerbs had been flattened by tank tracks, and the roads themselves were very often barely negotiable. Through the driving rain we saw abandoned homes, pile upon pile of rubble, and people who stared blankly at us.

In April 2002 the IDF mounted Operation Defensive Shield – a series of incursions into a number of West Bank towns. Tanks and armoured bulldozers swept into Nablus, and the resultant damage was the most severe the residents had seen for a long time. An estimate by Koichiro Matsuura, Director-General of UNESCO, put its cost at approximately $114 million. According to the Nablus Municipality, more than 70 people were killed, with hundreds injured; vital services such as electricity, water supplies and sewerage were badly affected; schools were damaged; and the Old City, which contained examples of Roman, Byzantine, Crusader, Islamic and Ottoman architecture, was hit by rockets, shelled by tanks and bombed by F16 war jets. Great swathes of ancient Nablus had been flattened by a major earthquake in 1927, making the further loss of historically significant buildings even more acute.

Naseer Arafat, a tall, dignified architect and planner with a passion for his home town, was to show us round. Having studied in the UK, he spoke impeccable English. The first place to which he took us was the 800-year-old al-Khadrah mosque, built originally as a Crusader church on a hill above the Old City. There was little visible damage, but Naseer told us that major repairs had been carried out so that the mosque could keep functioning. Before prayers started we spoke with the forthright local imam, Maher Kharraz, about what had occurred. 'The Israeli army attacked the mosque using bulldozers, and demolished part of it,' he told us. 'This process of destruction went on for one and a half hours, destroying both this old part of the mosque and the new extension. There were no terrorists or weapons here, and we do not know what the nature could be of the crime which justified this attack.' He was unequivocal in his interpretation of the operation: 'It was an attack against Islamic culture and history. The doors of the mosque are open 24 hours a day.' He paused solemnly. 'They could have simply entered through the door.' As he told it, it was a terrible tale of unnecessary damage sustained by a mosque that had served the town for centuries. And, if true, it represented a worrying change of focus by the Israeli army, who, as the young soldier at Rachel's Tomb had been at pains to explain, generally regarded religious sites as off-limits; now, we were being told that three other mosques had also suffered structural damage during the incursion. As we left I noticed a poster on the wall and asked Naseer what it said. He told me that there was to be a Hamas demonstration in the town square that lunch time against the war in Iraq. The bad weather would probably put many people off, but it was still somewhere to avoid.

We made our way down to the souk in the heart of the Old City, its narrow maze of streets hard for soldiers to penetrate. The rain was now turning to snow and so, passing the usual fabulous array of fresh produce that characterized Israel and the Occupied Territories, we took refuge in a whitewashed coffee shop where some ten elderly men in their keffiyehs were talking. They welcomed us in and, through Naseer, Dan asked them about the incursion. 'They attacked my house a number of times and smashed everything up,' said one. Another chipped in: 'There were dead bodies lying in the street outside my house. They destroyed our houses for the sheer fun of it – there were no fighters inside the houses. I used to work as a taxi driver on the road from Nablus to Tulkarm,' he went on. 'I have been sitting here for the last two years smoking. How am I supposed to earn a living?' The men were becoming animated and needed little encouragement to express their anger. 'How can I be expected to forget that they destroyed the house in which my ancestors had lived for hundreds of years?' another shouted. 'Very young men, like flowers, were killed and left in the street.' One of the earlier speakers returned to the debate: 'I want peace, but you have to give me back my house.' He gestured towards Dan. 'How would he feel if I took his house in London and kicked him out – would he be my friend if I did that to him?' The rhetoric was very powerful and, like all good rhetoric, hard to refute.

Outside once more, every shop's canopy distributed water on to our heads, while impromptu streams chased down the cobbled streets whose walls were plastered with posters of 'martyrs' – those killed by the IDF. A few shops were still trading – we passed a butcher who berated us for not being in Iraq to 'photograph the US and UK killing the people. Do you understand?' We certainly did. In the heart of the casbah Naseer pointed out the site of two soap factories, the Can'an and the al-Nabulsi, dating from the sixteenth or seventeenth centuries, which had been destroyed, he said, during the April 2002 incursion. For centuries Nablus had been famous for its soap, made from the superb local olive oil. Known in Nablus as Ground Zero, the site had been roughly levelled, and battered cars were parked or dumped among the piles of debris. It was a huge space, and around its edges we saw how the factories had literally been ripped out, gutted from the city, leaving the vaults of the surrounding buildings open to the air. It was truly shocking that, if the details we were being given were correct, helicopter gunships had destroyed these historic buildings, as well as seven equally old Ottoman houses nearby. Down a muddy slope from the site of the soap factories was another gaping hole, the site of Alwakala al-Gharbyyah, a caravanserai or merchants' meeting hall, dating from the Ottoman period. It, too, had been reduced to rubble. It was hard to imagine why such devastation had been perceived as necessary, even in the search for terrorists. Could it indeed be a conscious attempt to destroy history? Our spirits as dampened as our clothes, we retreated to a café.

Over tea and sticky baklava and *kunafeh*, a local delicacy, Dan asked Naseer what he knew personally about the incursion. Naseer chose to put it in a historical context. 'April 2002 was one of the many catastrophes this city has suffered from. In the great earthquake of 1927, about 50 houses were demolished. In April 2002 over 60 houses suffered the same fate, and more than 250 were damaged.' He described helicopter gunships attacking the town, tanks firing on the Old City from the surrounding hillsides, and soldiers using explosives to blast holes in the walls of houses so that they could make their way across town by passing through people's homes rather than using the dangerous narrow streets. The inhabitants had been left with huge holes in their properties, requiring much money and work to repair. When Dan asked Naseer why he thought this had happened, his anger was palpable. 'This question should be directed to the Israelis. Why did they attack the Old City? Why is the Palestinian cultural history attacked and targeted? I cannot find any justification for what happened.' But he believed that the Israelis had inadvertently achieved the opposite effect to that intended: 'It has opened the people's eyes to the cultural wealth they have here in the Old City.'

At that moment, the café owner brought out a poster bearing photographs or identities of all the people believed to have died as a result of the incursion. It turned out that eight members of his own family had been killed when their house was flattened. He had only been able to discover their fate when the curfew was lifted a week later, and their bodies were uncovered in the rubble. Before we left Nablus, Naseer took us to the site of the house in question, which dated from the sixteenth century. The man's grandparents had survived by hiding in a basement room, but the eight other family members had, allegedly, been crushed against the front door. It was an unimaginable scene, and an appallingly bleak conclusion to our trip to Nablus.

We were to return, though, another day. This time things were even more tense as a result of the continuing Coalition attacks on Iraq, and we felt very unwelcome. As we filmed in the main market square we were constantly questioned. Where had we come from? Why were we there? And, inevitably, why we were not in Iraq? At one point an American media crew drove past in an armoured car, and we wondered if we were underestimating the situation. People were angry and wanted to articulate their feelings, but at no stage did it feel personal or actively dangerous. Surely it was more conspicuous, and divisive, to trundle around town behind bulletproof glass?

As we walked through the Old City near its impressive al-Kabir mosque, built on the foundations of a Crusader church, and stepped carefully round the wooden carts of fresh garlic and spring vegetables outside shops with Iraqi flags fluttering overhead, by chance we spotted a breathtaking Crusader arch down a side alley. It typified the excitement of a town with such a rich history – one could just happen upon such hidden treasures absorbed into its very framework. While we were examining the arch's bold geometric patterns, a man asked if we wanted to look at his house nearby. Heidi, with her instinctive nose for a story, agreed, and he led us through the arch to a staircase that ascended to his house. It was over 350 years old, and Bashar Temimi said that his family had always owned and lived in the property. Off the main living room he showed us a room with shrapnel and bullet damage in its walls – sustained, said Bashar, during the April 2002 incursion. His family had been forced to leave for seven or eight days while the IDF occupied the casbah, and soldiers had been in his house causing considerable damage. When he took us down a level and outside, we realized the scale of the property. His family's house stood on top of the broken vaults of an old *hamam*, or Turkish bath, which had been partially destroyed during the great 1927 earthquake but had also suffered damage during the incursion. Bashar pointed to a house under construction 50 metres down the street which he said was replacing an Ottoman property destroyed by a bomb, the shrapnel from which had struck and damaged his own house. Bashar felt very strongly about the remains: 'Sometimes I feel that they talk to me, like a person,' he confided, adding that, though human beings were at the top of the pile, stones and places were essential to our place in the scheme of things, and that when they were destroyed memories too were lost, and these were the essence of mankind.

We went with Bashar down a narrow set of worn steps into the rooms below, passed outside the rooms into an alley, then re-entered the building in another part and found an amazing sight. There, in several vast chambers of the *hamam*, was another of Nablus's famous industries in full flow. Half a dozen men were hard at work rolling out sweets and, while the bath chambers were clearly discernible, instead of steam they were thick with a delicious sweet fug. This part of the building, too, had suffered during the incursion, though it had been patched up. Bashar, despite his faltering English, was eloquent in his analysis of what had happened. He believed that the IDF 'want to destroy our past, our memory, our roots, to cut us from the past'. His home spoke to him of preceding generations of family, and of the old city of Nablus, but he saw the IDF as trying to cut him and his people off from the area. 'In Nablus, thousands of years have been destroyed in a minute.' It was a depressing thought to take away with us.

On the edge of town we visited a place that spoke of the rage bubbling in Nablus, and of the shocking sacrifice of a sacred site to sectarian hatred. Joseph's Tomb, at the end of a bone-crunchingly ripped-up road, marks the traditional resting place of the patriarch, as detailed in the Book of Joshua, though some Muslims believe him to be buried in the Tomb of the Patriarchs. Whatever the truth, the site is recognized as a Jewish shrine and claimed by Ultra-Orthodox Jews as theirs in perpetuity due to having been bought by Joseph's father, Jacob – this despite the fact that it lies in Nablus, and that certain Palestinian archaeologists believe the site to be instead the burial place of a Muslim sheikh, Youssef Dawiqat, two centuries ago, and, even earlier, a Samaritan holy place. Before 2000, the tomb was housed in what the *Rough Guide to Israel and the Palestinian Territories* called a 'small, white-domed and entirely unspectacular building'. That certainly changed after October 2000, and then again in February 2003. When we drew up, scattering a gang of local schoolchildren – one studious-looking boy of about 11 approached and gravely announced 'My name is Omar. I have guns' – it was a bleak sight. Its most eye-catching features were the huge hole in its domed roof and the general disrepair of the exterior. As we got closer, our every movement scrutinized by local 'police', we saw that all the windows of the original building, and of newer outbuildings flanking it, had been smashed, the walls graffiti-ed with anti-Semitic scrawl, the ground strewn with rubbish and the complex's railings and doors thrown into the entrance area. As Dan picked his way down the steps, a huge rat scuttled away from the rotting debris. Daubed with spray-paint inside and out were Stars of David – whether done in derision or resistance was not clear. Inside, the dereliction and damage were even worse. The whole tomb chamber had been vandalized, the vault of the tomb broken up, and the walls bore the evidence of fire. Only the jagged light entering from the hole in the dome lifted the gloom that enveloped this unholy mess.

The story behind the chaos was unedifying. The tomb had become a focal point for local anger against the Israeli authorities, and attacks on it by local Palestinians had occurred sporadically for years before. Then, on 7 October 2000, a few days after the intifada started, the tomb and its IDF guards came under attack from a group of Palestinians. The soldiers agreed to pull out after the PNA promised to protect the site, but within hours the building housing the tomb had been attacked with pickaxes and iron bars, and Jewish prayer books were burned. The PNA quickly moved to restore the site, but in late February 2003, only weeks before we arrived, it was vandalized again: the large stone marking the grave was broken up. The mayor of Nablus was keen to restore it as a Muslim shrine, while the IDF hoped that a way might be found to allow Jews to return to worship there. As we left the town, avoiding the burning tyres in the road, our van stoned half-heartedly by local youths, it felt as though there was nothing that could reconcile these proud, ancient peoples.

Frustrated in our attempts to elicit comment from the IDF on the subject of the devastation in Nablus, we turned to Martin Weyl. This former director of the Israel Museum had written scathingly to *The Art Newspaper*, which had reported the damage in Nablus, refuting charges that the IDF had deliberately targeted Palestinian cultural heritage and speaking of 'non-existent damage' and 'misinformation' fed by the 'strong anti-Israel bias in the UN's various agencies which are largely controlled by a pro-Arab lobby'. We met Weyl, a neat, courteous man, at his modern apartment in West Jerusalem. He now admitted that some damage had occurred to historic buildings in Nablus, but 'not purposely, only in the heat of the moment because of the problems in there, and one has to be very sorry about it. But it's definitely the kind of damage that can be restored.' Dan asked him if he had been to Nablus to see it for himself. 'I haven't seen the damage,' Weyl replied, 'but I have received extensive documentation and photographs. It's a pity, but it's the price of war.' It amazed us that he had been willing to go into print with such vehemence based only on third-party accounts. And he rejected any suggestion that the destruction might have been a conscious IDF policy. 'I really think that is overstated. In Nablus, there were armed forces that fortified themselves in buildings of cultural value. Nablus is a nest of resistance, and so there were military not cultural considerations.' The Palestinians, on the other hand, were not so discriminating, according to Weyl: 'I can't really say this is reciprocal, and it's mainly the result of a difference between Western values and Islamic values, where cultural values are less pronounced.' Returning to the specific case of Nablus, Dan asked him what his response was to the UNESCO report criticizing the damage done to the Old City during the incursion. Astonishingly, Weyl proceeded to lambast UNESCO and its report on the basis that its officials had not been to Nablus to verify their facts. This seemed rather rich, as well as being untrue. In a subsequent telephone conversation Costanza Farina, head of the UNESCO office in Ramallah, confirmed that she herself had visited Nablus only days after the incursion. It was hard to know what to say to this urbane yet strident man, unshakeable in his belief in the integrity and honour of the IDF. Before we left, he expressed his pessimism with these bleak words: 'This conflict between the Western world and the Islamic world is going to grow bigger and bigger, with many human lives sacrificed, as well as cultural sites. Without any doubt.'

After that grim assessment there was only one place to conclude our trip. That Armageddon is a place comes as a surprise to many people, but its past is soaked in the blood and sweat of battle. These were the killing fields of the ancient world and, according to the Book of Revelation, they will be so again in the last great battle that will bring this world to an end. This is something people have feared for thousands of years, as the darkly prophetic verses of the Bible spell out: 'And he gathered them together into a place called in the Hebrew tongue Armageddon. And the seventh angel poured out his vial into the air; and there came a great voice out of the temple of heaven, from the throne, saying, It is done' (Revelation 16:16–17). Route 66, the road to Armageddon, is in fact a pleasant, undemanding straight one through pretty, rolling countryside. Megiddo, as Armageddon is now called, has witnessed many explosions of violence over the centuries due to its position on the strategic trade route from Egypt to Mesopotamia. In more recent times, the British fought the Turks there in World War I, and Jewish and Arab forces clashed in the 1948 war. Today the site is a huge archaeological park, with remains of palaces, a temple mound and an ingenious ninth-century BC water system. In the fading ochre light its appearance, fringed by palm trees, was more idyllic than apocalyptic as we wandered about its former streets, the sound of battle now long forgotten.

The war in Iraq was still being waged, and the Coalition forces were marching on Baghdad. Our worst personal fears had not been realized – no Scud missiles had been fired at Israel and there had not been any major incidents, or at least no more than there ever were in this troubled land. Yet the conflict was fanning flames that needed no encouragement, and at times the mood had been ugly in towns in the West Bank; the gap between the West and the Middle East, Jew and Arab, Christian and Arab, showed no sign of halting its slow, remorseless widening. The world's attention had been momentarily distracted from Israel but it would certainly return, bringing with it different perspectives and harsher scrutiny. Most people we spoke to on our trip felt that these were ominous, disturbing times, as though this latest military action carried with it a higher price than we yet knew. Izzat, our Israeli Bedouin driver, recalled that when we had been south of Jerusalem earlier in the week to see the dawn rise over the Dead Sea, we had seen Jupiter shining brightly in the sky. It reminded him of what his mother had once told him: that, according to Bedouin superstition, if you wake up and see this star something terrible will happen, as when the Yom Kippur War followed a sighting in 1973. Izzat himself had a sense of foreboding: 'This is going to be a crossroads, here in the Middle East, but also across the world. If you look back at what has happened over the last two years, we've had the Twin Towers, then Afghanistan, and now Iraq, even the SARS epidemic in Hong Kong. All the signs are not good, and I have a bad feeling about everything. It could well be apocalyptic.'

Our journey through Israel had revealed to us many things about human nature and its deadly ingenuity at carving divisions between sibling faiths. We had witnessed first-hand the rival claims to the Church of the Holy Sepulchre in Jerusalem, nearly prompting a diplomatic incident. We had not been permitted to enter the Temple Mount, but had seen the frenzy of possession that a lump of rock could generate in Jew and Muslim alike, and the peril in which sacred buildings could be put by fanaticism and hatred. In Hebron, one of the world's holiest buildings had been drained of much of its spirituality by politics and violence, and Rachel's Tomb was a depressing glimpse of a future with contested places of worship, fortified and mostly empty. And then there was Nablus. In the London *Evening Standard* on 15 April 2002, very soon after Operation Defensive Shield, the columnist A.N. Wilson had compared the destruction in Nablus to the destruction by the Taliban of the Buddhas at Bamiyan. Whether the IDF deliberately aimed to destroy Palestinian cultural heritage is contentious, but that had certainly been one of the effects. As with the Taliban's actions in Afghanistan, and the threatened archaeological sites in Iraq, the potential for the erasing of history remained high, and a people without a history, without roots, are a people not only without a past but also without a future. It would be wholly wrong to compare the IDF to any such evil, but when we finally got a response from them to our questions about what had happened in Nablus in April 2002 it took the form of an official fax, which denied knowledge of the events and damage we described. The statement, received on 3 April 2003, is reproduced here in full.

> The IDF makes every effort to safeguard public property, especially sites of historic or archaeological significance.
>
> Holy sites have a special status and it is general IDF policy not to return fire even if Palestinians fire on our forces from a holy place.
>
> Unfortunately, we were unable to verify claims as to damage sustained to the historic sites you mentioned or that such damage was caused by the IDF, due to the length of the time that elapsed since the incident.
>
> During Operation Defensive Shield, which followed the Passover eve terror attack in which 29 Israelis were killed, the IDF was forced to enter Nablus in an effort to arrest terrorists and disable terrorist infrastructure.
>
> We reiterate our commitment to respect holy places – even when terrorist [sic] use such places to launch attacks on us – and to safeguard historic and other public sites. Unfortunately Israel has been forced by the terrorists to pursue the war on terror in an urban environment, and in a built up area like Nalbus [sic], which the terrorist [sic] use as a base to preparing and launching attacks.

It was hard not to see such a denial as an attempt to brush off the episode, given that sites of historic significance were described in the statement as 'terrorist infrastructure', and a year was all it had taken for the IDF to erase the incident from their records and memories. The people of Nablus, whose homes were wrecked, whose heritage was bulldozed, are unlikely to forget so quickly.

There are already plenty of well-researched analyses of the politics of this region, and of the violence that has blighted its history, ancient and modern. Our remit was never to examine all the issues at stake, or to equate, for example, a suicide bomber with an army incursion; our narrow focus was the Israeli and Palestinian cultural heritage, and historic sites that are brought into the firing line or appropriated for violent ends. The progress of the much-vaunted roadmap for peace in Israel and the Occupied Territories, politically driven by the United States, may yet produce a solution, however fragile, to the apparently irreconcilable claims to this land; so far, though, all roads have seemed to lead to conflict. All acts of violence against people or property, regardless of creed or authority, must continue to be condemned as fully by those on the side of the perpetrators who must take responsibility for their actions, as by the victims. When we turn our guns on the bricks of our ancestors we are in effect turning them on ourselves and on the identity of future generations. What are, superficially, the bricks and mortar of past cities so often inform the lifeblood of our memories, and without them we are doomed to look on the world with less forgiving, less understanding eyes.

It was apt that we should have ended up in Nablus at a site now known as Ground Zero, taking us back to the terrible event that had in many ways set our various journeys in motion. The attack on the Twin Towers and the blowing up of the Buddhas at Bamiyan were epic statements of intent, both grandiose in their execution, the former appalling in its human cost. But it is important not to forget the smaller acts that do not generate as many column inches or command the airwaves so dramatically. Truth is vanquished when history is not respected, and to eradicate a people's heritage, even partially, is to strike at the foundations of their cultural identity: this was the truth behind the painful modern parable offered by this ancient land. Perhaps the end of the world will not be a colossal, bloody battle but a slow, painful squeeze of intolerance, faith against faith, nation against nation. Perhaps even now, as we hurtle through our lives, we are already on the road to Armageddon.

EPILOGUE

WITH HINDSIGHT, THE TIMING OF OUR TRIPS was to prove incredibly fortuitous; Afghanistan and Iraq have since seen a marked deterioration in their security situations. Afghanistan remains a deeply unstable, poverty-ravaged country, still not under effective control from Kabul. The drug trade continues to grow apace, and there are disturbing reports of an unholy alliance between the drug barons and Taliban insurgents. There have also been increasing numbers of attacks on peacekeeping troops and aid workers. Sadly, on 23 August 2003, *The Times* reported that pieces from the destroyed Bamiyan Buddhas were being sold to tourists in Pakistan at £1850 per kilogramme.

On the positive side the Bamiyan valley, and Ashur in Iraq, have been placed on UNESCO's World Heritage List and List of World Heritage in Danger, which should lead to the provision of crucial resources for their cultural protection. Also intriguing are rumours of a third, hitherto lost, Buddha at Bamiyan, a kneeling figure possibly larger even than the two destroyed by the Taliban – though experts are divided as to whether it should be searched for or left buried. However, the UNESCO restoration project, which is likely to take ten years, could well unearth a new treasure for the Hazara people. The British Museum, along with the Foreign and Commonwealth Office in London, has launched an initiative to establish and fund a conservation studio in the Kabul Museum. The Greek government has also offered to pay for the reconstruction of the museum, and the US government has made a donation, though not enough money has yet been received to reroof the building.

In June 2003, the *Guardian* reported that a group of French experts from the Guimet Museum in Paris had started to glue together King

Kanishka – his pantaloons had been found, though his right foot remained missing. As for the rest of the country, according to the British Embassy in Kabul, Ghazni has become a no-go area, with reports of heightened Taliban activity in the region. The Kabul–Kandahar road remains off-limits for Westerners, including aid workers and journalists, and even in the capital suspected terrorist incidents have increased noticeably. Ten thousand US troops remain in the region as a whole, intent on rooting out Osama bin Laden. The search continues.

In the aftermath of the Coalition forces' intensive military campaign in Iraq, considerable concerns remain about the security and safe keeping of the country's historic sites. Elizabeth Stone, the head of archaeology at Stony Brook University in New York, was widely reported as calling for armed patrols to combat gangs of marauding looters at the country's archaeological sites: 'I think you have got to kill some people to stop this.' As in Afghanistan, if left unchecked, this looting threatens to drain the cultural lifeblood of the country.

The Iraq Museum story rumbles on. At the one-off opening of the Assyrian Gallery in July 2003 for press and invited dignitaries, at which the golden treasures of Nimrud were displayed for the first time since their retrieval from the vaults of the Central Bank of Iraq, Dr Donny George expressed his hope that the whole museum would open to the public again within a year or two. A week or so later, at an international conference held at the British Museum in London, Colonel Bogdanos and Dr Donny confirmed the latest assessment that 40 major items had been stolen from the main galleries, of which ten had been returned. Approximately 13,000 excavation site pieces were believed to have been taken from the secure storerooms, of which 3000 had been returned. Of the 10,000 still missing, about 95 per cent were believed to be the result of inside knowledge. The British Museum was sending out a team of curators to Baghdad to help their Iraqi colleagues and to advise on conservation, while Bogdanos is in the middle of compiling an updated report on the situation, which is scheduled for release in autumn 2003.

Baghdad and beyond remain increasingly dangerous. On 5 July Richard Wild, a 24-year-old freelance British journalist who had been in Iraq for only two weeks, was shot and killed at point-blank range by an unknown assailant directly outside the Iraq Museum. He was the sixteenth journalist to be killed in the country since 20 March, when the war began. Two days earlier, a US soldier guarding the museum had been killed by a sniper. The sense that things would only get worse, which had grown as our trip progressed, was being borne out as Iraqi frustration at the lack of basic utilities and resources turned to anger and retribution, and deadly attacks against Coalition troops proliferated across the country. On 19 August, a huge truck bomb exploded inside the United Nations compound in Baghdad, killing the UN Special Representative, Sergio Vieira de Mello, and 22 others. The United Nations denied it would pull out of Iraq in response but aid agencies were less sure, and the International Committee of the Red Cross quickly announced a scaledown of its mission. On 26 August, Oxfam decided to withdraw its staff from Baghdad, fearing for their safety.

After the perceived success in overthrowing Saddam Hussein's regime, President George W. Bush, as expected, turned his attentions to Israel, and the much-vaunted roadmap. Israel started to dismantle a few roadblocks, though not quickly enough for its critics. Israeli security forces were withdrawn from Bethlehem on 2 July 2003, and agreed to withdraw from Jericho, though there remained an impasse over the other contested West Bank towns, where violent confrontations continue. On 8 June an Israeli was shot dead near the Tomb of the Patriarchs in an exchange of gunfire in which two Palestinians were also killed. Several weeks after the resumption of visits to the Dome of the Rock by non-Muslim tourists and non-kippa-wearing Jews, kippa-wearing Jews were also granted entry to the site. However, two weeks later Israeli police suspended visits for fear of Palestinian rioting, after Muslim claims that the so-called tourists were, in the words of Yasser Arafat, an 'invasion of extremists disguised as tourists, under the auspices of Israeli police'. And the Palestinian Prime Minister, Abu Mazen, denounced the decision to allow entry to Jews as 'pro-vocative'. Then, on 20 August, in this dizzying merry-go-round of events, more than 150 Jews were allowed by Israel police to visit the site.

The construction of the controversial security fence continues to attract international criticism. The fence, which divides the West Bank into two small, self-contained Palestinian regions, is seen as an Israeli model for new national boundaries and suggests a much-reduced Palestinian state. Israeli soldiers are reported to have fired 'non-lethal means of crowd dispersal', or rubber bullets, at protesters. Prime Minister Ariel Sharon insisted that construction would continue, despite the objections of the Americans who were considering financial sanctions against Israel in response. Sharon maintained that small 'wildcat' Jewish settlements in the West Bank would be removed, but was not to be drawn on a freeze on the construction of state-sponsored settlements. On 6 August, Israel released 336 Palestinian prisoners but just eight days later Israeli troops killed Mohammed Seder, the Islamic Jihad military leader in Hebron, following two Palestinian suicide bombings. In response, on 19 August, a suicide bomber blew up a bus full of Israelis returning from prayers at the Western Wall, killing 21 and wounding over 100. Two days later, Israeli forces killed Hamas leader Ismail Abu Shanab, leading to Palestinian militant groups calling off their truce. And so it goes on, the prospect of lasting peace growing ever dimmer.

And, inevitably perhaps, there is still feistiness in the centuries-old feuding at the Church of the Holy Sepulchre. Remarkably, at the end of May the *Guardian* reported that Eireneos I, a patriarch of the Greek Orthodox Church of Jerusalem, had accused Metropolitan Timothy of Vostron, a colleague and one-time rival for the patriarchy, of hiring a Palestinian hit squad for $500,000 to have him murdered. Only in Israel, one is tempted to conclude.

Anton La Guardia, in his impressive book *Holy Land Unholy War*, quotes Shimon Peres as telling him, soon after the signing of the Oslo Accords, that 'what we are trying to do is turn an omelette into eggs'. Phase 3 of the roadmap is due to conclude in 2005, and its tentative progress is to be greeted with cautious optimism. However, the culinary alchemy described by Peres will need to start soon if the rigid knot that is Israel and the Occupied Territories is to be sustainably unpicked. And, regardless of the political nudging and inching, it is hard not to see the Holy Land's historic sites as remaining a lightning rod for the Israeli and Palestinian peoples' competing claims for many years to come.

David Vincent, London, August 2003

ACKNOWLEDGEMENTS

The authors would like to thank the following for their valued contributions to all aspects of the productions: Basil Comely, who gave vital shape and support throughout; Sam Hobkinson, whose vision and art were instrumental in defining the shape and structure of the films; Nick Reeks, an invaluable companion and professional; Heidi Perry, whose intrepid vision and talent were so key in Israel; Guy Smith, for his good humour and tenacity in never taking no for an answer; and the following, in strictly alphabetical order: Philip Abrams, Thaer Ali, Dale Allen, Naseer Arafat, Read Khzal Asaif, Linda Blakemore, Jan Cholawo, Flick Crawford, John Curtis, Dr Mohammed Darwish, Khalil al-Dliamy, Simon Greenwood, Mark Harrison, Matthew Hill, Hedaer Hussein, Esther Jagger, Nick Jones, Gav Kerr, Ruthy Lustig-Dassa, Natasha Martin, Rob Paxman, Mel Quigley, Martin Redfern, Jane Root, Khaled Saeed, Billal Sarwray, Emma Shackleton, Ali Shafout, Becky Vincent, Stan Watt, and all those who waited at home.

In memory of Wilfred Thesiger, 1910–2003

BIBLIOGRAPHY AND SUGGESTED FURTHER READING

AFGHANISTAN

Byron, Robert, *The Road to Oxiana* (Penguin, London, 1937)

Carew, Tom, *Jihad! The Secret War in Afghanistan* (Mainstream Publishing, Edinburgh, 2000)

Chittick, William C., *Sufism: A Short Introduction* (Oneworld Publications, Oxford, 2000)

Doubleday, Veronica, *Three Women of Herat* (Jonathan Cape, London, 1988)

Dupree, Louis, *Afghanistan* (Princeton University Press, New York, 1974)

Dupree, Nancy Hatch, *An Historical Guide to Afghanistan* (Afghan Tourist Organization Publication Number 5, Kabul, second edition, 1977)

Elliott, Jason, *An Unexpected Light: Travels in Afghanistan* (Picador, London, 2000)

Esposito, John L. (ed.), *The Oxford History of Islam* (Oxford University Press, New York, 2000)

Ewans, Martin, *Afghanistan: A New History* (Curzon Press, London, 2001)

Ewans, Martin, *Afghanistan: A Short History of its People and Politics* (HarperCollins, London, 2003)

Girardet, Edward and Walter, Jonathan (eds), *Afghanistan: Essential Field Guides to Humanitarian and Conflict Zones* (Media Action International, London, 1998)

Griffin, Michael, *Reaping the Whirlwind* (Pluto Press, London, 2001)

Ignatieff, Michael, *Empire Lite: Nation Building in Bosnia, Kosovo, Afghanistan* (Minerva, London, 2003)

Ignatieff, Michael, *The Warrior's Honour: Ethnic War and the Modern Conscience* (Chatto & Windus, London, 1998)

Knobloch, Edgar, *The Archaeology and Architecture of Afghanistan* (Tempus Publishing, London, 2002)

The Koran, trans. Dawood, N.J. (Penguin Classics, London, 2001)

McCauley, Martin, *Afghanistan and Central Asia:*

A Modern History (Longman, London, 2002)

Marsden, Peter, *The Taliban: War, Religion and the New Order in Afghanistan* (Zed Books, London, 2001)

Newby, Eric, *A Short Walk in the Hindu Kush* (Hodder & Stoughton, London, 1972)

Norcliffe, David, *Islam: Faith and Practice* (Sussex Academic Press, Brighton, 1999)

Rashid, Ahmed, *Taliban: Islam, Oil and the New Great Game in Central Asia* (I.B. Tauris & Co., London, 2001)

Sikorski, Radek, *Dust of the Saints: A Journey to Herat in Time of War* (Chatto & Windus, London, 1989)

Toynbee, Arnold, *Between Oxus and Jumna* (Oxford University Press, Oxford, 1961)

Urban, Mark, *War in Afghanistan* (Macmillan, London, second edition, 1990)

IRAQ

Basmachi, Dr Faraj, *Treasures of the Iraq Museum* (Iraqi Ministry of Information, Department of Antiquities, Baghdad, 1975)

The Battle for Iraq: BBC News Correspondents on the War Against Saddam and a New World Agenda (BBC Books, London, 2003)

Christie, Agatha, *An Autobiography* (Collins, London, 1977)

Christie, Agatha, *Murder in Mesopotamia* (Collins, London, 1936)

Christie, Agatha, *They Came to Baghdad* (Collins, London, 1951)

Christie Mallowan, Agatha, *Come, Tell Me How You Live* (P. Chivers, London, 1984)

Dabrowska, Karen, *Iraq* (Bradt Travel Guides, London, 2002)

Dalley, Stephanie (trans.), *Myths from Mesopotamia: Creation, the Flood, Gilgamesh and Others* (Oxford Paperbacks, Oxford, 2000)

Hiro, Dilip, *Iraq: A Report from the Inside* (Granta Books, London, 2003)

Iraq State Organization for Tourism, *Iraq, A Tourist Guide* (General Establishment for Travel and Tourism Services, Baghdad, 1982)

Lloyd, Seton, *The Archaeology of Mesopotamia* (Thames & Hudson, London, 1978)

Lloyd, Seton, *Twin Rivers* (Oxford University Press, London, 1943)

Maxwell, Gavin, *A Reed Shaken by the Wind* (Longman, London, 1957)

Raban, Jonathan, *Arabia through the Looking Glass* (Collins, London, 1979)

Sandars, N.K. (intro.), *The Epic of Gilgamesh* (Penguin Classics, London, 1960)

Stark, Freya, *Baghdad Sketches* (John Murray, London, 1937)

Thesiger, Wilfred, *Arabian Sands* (Longman, London, 1964)

Thesiger, Wilfred, *The Marsh Arabs* (Longman, London, 1964)

Tripp, Charles, *A History of Iraq* (Cambridge University Press, Cambridge, 2000)

Winstone, H.V.F., *Gertrude Bell* (Jonathan Cape, London, 1978)

Woodward, Bob, *Bush at War: Inside the Bush White House* (Simon & Schuster, New York, 2003)

Young, Gavin, *Iraq, Land of Two Rivers* (Collins, London, 1980)

Young, Gavin, *Return to the Marshes* (Collins, London, 1977)

ISRAEL AND THE OCCUPIED TERRITORIES

Andrews, Richard, *Blood on the Mountain: A History of the Temple Mount from the Ark to the Third Millennium* (Weidenfeld & Nicolson, London, 1999)

The Bible, King James (Authorized) Version

Chomsky, Noam, *The Fateful Triangle: The United States, Israel and the Palestinians* (South End Press, New York, 1984)

Dalrymple, William, *From the Holy Mountain: A Journey in the Shadow of Byzantium* (HarperCollins, London, 1997)

Dimbleby, Jonathan, *The Palestinians* (Quartet Books, London, 1979)

Ellis, Marc H., *Out of the Ashes* (Pluto Press, London, 2002)

Elon, Amos, *Jerusalem: City of Mirrors* (Little, Brown, London, 1989)

Epstein, Isidore, *Judaism: An Historical Presentation* (Penguin, London, 1990)

Gilbert, Martin, *Israel: A History* (Doubleday, London, 1998)

Grossman, David, *The Yellow Wind* (Jonathan Cape, London, 1988)

Hellander, Paul et al, *Israel and the Palestinian Territories* (Lonely Planet Publications, Victoria, 1999)

Herzl, Theodor, *Der Judenstaat (The Jewish State)* (M. Breitenstein, Leipzig and Vienna, 1896)

Hiro, Dilip, *Sharing the Promised Land* (Hodder & Stoughton, London, 1996)

Hirst, David, *The Gun and the Olive Branch: The Roots of Violence in the Middle East* (Faber, London, 1977)

Jacobs, Daniel, *Israel and the Palestinian Territories* (Rough Guides, London, 1998)

Kenyon, Kathleen, *Archaeology in the Holy Land* (Benn, London, 1979)

Kenyon, Kathleen, *Digging Up Jericho* (Benn, London, 1957)

La Guardia, Anton, *Holy Land Unholy War* (John Murray, London, 2001)

Murphy-O'Connor, Jerome, *The Holy Land* (Oxford Archaeological Guides, Oxford, 1980)

Oz, Amos, *In the Land of Israel* (Chatto & Windus, London, 1983)

Praill, David, *Return to the Desert: A Journey from Mount Hermon to Mount Sinai* (Fount, London, 1995)

Roth, Philip, *Operation Shylock* (Simon & Schuster, New York, 1993)

Sachar, Howard M., *A History of Israel: From the Rise of Zionism to Our Time* (Knopf, New York, 1976)

Said, Edward, *Orientalism: Western Concepts of the Orient* (Routledge, London, 1979)

Said, Edward, *The Question of Palestine* (Routledge, London, 1980)

Said, Edward W., *The End of the Peace Process* (Random House, New York, 2000)

Segev, Tom, *One Palestine Complete: Jews and Arabs under the British Mandate* (Little, Brown, London, 2001)

Shlaim, Avi, *The Iron Wall: Israel and the Arab World* (Penguin, London, 2000)

Thubron, Colin, *Jerusalem* (Heinemann, London, 1969)

Twain, Mark, *The Innocents Abroad, or The New Pilgrim's Progress* (American Publishing Co., Hartford, 1869)

Weyl, Martin, *Treasures of the Israel Museum* (Israel Museum, Jerusalem, 1995)

Yadin, Yigael (ed.), *Jerusalem Revealed: Archaeology in the Holy City 1968–1974* (Yale University Press, New York, 1976)

INDEX